"Scot McKnight brings Romans to life in ways unmatched by traditional commentaries or textbooks. With eyes focused on the letter's first audience and later interpreters in peripheral vision, McKnight responds to today's readers' questions with the questions that Paul sought to answer for the believers in Rome. New connections and fresh resonances emerge from this well-conceived and well-written approach to Romans."

—**Mark Reasoner**, *Assistant Professor of Theology, Marian University*

"When you are axle-deep in mud, backward is the only way forward. McKnight lifts, spins, and energetically pushes in a new direction. Hang on tight. The church and academy are careening down an adventurous new path."

—**Matthew W. Bates**, *Associate Professor of Theology, Quincy University*

"Christians typically read Romans forwards but too often stop at chapter 8 or 11, thinking they have the good stuff—the abstract theology that informs our traditional debates. In *Reading Romans Backwards*, McKnight reminds us that Paul's final chapters are the crescendo of his letter, not an afterthought. He calls us to reckon with Romans as lived theology, pastoral counsel for cultivating unified communities of God's peace."

—**Timothy Gombis**, *Professor of New Testament, Grand Rapids Theological Seminary*

"To read Romans backwards with Scot McKnight is to experience the epistle as a pastoral intervention directed toward believing communities under stress. Read backwards, Paul's great insights concerning justification, grace, and faithfulness reveal themselves not as doctrines received from the sky but as Paul's active work as a missionary theologian. Accessible to students and pastors, this book will provoke scholars to examine our assumptions about Romans as well."

—**Greg Carey**, *Professor of New Testament, Lancaster Theological Seminary*

Text - Ch 3
RRB - ch

"*Reading Romans Backwards* sheds fascinating light on Paul's famous letter. Starting our reading with Romans 12–16 means the whole of Romans can be seen as a pastoral letter addressed to Jewish Christians and Gentile Christians in Rome, speaking about privilege and power, and replacing both with the peace of Christ at the heart of the empire. Working backwards creates a whole new set of connections and unwraps Romans as lived theology of the grace of God."

—**Paul Trebilco**, *Professor of New Testament Studies, University of Otago*

"Most scholars consider Romans the jewel of Pauline theology, but McKnight has recovered Romans as a *pastoral* letter that communicates a lived theology to a divided Christian community in Rome. By focusing on clues about the socio-historical context found especially in the last few chapters of Romans, McKnight offers a compelling reading of the letter as a whole. He brings the text to life in such a way that the reader can imagine what it was like to be in the room when Romans was first read aloud."

—**Nijay K. Gupta**, *Associate Professor of New Testament, Portland Seminary*

Reading Romans Backwards

A GOSPEL OF PEACE
IN THE MIDST OF EMPIRE

Scot McKnight

BAYLOR UNIVERSITY PRESS

Cover and Interior Design by Savanah N. Landerholm
Cover Art from Fresco depicting banquet scene (fresco), Roman (4th century AD) / Cimitero dei SS. Marcellino e Pietro, Rome, Italy / De Agostini Picture Library / Bridgeman Images.

First paperback printing in September 2021
Paperback ISBN: 978-1-4813-0878-6

The Library of Congress has cataloged the hardcover as follows:

Names: McKnight, Scot, author.
Title: Reading Romans backwards : a gospel of peace in the midst of empire / Scot McKnight.
Description: Waco, Texas : Baylor University Press, [2019] | Includes bibliographical references and index.
Identifiers: LCCN 2018058127 | ISBN 9781481308779 (hardcover : alk. paper) | ISBN 9781481310529 (web pdf) | ISBN 9781481310512 (kindle) | ISBN 9781481308793 (epub)
Subjects: LCSH: Bible. Romans--Criticism, interpretation, etc.
Classification: LCC BS2665.52 .M39 2019 | DDC 227/.1066--dc23
LC record available at https://lccn.loc.gov/2018058127

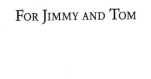

FOR JIMMY AND TOM

CONTENTS

Romans chapters:

12-16
9-11
1-4

Contents

III
A Torah That Disrupts Peace
Romans 1–4

IV
A Spirit Creating Peace
Romans 5–8

PREFACE   Ch's

Reading Romans forwards, beginning at 1:1 and closing the letter at 16:27, is both the best way to read Romans and its biggest problem. Reading Romans forwards often enough leads to fatigue by the time one gets to 9:1, and even more so by the time one arrives at 12:1. The impact of the fatigue is that the specific elements of the faith community in Rome as detailed in chapters 12 through 16 are ignored for how one reads chapters 1 through 8 or chapters 1 through 11. I am not proposing, then, that the right way to read Romans begins with chapter 12, but I do propose that a correction is in order and that fresh light can be thrown on chapters 1 through 11 by first taking a deep look at chapters 12 through 16. I call this reading Romans backwards: first, Romans 12–16, then 9–11, then 1–8 (since they work together in a special way). This is against everything my English-teacher father taught, but I have my reasons as the book will show.

A word about the kind of book this is. The contextual reading I offer has similarities to Peter Oakes, who imagined how a household in Pompeii might have heard Romans. I have imagined how the Strong and Weak heard this letter. I am an academic "son" of Jimmy Dunn, I have learned much from Tom Wright, and I consider myself steeped in the new perspective on Paul. But we are not all alike. *Reading Romans Backwards* bears similarities to the studies of others, most notably Paul Minear, A. J. M. Wedderburn, Philip Esler, and Francis Watson.[1] In addition, one surge of studies that began with Stanley Stowers' rhetorical approach that flowed into finding an exclusive gentile audience for Romans, as for instance in Matthew Thiessen, and another surge with the apocalyptic school and Douglas Campbell's intricate reinterpretation of Romans 1–4 pushed me to reread Romans all over again and again and again. My apologies to these scholars and many others for not interacting more directly, but this is not that kind of study. This book is about how I read Romans and not about how I read Romans in interaction with the mountains of scholarship about Romans. Because of this I don't weight possibilities and probabilities but rather expound what I think is the best view. Time after time I was aware of alternative explanations, but this is not a book of interaction with scholarship. Rather, I am exploring an approach to reading Romans, and at times I will make some bold suggestions that would require much further work to demonstrate adequately. But, again, this book attempts to hear Romans through the (imagined) ears of the Weak and Strong.

Western Christianity has been shaped by Romans like no other book in the Bible: Augustine, Luther, Calvin, Wesley, Edwards, Hodge, and Barth. Each forged his ideas as Romans worked its transformation. Add to these seminal thinkers, noticeably absent of minority voices, the massive commentaries undertaken in English the last fifty years, including C. E. B. Cranfield, J. D. G. Dunn, N. T. Wright, R. Jewett, and R. N. Longenecker. Romans, too, has featured in all major studies of Pauline theology, and I think of W. D. Davies, H. Ridderbos, E. P. Sanders, J. C. Beker, J. D. G. Dunn, N. T. Wright, and D. Campbell. Paul is just as important in Protestant Europe, which only intensifies the density of scholarship. In writing his massive two-volume study of Paul's theology, N. T. Wright had to write another volume on recent interpreters of Paul. All this is to say that interaction with these will not be found in the pages or footnotes of this study.

For decades I have read and listened to scholars and heard preachers on Romans 1–8, and one would think, after listening or reading, that those meaty chapters were written for a theological lectureship rather than to a local church or a set of house churches in Rome in the first century when Nero was emperor and Paul was planning his future mission to Spain. One would think the listeners were theological savants geared up for the latest theory of atonement or soteriology or salvation-history. I developed in my personal reading of Romans and in the occasional lectures on Paul a strategy: reading Romans 12–16 before reading the rest. At times I would begin a talk on Romans by sketching the Strong and the Weak in Romans 14–15 just to keep the context of Romans in mind. What follows is an exploration of Romans when one reads it backwards. One might say there are two primary orientations to reading Romans: a soteriological one that finds the message of redemption as the center of the letter and another reading that locates the center in an ecclesial setting—namely, the message of reconciliation and living in fellowship as siblings. The two are related; they are not dichotomies. If the soteriological reading has dominated much of Romans scholarship, there is clearly a trend today to see a shift toward the ecclesial readings. This book is an essay that will side with an ecclesial reading of Romans. I have pursued my own approach, occasionally mentioning others, but by and large that kind of discussion is for another day and another book.

I am grateful to Carey Newman at Baylor University Press once again for his encouragement and enthusiasm for this book, and to the expert editing of Dan Khan, both of whom made this book better. I am grateful to Justin Gill, my graduate assistant, for compiling the indices with care.

I dedicate this book to Jimmy Dunn, my *Doktorvater*, and to Tom Wright, my friend, two of the great Romans scholars of our generation.

INTRODUCTION

LIVED THEOLOGY

Americus, Georgia, 1950, Rehoboth Baptist Church. August 13 to be exact. The precipitating problem is that Clarence Jordan's Koinonia Farm, just down the road from the church, brought to church a visitor, an Indian Hindu named R. C. Sharma. The problem was not that he was a Hindu and therefore in need of hearing the gospel but that he had dark skin. On August 13, the congregation voted—two-thirds—to expel Clarence and his wife, Florence, along with all other members of Koinonia.

> The central argument of the resolution was that they "have brought people of other races into the services of Rehoboth Baptist Church, and have done this with the knowledge that such practices were not in accord with the practices of other members."

The vote took place, the whole church was hushed into silence, and "then someone began to sob, and soon others joined. For five minutes, the congregation cried quietly. Then they got up and, one by one, they began to go out the door."[1]

In the midst of that congregational event at Rehoboth Baptist is where we need to be if we seek to understand Romans. It is foolish to look down our convictions onto the debates in Rome in the first century and to think ours are worse or better than theirs. Why foolish? Because our issue is their issue: the issue is the inability of the Privileged and the Powerful to embody the gospel's inclusive demand and include the Disprivileged and the Disempowered. The mirror of this issue is the Disempowered claiming their own kind of Privilege and Power. There is no reason at this point even to raise the specter of racism, for that only aggravates the symptom: the reality is Privilege and Power used to create and enforce various forms of injustice, including racism.

Romans is about Privilege and Power.

Paul's gospel deconstructs Power and Privilege.

Paul's lived theology turns power upside down and denies privilege.

Paul's lived theology is about Peace in the empire, and it is a radical alternative to Rome's famous *Pax Romana*.

Romans 12–16 is lived theology, and Romans 1–11 is written to prop up that lived theology. Romans 12–16 is not the application of Paul's theology, nor is Romans a classic example of the indicative leading to the imperative. What Paul had in focus was the lack of praxis, the lack of lived theology, the lack of peace in Rome, and he wrote Romans both to urge a new kind of lived theology (12–16) and to offer a rationale (1–11) for that praxis.

The theologian's Privilege and Power have made Romans about theology abstracted from the Peace it seeks to create. Romans is about theology, but it isn't mere theology—it isn't abstract theology. If you will, the theology of Romans is about a way of life, about lived theology. Romans advocates for a *via vitae*, both for the individual and for the community of faith in Rome. As is the case with some, if Romans is seen as theology with little to no emphasis on its *via vitae*, then its message is stripped of its own deconstructing powers. We'll get to this shortly, but it should be said now that there will be no letup on this point. From beginning to end of this letter, or from End to Beginning, the letter deconstructs Privilege and Power and replaces with Peace.

To say it again, it is for many an irresistible temptation to make Romans abstract systematics, theology, or philosophy. A theodicy if you will. A systematic theology if you will. A long day's discussion under the stoa in Athens if you will. An exploration of how God can somehow maintain integrity and holiness and still be full of grace and love and then justify, sanctify, and glorify sinners while maintaining covenant with Israel. Romans 1–8 or 1–11 becomes Christianity's first abstract theology. Those chapters become timeless theology, their ties to the house churches of Rome ripped from their hooks. Many are so worn down by this approach to Romans that by the time they reach chapter 12, they breeze through the rest as compulsory, unimportant information. The best of commentaries barely escapes this temptation, so I have chosen to read Romans backwards in order to demonstrate that this letter is a pastoral theology about Privilege and Power in search of Peace in the empire.

Romans 12–16, it will be argued, reveals the pastoral context of Romans. I move then to Romans 9–11 because it is a revelation of the narrative at work in the entire letter and one that has special relevance in the lived theology of Romans 12–16. Only after comprehending Paul's pastoral aims and narratival assumptions can we see the theology of Romans 1–8 for what it is: pastoral theology aimed at justifying the lived theology of peace in chapters 12 through 16. In reading Romans backwards, I am not discounting the brilliant connections made in reading Romans forwards. Those connections still obtain. What I hope to show is that working backwards creates another set of connections: to the lived theology of Romans.

The lived theology of Romans emerges out of Paul's two decades of gentile mission, much of it hard-fought and some of it learned in prisons along the way or explained on the run. Everything Paul writes comes from that mission, not from a library, and what Paul has learned out of that lifetime of gentile mission experience comes to the surface in Romans. At times, Paul jumps topics as if he were turning his head from one person at the party to another, and then he shifts his feet a bit and butts in on another conversation with a zinger or two, returning back to the original conversation with utter fluency. Thus Romans appears at times to be a pastiche of Pauline pieces as much as it is a linear argument.

I
A Community Needing Peace
Romans 12–16

1

PHOEBE—THE FACE OF ROMANS

(16:1-2)

The apostle Paul is one of the most influential thinkers in the history of the Christian world, and most influential among his writings is his Letter to the Romans. This oft-claimed patriarchal male asks a wealthy, influential female, Phoebe, not only to deliver his prized letter but also to read it to each of the five or six (or more) house churches in Rome. Letters in Paul's world were the embodied, inscripted presence of the letter writer, in this case Paul. He chooses a woman to embody his letter, which means the face of Paul is experienced as the face of Phoebe. Before anyone hears the letter, they encounter the body of Phoebe in their midst.[1]

How did she get to Rome? Inasmuch as her home, Cenchreae, was Corinth's major port on the Saronic Gulf on the Aegean Sea, Phoebe may well have traveled by boat around Greece and under Italy, by Sicily and up to the Roman port Ostia, where she could take a boat up the Tiber to Rome. Wind and weather were always factors for the Mediterranean. Alternatively, she may have walked the road up the east coast of the Adriatic and then down to Ravenna and then to Rome. We don't know. At least I don't.

Why Phoebe? She's a "sister," a term Paul uses elsewhere for women in Christ, and she's a gentile convert sister. Phoebe means "Titaness," and this indicates she was converted to Christ from a pagan background, as no self-respecting Jewish family would name their daughter after a pagan god/ goddess. She's like Apphia, also a sister (Phlm 2), and like other traveling missionaries called "sister wives" (1 Cor 9:5, my translation).[2] This becomes more explicit in 1 Timothy 5:2, where Timothy is exhorted to speak with "younger women as sisters." Paul's favorite metaphor for Christians is that they are "siblings." Siblings in a family are marked by love, by harmony, by forgive-ness of one another, but also by order and even hierarchy.[3] If the metaphor "sister" means anything, it means a new social reality is at work among the

3

house churches throughout the Roman Empire, for in that world one's identity was one's status, and one's status was determined most by one's family, one's connections or patrons, one's wealth, one's success in military expeditions, or one's sheer ambition to climb up the pervasively present *cursus honorum*, or the social path to public honor. This path to glory, the cursus honorum, was as invisible as it was influential in society. But for Paul, redemption in Christ obliterates the quest for special public honors, and in their place he concentrates on siblingship. With the term "sister," Paul creates a new society of siblings, one designed to obliterate Privilege and Power as ancients knew it.

Phoebe is also a "deacon." The Greek term *diakonos* can be used more generally for a "servant": Roman officials are servants (Rom 13:4); Christ is a servant (15:8); Paul and his minister associates are servants (Col 1:7; 1 Cor 3:5; 1 Tim 4:6) as also are counterfeit ministers (2 Cor 11:15). But the term, especially when connected to a church (as Rom 16:1 is), brings to mind the more official recognized ministry or office of "deacon." Thus, already to the Philippians, Paul speaks of "bishops and deacons" (Phil 1:1). The term "deacon" comes to surface noticeably in the Pastoral letters where we have a list of qualifications for deacons (1 Tim 3:8-13). That Paul connects Phoebe's diaconate with the church of Cenchreae seems then to mean she has the more official role of being a deacon in that church, which means she is marked by Christian character and has gifts of leadership. The meaning of "deacon" for Phoebe then is closer to those who are coworkers and coservants with Paul. Thus, she stands alongside Apollos and Tychicus and Timothy and Epaphras, those "ministers of a new covenant" (2 Cor 3:6; 6:4; Eph 3:7). As is the case with Nympha (Col 4:15), it is likely that the house church of Cenchreae meets in Phoebe's home and that she is both patron and leader of the church.

Phoebe was a woman of *wealth*. Paul uses a wildly popular term, "benefactor." More than any term in his world, a benefactor gained a person public honor in the Roman cursus honorum. City officials only got their positions because of their wealth and obligation to provide for a community. How so? Food and provisions when needed; public feasts as well as providing funds for athletic contests. But Phoebe turned at least some if not all of her donations toward churches and Paul and his planned mission to Spain (Rom 15:23-24). To do the work of an apostle required time for prayer, for study of the Scriptures, and for pastoring, meeting, talking, and discussing, and more time for traveling and starting new churches—add to this Paul's time in prison, where support came from friends (not the prison system and taxation). To do all this, Paul needed patrons, and Phoebe is one of them. Paul adds that Phoebe was a benefactor "of many."

The house churches of Rome, however, did not encounter Phoebe as a deacon or benefactor. They encountered her as a *commended sister worthy of hospitality and fellowship*: "I commend to you . . . Phoebe." There is more here than meets the skimming eye: the commendation reveals Phoebe as the letter carrier, or courier. Pseudo-Demetrius speaks of the courier in terms strikingly like our verse: "who is conveying this letter to you," and "You will do well if you deem him worthy of hospitality both for my sake and his."[4] The courier had other responsibilities: to pass on personal information from Paul to the churches at Rome, especially to those like Priscilla and Aquila who knew him. As well, the courier's task was to deliver the letter, probably also to read the letter, interpreting as she read and answering questions (and surely they had them!).

More needs to be said about reading the letter. The courier Phoebe *performed the letter*, and I assume to each house church (but it is possible she read it only once). (The issue, as we will see below, is if the second-person greetings of 16:3-16 imply the letter was sent only to one house church.) Writers like Paul didn't hand letters over to schmucks to stumble their way through the letters. He (and his coworkers) mentored the readers so they could read the letters in a way that made Paul seem present and his lived theology compelling.[5] How was such a letter read? The standard elements of reading as performance included gestures at the right time and to the right segment of the audience (when Phoebe read "Strong" or "Weak," she looked them in the eye, or, if she thought they needed it, the opposing group in the eye!); inflection of the voice (here pastoral, there admonishing, here softening, and there exhorting); acting out specific elements of the letter; pausing and speeding up when needed; making eye contact at crucial moments; and having "ad-libbed" if she thought the audience needed it. How to read the letter would have been discussed by Paul as well as Timothy, Tertius, and Gaius (16:21-22). She no doubt practiced in their presence. Some think she had the whole letter memorized and performed it from memory.

We start here, then, with our reading of Romans: with the face of Phoebe, in our presence, performing the letter in such a way that each person in the churches senses Paul's presence.

2

THE GREETINGS AND
THE HOUSE CHURCHES OF ROME

(16:3-16)

Rome was a jumble of homes with twisting, turning paths on which one saw immigrants inquiring for residence and merchants finding a sale and the wealthy searching for even more status and intellectuals finding a conversation and politicians plotting power that privilege provided. Not just the Tiber but the whole world flowed—so they thought—through Rome. That throng of immigrants was led by slaves, many captured in foreign military campaigns. Some arrived loaded with ambition, others were buoyed by the chance of fame or fortune or a chance to find better work, some entered Rome on a quest for learning from leading philosophers, while yet others found their way to Rome because of friendships.[1] By the time of Paul's letter's arrival, an increasing number of provincial (i.e., from the provinces) leaders were becoming senators in Rome itself. Some (Athenaeus) liked this; others (Juvenal) didn't; all recognized numerous tensions.

Surely the churches in Rome had some wealthy and more poor from the provinces, and not a little of the bubbling tensions in Rome would have emerged in the churches. There were at least five house churches in Rome to whom Paul wrote this letter, and before each Phoebe may well have read the entire letter. The impression Phoebe got was that it was a diverse lot of believers, well represented as it was by women and slaves or former slaves with their touch of tarragon being a few high-status persons. Jewish believers were also noticeable. The jumble of Rome was mirrored in the churches.

JEWISH CONNECTIONS IN ROME WITH JESUS FOLLOWERS

If we examine all the evidence—archaeological, numismatic, literary—can we determine where the earliest house churches were located in Rome?[2] The

7

answer is yes, within reason. Snaking north to south through Rome is the Tiber River. West of the Forum and south of today's Vatican (a first-century term too) was the port area of the Tiber called the Trastevere (trast-EH-ver-eh). House churches were located here in the first century. South and slightly east of the Forum, on a main road through the heart of first-century Rome called Via Appia, was another dwelling place for followers of Jesus. Between the two, in an area called the Aventine, where more and more senators were forming their homes, was a third location for a Christian presence, but the evidence is not as abundant. North and slightly west of the Forum was Mars Field, and along its eastern side is the Via Lata/Flaminia, yet another area where Christians lived.

We can know a little more about the Christians from what we know of these areas. The Christian presence *emerged out of Jewish synagogue gatherings.* Further, inasmuch as these locations were *dense populations* of mostly poor and immigrants, we know the followers of Jesus were probably poor. The Trastevere in particular was composed of workers connected to the harbor and trade and transportation like sailing. Trade would create shopkeepers and those who tanned skins (with their putrid odors). As home to travelers, the Trastevere was filled with foreign religious shrines and adherents. What we known of the area along the Via Appia was that it was filled with transportation vehicles as well as workers and porters and craftsmen. The Aventine Hill, however, was mixed with upper-class Romans and their slaves and workers. Mars Field is more or less the same as the Aventine population. All of this to say: the Christians of Rome were located among the poor with possible connections with some high-status individuals.

At the time Paul wrote this letter, Nero had excited hopes for more trade and jobs *by reducing taxes* so some immigrant followers of Jesus as well as local Roman believers may well have been employed in Nero's numerous, often vain, building projects.[3] He sought to revive the Augustan era's monumental architecture. Just north of the Trastevere, under what is now the Vatican, Nero completed the circus originally started by Caligula and, to make it easier to attend his own performances (acting, singing, and chariot racing),[4] built a bridge across the Tiber. We may be so bold as to make the suggestion that some in the Trastevere may have worked on the circus. Christians living along Mars Field could have found employment building the wooden amphitheater Nero constructed on Mars Field, while those nearer the Aventine Hill or Appian Way may have found work opportunities in his reconstruction of the marketplace called the Macellum on the Caelian Hill. Not long after this letter's arrival, Nero's grotesque and expansive *Domus Aurea*, the Golden House (which opened with a 120-foot column, on top of which was a statue of Nero morphed with the sun god or, perhaps, Apollo), began construction, and some may have been engaged in that project.[5] Large portions of this construction were dismantled by Vespasian and reused for other constructions, like the Colosseum.

The dwelling places of the Roman Christians were at least sometimes apartments (tenements, *insulae*)[6] and not in a house (*domus*) or on villas, though there were single-family dwellings in each of these areas where Christians were found in Rome. Earliest Christianity in Rome was predominately Jewish, and it is probable they were in the middle of the problems that provoked Claudius. Still reeling from his wife Messalina's affair (or marriage or whatever happened)[7] and the publicity of marrying his niece Agrippina the Younger, and seeking to show his own *bona fides* to Roman religion and traditions, he cut the knees out from under the Jewish troublemakers in Rome by exiling them. We read about this in Acts 18:2 when it says "because Claudius had ordered all Jews to leave Rome." An early Roman historian adds to Acts 18:2 that the Jewish "disturbances" were "at the instigation of Chrestus."[8] The terms "Chrestus" and "Christus" are so alike that the historian's "Jews" were probably our "Jewish Christians."[9] In the middle of this group of Jews expelled were Priscilla and Aquila. But then Claudius died. Under the very young seventeen-year-old (at accession), Nero Claudius' decree was forgotten, so some of the expelled returned.

The return of these Jewish Christians created *tensions*, for it seems nearly certain that the expelled returned to lesser roles and status. During their exile, the gentile Christians formed a new Christian culture, and it was not a Torah-observant culture. It is then entirely reasonable to theorize that the earliest Christians of Rome were Jewish, with some God-fearing gentiles joining them (e.g., Acts 13:43, 50; 16:14; 17:4, 17; 18:7). Jews knew Godfearers were not as fully Jewish as they were, and this gave the Jewish believers a sense of Torah-observance privilege, and my suspicion is that the Weak of Romans 14–15, who will be described in chapter 3, absorbed that worldview when they became convinced Jesus was their Messiah. But that worldview shifted when they were no longer around and the then-in-power gentile (Strong) believers formed a non-Torah culture. We'll get to this tension soon enough, but for now it is worth repeating that Privilege and Power were at the very core of the Roman house churches and Paul faced both head-on.

A TYPICAL HOUSEHOLD

Space determines. A church meeting in a long basilica with a central altar and offset pulpit and seating or standing space for hundreds facilitates specific kinds of actions (sermons to lots of people) and audience responses (listening, agitating a crowd into reactive responses). Basilicas make possible the development of a commanding preacher—think John Chrysostom or Ambrose or Basil the Great. The believers listening to Phoebe read Romans were not in a basilica as that didn't happen until Constantine and after. Rather, the Roman followers of Jesus were in houses, some smaller and some larger. Space determines. House churches made conversations common, made questions and answers common, and made speakers less the orator and more importantly a sibling. What all this does mostly is remind us that our Sunday-morning worship services are not first-century church gatherings. If space determines, for listening to Romans, we need to think more about church-in-a-house or a living room or around a kitchen table.

What we know about who lived in households in Italy—Rome, Pompeii—at the time of Paul is sufficient for us to offer a brief sketch of who might be in a house church and what kind of diversity it might create. Remember again, one didn't have to be a "member" to be in a house church. No, if you were in the house, you may well have been part of the gathering, and remember too that households were businesses as much as homes. Who was there? Approximately (but no more than) thirty people centered around the householder, who may well have been a craftworker and his immediate and extended family. Others may have been those who rented a room from the craftworker, while yet others were converts but not directly connected to the householder. Add into this mix slaves and dependents and some homeless.[10] If we add some Jewish believers along with some Jewish slave or free or immigrant believers to this sketch, we will be about as close as we can get to what a first-century household in Rome looked like. One likely place for the gathering was the home's atrium, which served also a waiting room for those doing business with the householder—not, in other words, your typical Sunday-morning church. House churches may best be understood in modern terms as a gathering of believers in a designated space of a private business. It was as much "public" space as it was sacred space.

The House Churches of Rome

There are three sorts of greetings: first person, second person, and third person—that is, I greet You, or I greet Others through You, or Another greets You through Me. The formula for greeting these people in Romans 16:3-16[11] is a second-person greeting (fifteen times!). Which means those greeted are not the direct recipients of this letter, though (as most assume) they are at least indirect recipients and thus the extended audience of the letter. Some have suggested that the second-person greeting implies those greeted are not the audience of the letter at all, and the audience is to be detected apart from these greetings. I disagree.

In addition, it is reasonable to infer that those greeted mirror the makeup of the Roman house churches (thus, both Jewish and gentile believers). Greeting one another symbolized the fellowship of the church and entailed acts like kissing (16:16), embracing, and even washing feet. This greeting is the origin of the Christian tradition of "passing the peace."

The Households

The separate house churches are designated by "house" (16:5), by "family" (16:10, 11), and by "with them" (16:14, 15). I separate Prisca and Aquila's, since it alone is called a "house" (16:5), I see their household as the leading location, and I lean toward seeing the "residences" as made up of mostly slaves or freed slaves. The "residence" of Aristobulus could well be an estate or larger household and perhaps had special Jewish connections (Herodion is in that household). One should not be afraid to see in these various households leaders who could be voices of tension with other household leaders. Each household will have developed its own culture and leaders, perhaps already called presbyters and bishops, and distinctive approaches.

- ❖ Household of Prisca/Priscilla and Aquila (16:3-5a)
- ❖ Residence of Aristobulus (16:10)
  Perhaps grandson of Herod the Great, who had died in the 40s but whose household continued; perhaps a Christian slave came with him and helped found the church in Rome.
- ❖ Residence of Narcissus (16:11)
  Perhaps the home of the deceased Roman administrator either under Claudius or, less likely, under Nero.[12]
- ❖ Residence of Asyncritus and others (16:14)
- ❖ Residence of Philologus, Julia and others (16:15)

We do not know where the rest of the names are to be located, though one could easily add another two or more households and suggest there were eight (or even more) house churches in Rome. These believers could not and did not all gather in one location for instruction and worship. They gathered in homes designated by the name of the paterfamilias, and it is reasonable to think then that house churches dependent upon a paterfamilias naturally evolved into leadership.

How large were these house churches? One estimate is a maximum of forty, while others think these, or at least some of these, are tenements, which would suggest much smaller numbers. We can guess there were fewer than two hundred and probably closer to one hundred Jesus followers in Rome at the time of this letter. But what is clear is that no matter where Paul founded a church, the dainty game of status was played. At times with a heavy stick. Power and Privilege was the way of Rome, the way of the world, and the way of the Christian who was not Christoform. A greeting from Paul was enough to swell the chest of some and to raise the blood pressure of others. ☺

The People

At times some suggest Paul did not know the house churches of Rome, because he had never been to Rome. Not so. Paul clearly knows some of the twenty-six names, plus Rufus' mother and Nereus' sister as well as "brothers and sisters." The expulsion of Jews and Jewish Christians from Rome by Claudius in AD 49 led some of these persons into Paul's circle. Those known to Paul include Prisca and Aquila, Epaenetus (fellow Ephesian and possibly a freedman), the gospel laborer Mary, Ampliatus, Urbanus, Stachys, Persis, and Rufus and his mother. He may well have known Andronicus and Junia (who could be relatives of Paul or simply fellow Jews), Apelles, Herodion (again, either a relative or a fellow Jew), and probably Tryphaena and Tryphosa, whom Paul dubs "workers in the Lord." My suspicion is that those named are leaders in the house churches of Rome. I would suggest that the churches were planted by the likes of Prisca and Aquila, Mary, Andronicus and Junia, Ampliatus, Urbanus, Stachys, Apelles, Tryphaena, Tryphosa, Persis, and Rufus.

The tradition of translators to turn Greek or Jewish names into their Latin-based equivalent—Narkissos becomes Narcissus—obscures a hidden reality of the Roman house churches: there are Greek names, Latin names, and Jewish names. Thus, there are seven (probable) Jews named with one's "mother" added: (Mary [Miriam, Mariam], Andronicus, Junia, Aquila and probably Prisca, Herodion, Rufus and his mother, of Mark 15:21 fame?), and there are just a few Latin names (Ampliatus, Julia, Urbanus). The others have Greek names in spite of the standard Latin spellings in our translations. Thus, we can guess that the most common language of the house churches was Greek, the second-most common Aramaic or Hebrew, and the third-most common Latin.

Women's leadership at Rome is obvious: Prisca, Mary, Junia, Tryphaena and Tryphosa (perhaps sisters), Persis, Rufus' mother, Julia, Nereus' sister, as well as the sisters in the household of Asyncritus. Prisca—known to Luke as Priscilla (the diminutive form)—was an itinerant missionary church planter with her husband, Aquila, and was fellow tentmakers with Paul, and they were a courageous couple willing to relocate for gospel work in the Pauline mission. They were from Pontus but relocated to Rome and then following the expulsion of Claudius are found in Corinth, Ephesus, Rome, and again in Ephesus on mission.[13] That Prisca is mentioned on a number of occasions before her husband probably speaks to her status in the Roman world, and archaeological evidence takes us back to the early second century AD to high-status property in her name. Prisca taught Apollos along with her husband (Acts 18:24-6). Theirs is the only actual house mentioned by name ("the church in their house" in 16:5).

The story of Junia has been told over and over, but these are the pertinent facts: Junia was a woman, she was a fellow apostle with her husband, she was a highly esteemed apostle, her name was changed in the course of church history to Junias because it was thought no woman could be an apostle, there was no such masculine name Junias, and it took until the last quarter of the twentieth century for Junia to recover (fully) her female status in the church! It is worth thinking that Andronicus and Junia, along with Prisca and Aquila as well as Mary, were the primary gospel agents in the city of Rome.

If the women are clearly prominent in the house churches of Rome, and that means Phoebe's voice would have been a common sound, it seems likely that slaves were also prominently engaged in the gospel work. Some believe that "household" (in Greek, "those of") in the Household of Aristobulus and the Household of Narcissus is an indicator of slaves. Whether "those of" indicates slaves or not, the presence of slaves in the house churches of Rome is certain. A few scholars consider Aquila a Jewish freedman, and, if this is the case, we have a high-status Roman woman married to a former slave. The famous lines of Galatians 3:28—"no longer Jew or Greek ... slave or free ... male and female"—are a reality in the churches of Rome. Others, such as Ampliatus and Asyncritus (and the whole church meeting in his residence) as well as Julia and Nereus and his sister, could be slaves or freedmen.

Diversity shaped every moment of the Roman house churches, but Paul sought for a unity in the diversity, a sibling relationship in Christ that both transcended and affirmed one's ethnicity, gender, and status. Paul was never non-Jewish, and he often affirmed his Jewishness (cf. Rom 9:1-5; 11:1; Phil 3:5-6), but he also celebrated sibling relationships that transcended his

Jewishness (Gal 3:28 with 1:13). Every person in each of the house churches in Rome had formed an identity apart from Christ and then in Christ, and the emphasis on "in Christ" or "in the Lord" in the names is as emphatic as it is often unobserved.[14] Life for the Christians in Rome is life in Christ, which they share with others throughout the Pauline mission churches. What they share now is a sibling relationship. For those in Christ, then, the ideal vision is Christoformity. That pattern meant saying some No's to their former identity and some Yes's to their identity as siblings in Christ. "Easier said than done" leads to our next observation about social realities in the Roman churches.

3

STRONG AND WEAK

(14:1–15:13)

Perhaps the most significant contextual factor in reading Romans is coming to terms with the identity of the Strong and the Weak in Romans 14:1–15:13. To anticipate where we are headed, this means the most significant contextual factor is about the believers in Rome learning to be siblings with every other believer. The instructions to the Weak and the Strong are the core of Paul's lived theology, and the aim of the entire letter. That claim changes how we read Romans.

Some Options

One might consider the Strong and the Weak, as is the case with persons in the parables of Jesus, as *literary figures* rather than actual groups in Rome. If so, these literary figures derive more from what Paul says in 1 Corinthians 8–10 than from actual realities in Rome. The length of our passage and the directiveness of the words make this consideration all but impossible. The Strong and the Weak, then, are *real groups* at odds with one another. The Weak could be Jewish believers, and the Strong gentile believers, or perhaps each term includes a mixture: the Weak are mostly Jews, and the Strong mostly gentiles.

Long ago a case was made not for two but for five distinct groups in Rome:[1] *Weak* judgers of the Strong, *Strong* despisers of the Weak, *Doubters* to whom the Weak and the Strong appealed, *Weak* who did not judge the Strong, and *Strong* who did not despise the Weak. Dividing the Roman Christians into five groups is too fine of a line to draw, but the general impression of alternative viewpoints is hard to deny. Clearly, there are the Weak and the Strong, but it is unlikely that everyone declared allegiance to one of two parties. That some Strong were stronger than others or that some Weak were weaker than others is commonsensical, and that there may well have been some undecided is just as reasonable. Simplistic dismissals of such a scheme is not wise.

A Common Mission Problem

To define Strong and Weak, we need to start with Paul's mission, which was to establish churches in the Roman Empire made up of Jews and gentiles, slaves and the free, males and females, Scythians and barbarians. In the providential plans of God, the church was the Body of Christ that expanded Israel's borders to include gentiles in the one true family of God under the world's one true Lord, King Jesus. Paul observed—in each mission community he established—tensions between what he here calls the Weak and the Strong. His fear was denominations—one Jewish, one gentile—and his message was peace among the Weak and the Strong. There is then nothing surprising in the Roman households to discover social tensions between various groups, and often enough they were between Jewish and gentile believers.

The Bible on Their Side

The Weak, if we assume for the sake of argument that they were a Jewish group of believers in the Roman house churches, had the Bible and history on their side. The point cannot be emphasized enough. How so? Jews believed God had elected them from Abram/Abraham on; had formed covenant with them and rescued them from slavery in Egypt; had given them the Torah as their revealed constitution for all of life;[2] had commanded them to circumcise all male covenant members; had gone before them to defeat their enemies; and had given them the Land as a place in which to observe the Torah faithfully. When Israel sinned, that same covenant God provided a means of atonement in the sacrificial system but also, if they did not repent, their God disciplined them and even exiled them—Egypt, Assyria, Babylon. God had given the bold covenant markers, like circumcision and food laws, and these prescriptions in Torah were to be followed faithfully.

Torah observance then was central to Jewish identity because it was so scriptural, and therefore observance was important to the Weak's own identity even as believers in Jesus as Messiah.[3] Whether or not one calls this "covenantal nomism"[4] is not the point, for Torah observance shaped the identity of the Weak in Rome.[5] If one grew up embracing this narrative of life and if one lived its theology, and if one thinks Jesus is the Messiah of that narrative, then it is not hard to imagine one will think one is in the right group all along. How could the Weak not think they were God's elect? But this identifies the Weak with Jewish believers, and we need to establish this now because it is contested.

Identifying the Weak and the Strong

The place to begin is 1 Corinthians, where we see these terms—"Strong" and "Weak." Thus, Paul warns the Corinthians in these terms: "But take care that this liberty of yours does not somehow become a stumbling block to the weak" (8:9). Romans was written at about the same time as 1 Corinthians, but more importantly Romans was written from either Corinth or its port city, Cenchreae. This makes it very unlikely that "Strong" and "Weak" will have radically different meanings in Romans and 1 Corinthians.[6] This leads to a starting point: the evidence in Romans 14–15 is less precise (days, food in general) and the language of 1 Corinthians more precise (food offered to idols). Next, the language of Romans does not substantively contradict the language of 1 Corinthians even if nuanced differences can be detected. Furthermore, the exhortations of Paul to both congregations focus on tolerance and unity and self-denial, or Christoformity, and the religious worlds of Rome and Corinth were more or less the same to the Jewish eye. Thus, a conclusion: *it is most probable that that controversial food of Romans 14–15 was nonkosher food, and I would suggest it is likely that it was food offered to idols and sold in the market*. We can't know for sure, but this seems most likely to me. As 1 Corinthians 8:7 puts it, "Since some have become so accustomed to idols until now, they still think of the food they eat as food offered to an idol; and their conscience, being weak, is defiled." The Weak want kosher food; the Strong have no such scruples. Eating together is now a problem. Not a lot stands with this starting point, but it seems justifiable.

Overall it makes most sense to see the Weak as Jewish believers and the Strong as gentile believers. That is, Weak and Strong are ethnic labels as well. Yet, the passage just cited might suggest the weak are former pagans who had been "so accustomed to idols" that eating food offered to idols was participation all over again in idolatry and it unnerved them spiritually (1 Cor 8:7). Hence, one cannot simply assume Weak is entirely Jewish, and the language of Romans keeps the door open to seeing Weak as not just Jewish. The Weak in Romans are weak "in faith" or "in conscience." Either way, weakness then is matter of faith and conscience and not just ethnicity and Torah observance (1 Cor 8:12). The Strong, then, eat anything and everything without scruples (Rom 14:2, 15, 20-23). Let's look a little more closely at what Romans says.

There are a number of considerations that lead to the conclusion that the Weak in Rome are at least predominately Jewish believers and the Strong predominately gentile believers. (I don't believe Paul ever addresses Jews in general in Romans; his concern is always with fellow followers of Jesus.) Remember that the churches began in connection with synagogues in Rome. Remember too there are Jewish names in Romans 16: Mary, Andronicus, Junia, Aquila, and probably Prisca, Herodion, and Rufus and his mother. Significant households appear to be led by Jewish believers. There are on the other hand more gentile names mentioned than Jewish names in Romans 16. We can add another consideration: in Rome, Jews were well known for avoiding pork, not to mention observance of other laws (Sabbath) that landed them on the rough side of ridicule and even expulsion.[7] In addition, one must also consider how this letter is constructed: in Romans 1–4, there is a strong emphasis on Jews (and I will contend it is stronger than many argue), while Romans 5–8 adopts significantly different language and appeals more directly to gentile believers (which I will argue as well), and one cannot make sense of anything in Romans 9–11 without thinking Jew-gentile relations in the church are at the forefront of Paul's thinking.[8] It would be beyond odd for Paul to get to the lived theology passages at the end of Romans and not have that Jew-gentile dynamic in play. In support of an ethnic core to Strong and Weak is also how our larger section (14:1–15:13) ends: it climaxes with a series of quotations from the Old Testament proving the inclusion of gentiles in fulfillment of the promise to the patriarchs (15:7-13). Paul finishes here because, from 14:1 on, Paul has been talking about the Jew-gentile issue as a way to address Christian issues. One more consideration—if we recall the discussion about the edict of Claudius to expel Jewish believers and their likely return in the early days of Nero, and if we date Romans right in that time period, then tension between returning Jewish believers and the now empowered gentile believers is all but a certainty.

What clinches the ethnic core to the Weak and the Strong label is that the specific issues the Weak have are naturally translated into typical halakhic topics and rulings. Notice that Paul says "nothing is *unclean* in itself" (14:14). He uses this term (in Greek, *koinon*) three times in this verse, and it can just as easily be translated "common" or what Jews today call *traif*. Nothing is common; nothing is *traif*; all foods are kosher. And Paul uses yet another typically Jewish term: "clean" (*katharos*, 14:20) or "kosher." In fact, Paul says he thinks all foods are "clean." What we hear in our passage is not only about food *but also about other Torah observances*: sacred days (14:5-6) and circumcision (15:8). It is all but certain then that there is an ethnic connection to the term "Weak." It is not as clear that "Strong" is exclusively gentile, and more will be said about that below.

Some Jewish followers of Jesus were offended by what was available to them as food and so, like Daniel, went vegetarian (Rom 14:2).[9] This tension should be expected: everywhere the gospel went, the issue of food and Sabbath were decisive symbolic markers of faithful observance of the Torah (Gal 2:11-14; Acts 10:13-16; 11:3; 15:19-21). For a letter to begin on the Jew-gentile theme and then flow into a long section on Israel's story and the gentile believers, and then to shift topics and drop that concern, only to bring it up at the end of our passage, beggars narrative coherence. Ethnicity, then, is at the heart of both the tension in Rome and the gospel message itself. One's theology and one's ethnicity cannot be segregated, and neither can one's ethnicity and one's identity be separated.[10] There is, then, a dialectical relationship between ethnicity and theology throughout the entire letter.

The tension between the groups bubbled over the top of the pot often. The language Paul uses reveals that the Strong *despised* the Weak and that the Weak *sat in judgment* on the Strong. Paul's words carry the message well: "Those who eat must not despise those who abstain, and those who abstain must not pass judgment on those who eat; for God has welcomed them. Who are you to pass judgment on servants of another?" (14:3-4). And in 14:10: "Why do you pass judgment on your brother or sister? Or you, why do you despise your brother or sister?" Josephus tells us that Claudius instructed Jews in Egypt not to "despise" the religious practices of others "and not to show a contempt of the superstitious observances of other nations, but to keep their own laws only."[11] Lived theology works like this because embodied life is theology!

The Strong's language is fierce (14:3, 10): the Greek term *exoutheneo* means "to disdain," to treat someone as having no status or merit or worth, and to perceive someone as beneath one's consideration. The Weak's language answers back (14:3-4, 5, 10, 13, 22): the Greek term is *krino* and means to sit in judgment on someone or something and has the sense of playing the part of God in rendering a person's condemnation. This same kind of language describing the Weak here is used in Romans 2 (2:1, 3, 27), where the same strong evocations are at work. In both Romans 2 and 14, the act of judging assumes the role of the divine (cf. 2:3, 12, 16; 3:4, 6; and 14:3-4, 10). This verbal competition brings into expression as it also calls into question the "lived theology" of the Strong and the Weak. Their life excludes the other, that kind of life is their theology, and it is a life of verbal crucifixion of the other.

Both of their takes on the issues are convincing to themselves. The Strong are liberated from Torah observance, while the Weak are faithful to Torah observance. One suspects the behaviors of the Strong are found in the following: "Some believe in eating anything" (14:2), and "others judge all days to be alike" (14:5), and "Everything is clean" (14:20). But I hear an echo or more of the same kind of lived theology in the expressions of Romans 6: "Should we continue in sin?" (6:1), and "do not let sin exercise dominion in your mortal bodies, to make you obey their passions. No longer present your members to sin as instruments of wickedness" (6:12-13). As well as here: "Should we sin because we are not under law but under grace?" (6:15). If the Strong "eat," the Weak "abstain" (14:3) even to the point of having to eat only vegetables (14:2, 21) and avoiding polluted wine (14:21). Lived theology for the Weak means Torah observance; for the Strong it means liberty. They are fully convinced and completely at odds with one another.

Defining Weak and Strong

It is time to draw the threads together. The Weak are Jewish believers who are in the stream of God's election, who know the Torah, who practice the Torah and still probably attend synagogue, but who sit in judgment on gentiles, especially the Strong in the Christian community in Rome. We will add to these elements as we read Romans backwards, but for now these six points are clear. The Strong are predominately gentiles who believe in Jesus as Messiah or king, who do not observe Torah as the will of God for them, and who have condescending and despising attitudes probably toward Jews but especially to Jewish believers in Jesus. This understanding of the Strong, too, will expand as we read Romans backwards.

The tension in Rome cannot be reduced to theological differences; the tension is at the level of lived theology and status. The irony of the Strong and the Weak in Rome is that both claimed Privilege: the Weak claimed their covenant heritage (cf. Rom 9:4-5 with 2:17-21), while the Strong claimed their higher status in the city of Rome (15:1). We can add a singularly important element to our definitions of Weak and Strong. If the food is the unclean food of the pagan temple, if there is an ethnic reality to the Weak (Jewish) and Strong (predominately gentile), there is also a *status issue*. Here we move from the claim of Privilege to that of Power. Romans 15:1 reads in the NRSV: "We who are strong ought to put up with the failings of the weak, and not to please ourselves."

The terms that deserve some scrutiny are "strong" (*dunatoi*), "failings" (*asthenemata*), and "weak" (*adunatoi*). The NIV falls in line with the NRSV, but it is the CEB that brings us into the thick of the social realities in Rome: "We who are *powerful* need to be patient with the weakness *of those who don't have power.*" Yes, that's right: the term behind the NRSV's "strong" and behind its "weak" is a cognate and translated more accurately in the CEB. Paul contrasts the *Dunatoi* and the *A-Dunatoi*. The powerful vs. the unempowered (or disempowered) or, to turn this into spatial categories, those who may well have lived in a home (*domus*) and those who most likely lived in apartments (*insulae*). *Dunatoi* and *A-Dunatoi* are status terms in the Roman world (where status was everything). That is, in Rome one knew the elites (senators, equestrians) from the nonelites, and the competition among the elites was beyond noticeable. In fact, around this time, Claudius—who revived the office of censor, whose responsibilities concerned raising the morality and another reviving ancient sacred rites of the city of Rome—had issued a strong edict about respecting those of high status.[12] Along with these was Claudius' persistence on expanding and enhancing citizenship. One has to wonder if perhaps the Strong had these Claudian concerns, or a threat of their not being able to achieve them, in their corner.

Notice it is the Strong who are told to "welcome" (14:1; 15:1, 7). Why? Power and privilege and status and location are on their side. It is the Weak who need to be welcomed. The act of the Strong welcoming the Weak is a Christoform act of crossing boundaries and turning no status into in-Christ-status. It is to say, "Because we are Strong and have Privilege and Power, we will not broker our Power to divide the faith community, but we will disempower ourselves to empower each sibling at the table and so live out the gospel of Christ."

To summarize now: The Weak are predominately Jewish believers who are in the stream of God's election, who know the Torah, who practice the Torah and still probably attend synagogue, but who sit in judgment on gentiles, especially the Strong in the Christian community in Rome, even though they have no status or Power. We will add to these elements as we read Romans backwards, but for now these five points are clear. The Strong are predominately gentiles who believe in Jesus as Messiah or king, who do not observe Torah as the will of God for them, and who have condescending and despising attitudes probably toward Jews but especially to Jewish believers in Jesus, and all of this is wrapped up in the superior higher status of the Strong in Rome. Another item comes next: Paul is among them, and this slightly reconfigures the ethnic connection for Strong.

What about Paul? Strong or Not?

Attempting to assign Paul to Weak or Strong is worth our effort. If Paul is Strong, then his language about the Weak borders on patronizing and at least smacks of bias in description. It is not possible to call out someone as "Weak" as a compliment. If Paul is Strong, then he has taken sides. It appears he has done just that. First, his working principle stated in 14:14a and 14:20—"I know and am persuaded in the Lord Jesus that nothing is unclean in itself," and "Everything is indeed clean"—is characteristic of the Strong, not the Weak. Second, at 15:1, Paul includes himself among the Strong when he says, "We who are strong." Perhaps most noticeable is that Paul's posture toward halakhic rulings and Torah observance is one of *tolerance*, not observance or endorsement. To say it is a matter of personal conviction, faith, or conscience (cf. 14:5) and to say that whichever view a person takes is done before God (14:6) is the lived theology not of the Weak but of the Strong. One might add here, too, that handing this letter over to Phoebe, a pagan convert who I must assume was on Paul's side, is to hold up as a model a gentile believer.

Again, Paul's *grounding* for his arguments is not "The Torah says." Rather, he speaks of God's welcome in 14:3b; of living before the Lord in 14:7-9 (live before the Lord); of God, not humans, being the final judge in these matters in 14:10-12; of avoiding all stumbling blocks for one another in 14:13-23; of the kingdom being comprised of not food and drink but joy in the Spirit in 14:17; of peace being the arbiter in 14:19; and, once again, of decisions on food and days and drink and Torah observance being a matter of personal conviction, and he exhorts them to make up their mind so as not to be a doubtful state in 14:22-23. What matters to Paul is his mission to spread the gospel about Jesus in the Roman Empire and to bring into one unified family both Jewish and gentile believers (15:7-13, 16-31; 16:25-27). His lived theology emerges from his mission (1 Cor 9:19-23). Paul sides with the Strong on at least the dividing issue in the Roman house churches: he does not think Torah observance is necessary for the lived theology of the Christians in Rome.

Yes, Paul is an equal criticism kind of apostle: he has harsh words for both Strong and Weak and encouraging words for both Weak and Strong. What is noticeable for Paul (and this is one element of Paul that baffles me when I hear people say nasty things about Paul's teachings) is this: *he does not expect everyone to be on the same page*. If the Weak want to avoid pork, that's fine with Paul; if the Strong want to eat pork offered to idols, that's fine, too. If there is anything distinct about Paul's lived theology, it is right here: he may be Strong, and he may think Torah observance is not necessary even for

Jews who believe in Jesus, but he does not demand that all Christians have the same lived theology when it comes to Torah observance. Which means what he is against is demanding uniformity on this issue of Torah observance. The operative terms for Paul, and we will get to this below, are *Welcome one another to the table as siblings!* The whole letter is found in that imperative.

4

ZEALOTRY

(12:14-21; 13:1-7, 8-10)

Barely noticeable unless you read slowly are a couple of expressions in Romans 13:1-4, and only by giving them space to play themselves out do their implications come to the fore. I'm looking at "whoever resists authority" and "those who resist" when tied to "no authority except God" and "be subject" and "instituted by God." Add to this "no fear of the authority" and "do what is wrong." These are terms drawn from civil society's self-perceptions of order, civility, citizenship, and justifiable authority for discipline and punishment. Paul suddenly turns in chapter 13 from general terms about how the Christians of Rome are to treat one another as well as the wider public to language about the empire, the emperor, and resistance. When he is done with these themes, he shifts to taxation. We are meant to combine resistance of authority with taxation, and it makes the reader wonder who might be tempted to resist taxation.

I venture that Paul has in mind once again one of the groups in Rome—namely, the Weak. What I want to say before I make my case is that "Weak" does not represent "Jews" in general. No, the Weak are Jewish believers who are in the stream of God's election, who know the Torah, who practice the Torah and still probably attend synagogue, but who sit in judgment on gentiles, especially the Strong in the Christian community in Rome, even though they have no status or Power. We add now to this description: the Weak were tempted to resist taxes paid to Rome on the basis of their zealotry tradition. I want to contend the Weak of Rome are tempted by the zealotry option, an option provoked not only by Claudius' severe taxation laws but also by the Strong, who are less than wholeheartedly committed to Torah observance and are flouting the sacred laws of Moses. The Weak, then, are in their own eyes courageous, while in the eyes of the Strong they are foolish and also unbending. So what is the zealotry option?

Paul knows a Zealot when he sees one because he was one. He says of himself that he was "far more zealous" than his contemporaries and that zeal led to violence against Jesus' followers (Gal 1:13-14; cf. Phil 3:6). In Acts we read he was "zealous for God" (22:3). Passionate commitment to Torah, observation of those flouting the Torah, zeal, violence, persecution. That's the map of zeal, but it's deeper than Pharisees like Paul. Israel's God is Zeal in being and motion: "I the LORD your God am a jealous God" (Exod 20:5). God's own zeal—the terms "zeal" and "jealousy" are connected in both Hebrew and Greek—provokes Israel's heroes in the faith to zeal. The paradigm is Phinehas (Num 25:6-13), but there are others.[1]

The term "zeal" is not found in Romans 13:1-7, and that at least tosses some dust in the eyes of those zealous to find zealotry here. Caution respected does not mean caution rules. Telling a group in Rome not to resist, to submit, to respect authority, and to pay taxes sounds too much like a response to planned resistance if not a temptation to rebellion and revolution. I suggest, then, that Romans 13:1-7 emerges from the Weak returning to Rome to find themselves not only displaced but with the added problem of increased taxation. In other words, it is less likely that the Weak were turning to physical violence or armed rebellion than resisting taxes. Resistance to Rome by not paying taxes was for them lived theology. I have used the expression "lived theology" a number of times, and it is time now to describe the lived theology Paul had in mind for the Romans.[2]

5

CHRISTOFORMITY—PAUL'S VISION FOR A LIVED THEOLOGY OF PEACE

(14:7-9; 15:3, 5, 7)

The social realities at work in this letter of Paul to the Romans form the context into which Paul forms a lived theology for the house churches: they will encounter this performed letter in the face of Phoebe, they will know the quotidian realities of life in Rome, they will know who lives where and who worships in which home, they will know who the Strong are and who the Weak are, and they will know the temptation to resist taxation. Paul forms a lived theology for precisely that context. I claim that lived theology is the aim of Paul's letter and that Paul's so-called theology sections (chapters 1–8 or 1–11) are as much shaped by his vision of lived theology as the other way around. All of Romans is in dialectical relationship. The claim then is that lived theology is theology and not application, implication, or even ethics—a separate and final section of theology proper.[1] Any reading of Romans that drops 12–16 into anything less than front and center misreads Romans.

The themes of lived theology of Romans 12–16 are not segregated into thematic units but interwoven throughout the entire section. In what follows, I will develop these themes synthetically, putting forth the central theses of the lived theology for Roman house churches. The central idea is Christoformity, and it finds expression in an embodied God orientation, a Body-of-Christ orien- 1, 2, tation, and a public orientation. The result of Christoformity for lived theology 3 is that Power and Privilege are turned toward Peace in the heart of the empire.

CHRISTOFORMITY 12:2

Lived theology is Christoformity, the process of being conformed to Christ. The central themes of two early Christian hymns (Phil 2:6-11; Col 1:15-20) lead directly to his view of Christoformity. Christ is the paradigm, the *eikon*

27

(image) of God, the fundamental revelation of who God is, and this God-in-Christ revelation is one who *because* he was God chose not to stay put but entered missionally into being a human even to the degrading status of one crucified.[2] That missional incarnation created redemption—both removing sin by an atoning death and raising humans to new life by the power of the resurrection—and led the Son of God back to the Throne of God through the ascension. Now on the Throne, the Son rules all creation and promises to bring all of creation to its final liberating redemption. Christoformity then is to enter into that story in union with that person, to be "in Christ," and to live a Christoform life. One might say the lived theology is "Christopraxis."[3] Thus, because of union with Christ, the Roman Christians are not to seek their own life but to seek the life of God-in-Christ for the redemption of others. "Union with Christ" may suggest something on the order of a mystical encounter or an inebriating, intimacy with God-in-Christ. Not for Paul: union with Christ is transformative into Christoformity.

Paul doesn't open up Romans 12:1 or any of his letters by saying, "The essence is Christoformity," so one must recognize the term as part of constructive theology. But there are very clear indicators that the heartbeat of lived theology for him was Christoformity. Two separate passages in Romans 14–15 ground lived theology in the pattern of Christ. Thus, Romans 14:7-9 teaches that Christ's death led to his resurrection, which led to his ascension and rule. So those who live or die "live to the Lord" and "die to the Lord." In such a manner, Christ is "Lord of both the dead and the living." But 15:3, 15:5, and 15:7 are more explicit. The Strong are not to please themselves but to use their Privilege and Power for others. Why? Because "Christ did not please himself." Even more, Christ's choice was not to please himself; instead (now quoting Psalm 69:9) he chose to let the "insults" fall on himself. Rather than claiming his Privilege and Power, Christ chose a life for others. The Strong are then to live a life shaped by pleasing others. If they do, they will find "harmony with one another, *in accordance with Christ Jesus*" (15:5). The Strong and the Weak are each brought into the room to hear Phoebe say, "Welcome one another" (15:7). Why, or how? "Just as Christ has welcomed you, for the glory of God." Here we see lived theology as Christoformity. As we will see in Romans 8, Christoformity is the explicit goal of all redemptive history: "For those whom he foreknew he also predestined *to be conformed to the image of his Son*, in order that he might be the firstborn within a large family" (8:29).

Christoformity becomes the core theme of lived theology. Taking on a Christoform identity is the aim of Paul's Letter to the Romans, and it takes on three separable themes: a God orientation, a Body-of-Christ orientation, and a public orientation.

6

CHRISTOFORMITY IS
EMBODIED GOD ORIENTATION

(12:1-2)

An embodied God orientation involves everything the ancient world included in what we call "religion," but two central elements we will call attention to briefly are sacrifice and prayer. I will focus on the sacrifice. These may be the most famous lived-theology words ever written by the apostle Paul:

> I appeal to you therefore, brothers and sisters, by the mercies of God, to present your bodies as a living sacrifice, holy and acceptable to God, which is your spiritual worship. Do not be conformed to this world, but be transformed by the renewing of your minds, so that you may discern what is the will of God—what is good and acceptable and perfect. (12:1-2)

A few observations are in order.

EMBODIED SACRIFICE

The sacrifice is offered, *first*, because of the transforming power of God's mercy and grace. The word "mercy" is English for more than one Greek word, and Romans 12:1's "by the mercies of God" is *oiktirmos*, a term that both echoes "I will have compassion on whom I will have compassion" (9:15) and forms an element of Paul's theology of two foundational terms: love and grace. The sacrifice of the Romans to God and to one another happens only because of God's goodness to the undeserving, to the idolatrous, to the disobedient, and to the sinful (11:30-32). Both Weak and Strong can offer themselves to God only because God has been merciful.[1] *Second*, the *sacrifice* Paul has in mind is radically new. Instead of offering animals and grains to the gods in local shrines and temples or in the temple in Jerusalem, Christian sacrifice is an *embodied* way of life offered to the invisible but ever-present God. What they *do* is their sacrifice: when they speak, listen, embrace, eat, drink, love, have sexual relations, guide children, offer wisdom, work, garden, pay taxes, offer visible expressions of care, respect, approve and disapprove, pray, participate in fellowship and worship and instruction ... one could go on. Their sacrifice is their embodied life.

This sacrifice, *third*, is *spiritual worship*. The Greek word behind "spiritual" is built on *logos* and is *logikos*, which literally might be rendered "wordy," but other translations include "rational," "logical," and "spiritual." The translation "spiritual" quickly runs against the grain of the verse: instead of embodied sacrifice, it seems to become disembodied sacrifice. A closer look at the term *logikos* in Romans connects it to the word *logos*, which refers to spoken words (3:4; 9:6, 9; 13:9; 15:18). *Logos* in Romans, then, is preeminently a gospel term. The term, I suggest, points us at an embodied, gospel-based worship. Thus, "spiritual," "logical," and "rational" are inadequate translations that create more confusions than clarities. A *logikos* worship is embodied gospel-formed worship. If *logikos* is connected to word/gospel, and gospel is connected to Jesus as God's Son (1:3-4), then *logikos* worship is Christoformity. There's more to be said: their embodied gospel-shaped life *is* their worship. Unlike moderns who use the term "worship" only for the singing portions of Sunday services, their embodied daily life *is* their worship. Once again, Paul is replacing ordinary Roman acts of sacrifice in their home or on the public altars with their embodied Christoformity.

An embodied sacrifice and worship, a lived theology, redefines not only sacrifice but, *fourth*, also "holy." The word "holy" describes God and anything in God's presence, and as such it also describes anything devoted to divine space. Holiness thus evokes a way of life in which God is present in Christ, and thus once again holiness connects to Christoformity. If their embodied way of life is holy, *fifth*, their embodied existence is no longer *conformed to this world* but is *transformed* because of the Spirit's presence (2 Cor 3:18; 4:16–5:5). Their nonconformity to the world is transcended by their conformity to Christ. In speaking here of the "world," Paul has in mind *the world as transitory*.[2] The present transitory age for Paul is the unredeemed world in alliance with the powers and principalities, all in rebellion against its one true Creator, God, the Lord Jesus. For the Romans, it especially means the way of the empire: of embattled competition for honor and status and glory, of idolatries formed in the dust of suppressing knowledge of God as Creator, of sexual indulgence outside the Creator's norms, of rebellion against Roman authorities, and most especially of any life that is not determined by love. Among the Strong and the Weak of Rome, it was experienced as derisive treatment of one another.

Holy Roman Christians are no longer Roman in their embodied way of life, *sixth*, because they are being transformed and renewed in their *minds*. Better yet, the many bodies that become a singular sacrifice also become one *mind* ("mind" is singular in Greek). New creation theology impacts the mind (2 Cor 5:17). The mind, though created by God and designed to worship God and direct humans into love and holiness and justice and peace, is corrupted and corruptible (1:28; 7:25). The mind is a discerning faculty (14:5), and, through an embodied life directed by the Spirit, the mind can be redeemed to become holy and loving and thus morally discerning. Noticeably, if the Weak or the Jewish believer may want to contain the will of God in the Torah (2:18) or the Strong in maintaining status, for Paul this will is known through new creation's mind-transformation. The redeemed, Spirit-prompted mind knows what "is good and acceptable and perfect." But these dimensions of the mind are to become a singular mind in the Body of Christ.

To sum up: this sacrifice is a dual action of God orientation and away-from-the-world orientation. To turn to God, to embody a life that is sacrificial worship, is to turn from the way of Rome, to turn to Christoformity.

PRAYER

God orientation is not only an embodied life of sacrifice; it is a life of prayer. Three times Paul erupts into prayer: 15:13; 16:20; and 16:25-27. I suspect when Phoebe read these prayers, she invited others to assume the postures of prayer. If they praise and pray with their mouths and hands and knees and head as Paul does here, if they practice this along with Phoebe's reading of these prayers and praises, they will orient themselves toward the God of the gospel. Most importantly, if they respond—as they should—with "Amen," Paul's prayers become theirs (11:36; 15:33; 16:27; with 1:25; 9:5).

The *God* of these prayers is described in these benedictions as the "God of hope" or "who gives hope" (15:13), of "peace" (15:33; 16:20), and the closing benediction to the letter expands what is said of God: "able to strengthen you" (16:25), "eternal" (16:26), and "wise" (16:27). Christian prayers sometimes get short on what is said *about* God. The Collects of the church, and I am most familiar with those prayers of the church in *The Book of Common Prayer*, begin by addressing God and then speaking to and about attributes of God. Thus, for the Second Sunday of Advent, "Merciful God" is followed by "who sent your messengers the prophets to preach repentance and prepare the way for our salvation." And a Collect for church musicians and artists goes like this: "O God, whom saints and angels delight to worship in heaven."[3] This church tradition of signaling divine attributes at the onset of a prayer is rooted in the Psalms and the prayers of the Bible like these benedictions in Romans.

Paul's *requests* for the Romans are general Christian virtues that matter most to him—thus: "May the God of hope fill you with all joy and peace in believing, so that you may abound in hope by the power of the Holy Spirit" (15:13). He prays for joy, peace, and hope, and those who adopt his gospel vision will pray the same for others. The middle request, peace, has in mind reconciliation and fellowship between the Strong and the Weak.

Paul also asks both the Weak and the Strong to *intercede* with the Father (through the Son, in the Spirit) for him (15:13, 30), as he does in other letters (1 Thess 5:25; 2 Thess 3:1-5; Col 4:2-4; Eph 6:18-20). He asks them to intercede for him that he may be "rescued from the unbelievers in Judea" and that his "ministry to Jerusalem may be acceptable to the saints." The hope of his request is that beyond the acceptance of the collection, he may both "come to you" and "be refreshed in your company" (15:31-32).

The *benediction* or *doxology*[4] of Romans emerges from the immensity of God and the desire in liturgical contexts to be poetic. One finds similar poetic moments in Romans (cf. 4:25; 8:31-39; 11:33-36; and 15:13):

> Now to God who is able to strengthen you according to my gospel and the proclamation of Jesus Christ, according to the revelation of the mystery that was kept secret for long ages but is now disclosed, and through the prophetic writings is made known to all the Gentiles, according to the command of the eternal God, to bring about the obedience of faith—to the only wise God, through Jesus Christ, to whom be the glory forever! Amen. (16:25-27)

This doxology highlights themes of Paul's theology in Romans (as well as that of Colossians and Ephesians). If this doxology is original to the letter and if a doxology at the end sums up the letter's themes, then this letter is about the inclusion of gentiles in the one family of God, Israel expanded—which it is, and Romans 12–16 brings to the surface the tensions of the churches of Rome that need to embrace the grace God has for both the Weak and the Strong. Paul praises the God of this plan for history, but to whom does "to whom" in the last line refer? One can't get back to the Father except through the Son, in grammar and revelation. The very pattern of Paul's prayers is also Christoform.

Finally, prayer in Romans is *proto-Trinitarian*. Directed to God the Father (15:13, 30, 32, 33; 16:20, 25, 27), the prayers occur through the Son (15:30; 16:27) and in the Spirit (15:13, 30; cf. 14:17; 15:16). The Son's location in the godhead is secured when one speaks of the "grace of our Lord Jesus Christ be with you" as a Christian benediction in parallel with the "God of peace" (16:20).[5] Prayers are offered not to the Son or to the Spirit in the New Testament but only to the Father through the Son in the Spirit.

Lived theology is the aim of Romans, and lived theology begins with an embodied life that is oriented toward God. Because it is oriented toward God, this lived theology also has an embodied Body-of-Christ orientation.

7

CHRISTOFORMITY IS EMBODIED BODY-OF-CHRIST ORIENTATION

(12:3-8; 14–15; 16:17-20)

A God orientation can easily get lost in the upper reaches of individualism, solitude, or mystical devotion, but, for Paul, God orientation is an embodied life with others. The church, the Body of Christ, is that embodied life with others.[1] The themes in Romans 12–16 take us to the heart of lived theology in Romans.[2] Phoebe's readings of Romans created the most tension in what she said about the Strong and the Weak and in how Paul wanted them to live, and I will focus on five themes designed specifically for that very audience.

BODY LIFE

To live an embodied life for God is to live with other bodies in the Body of Christ (12:3-8). The danger in that Body then is a danger in the Body today: "not to think of yourself more highly than you ought to think" (12:3). One might translate this as not to be "superminded."[3] Surely, Paul has in mind the Strong who know, indwell, and are jealous of their status in the Roman Empire. Surely, he, too, has in mind the Weak's claim of covenant priority. Each could and did play the Privilege card. It is noticeable, after Paul's much-memorized God orientation thesis in 12:1-2, that he immediately speaks of supermindedness. Why? Readers will not hear the words from Phoebe until 14:1–15:13, but readers of Romans know that supermindedness was flourishing in Rome among both the Weak and the Strong. Supermindedness was about the claim of Power and Privilege. Which is why they both need a God orientation that moves directly into a Body-of-Christ orientation. Paul opens this paragraph by speaking to "everyone," both Weak and Strong (12:3). Instead of protecting and claiming social, ethnic, or gift status, Paul exhorts the Christians in Rome to use "sober judgment," and that means thinking of oneself "according to the measure of faith God has assigned."[4] The term "faith" surprises, for in context it means "spiritual gift" rather than how much personal faith a person has. The antidote to supermindedness is to see oneself through God's assignment for one in the Body of Christ.

Why call the church a "body"? Romans and Greeks used "body" (*soma*) for the body politic, and the term "church" (*ekklesia*) was used for the gathered citizens (*demos*) in a political assembly. It was impossible for these terms not to have political overtones. Combine "church" with "body," and we are confronted with a Pauline claim: the local house churches were an alternative body politic. Add to this that the Spirit creates and animates this body, and that it is the Body *of Christ*, and you now have a new "emperor," the Lord Jesus, and a new Spirit-Power at work. One has here a Spirit-prompted embodied people under King Jesus. The Strong can't do it alone; the Weak can't do it alone; together they can embody the sacrifice to become God's design for humans in this world. Apart from the Spirit, they spend their energies judging who has Privilege and Power; with the Spirit they can find the true version of Rome's biggest claim, *Pax Romana* ("Roman peace"), "Peace in the Body of Christ." Peace is achieved in the Body through spiritual gifts.

But what are these diverse gifts of the Spirit? In different contexts Paul lists different gifts (e.g., 1 Cor 12:12-31; Eph 4:11; cf. 1 Pet 4:10-11), but here to the Romans he mentions prophesying, ministering, teaching, exhorting, giving, leading, and being compassionate. Each, it needs to be noted, is a "function" (*praxis*, 12:4), which is to say each gift is something practiced or done, not something owned or possessed. The gifts are what happens when the Spirit of God takes the sacrifice of an embodied Christian and uses it for the good of the Body of Christ. Prophets speak revelations from God to the people of God "according to the rule of faith" (my translation; Greek, *kata ten analogian tes pisteos*; cf. 1 Cor 12:29, 32);[5] those ministering serve the Body of Christ in a multitude of ways; those teaching mentor believers into wisdom and maturity; those exhorting inspire others to courage, to self-sacrifice, to love, to holiness, and to obedience. Paul adds giving because he is so intent on the collection for the poor saints in Jerusalem (15:16, 25-33). He comes next to leading (also at 1 Thess 5:12)—which means being out in front of others who trust and follow such a person (on the basis of calling, position, and example) in the direction of communal Christoformity—and being cheerful (the Greek term is cognate with our term "hilarity") in compassion, which taps again the key of giving as it moves the person toward those in need. Surely, the apostle has in mind especially the Strong when it comes to compassion on the Weak. The gifts are assigned not to the Strong *or* to the Weak but to *both* the Weak *and* the Strong.

This passage illustrates that the gifts Paul mentions in his various listings are shaped by the needs of particular congregations.

GENEROSITY

Genuine Christoformity, it needs to be recalled, is a "not Y but Z" kind of life: not self-status and self-pursuit but other-status and other-orientation.[6] Generosity toward others flows from the way of Christ as fjords flow from the oceanic waters in Scandinavia. That ocean is God's superabundant and generous grace, and that such surprising divine generosity overflows into Christian generosity. Paul's theology of generosity is shaped by his gentile mission and its dependence on the Jerusalem church and by the role he wanted Rome to play in that mission.

We need to understand that Paul's *mission map* (15:19, 28)[7] is rooted in divine mission, which he here describes in priestly terms: "because of the grace given me by God to be a minister of Christ Jesus to the Gentiles in the priestly service of the gospel of God, so that the offering of the Gentiles may be acceptable, sanctified by the Holy Spirit" (15:15b-16; cf. 1:5; 12:3). The language could not be more suggestive: the gentiles offer themselves to God in the collection's funds (15:25-33) because the Holy Spirit has made them *kosher* for the temple itself.[8] His desire is that this offering would be accepted both by God and by the church leaders in Jerusalem (cf. 15:31-32). Generosity crops up because of Paul's *plans*. Now that he has gone from Jerusalem to Illyricum he is ready to go through Rome to Spain (15:22-24). Since his mission is to plant new churches and not invade the mission locations of others (15:20), his plan is a brief stay in Rome. What he didn't know was that he would get to Rome in shackles, nor did he know that it would occur much farther down the road than he planned.

In the context of that mission map and those plans, the tangible expression of generosity Paul had in mind concerned *the poor saints of Jerusalem*. As Paul puts it, "I am going to Jerusalem in a ministry to the saints" (15:25). Paul describes the collection here with three terms: *diakonia* ("ministry"), *koinonia* ("share their resources"), and *karpos* ("what has been collected," or, better yet, "sealed to them this fruit"). From the very outset of the Pauline mission to the gentiles, Paul was urged to remember the poor saints of Jerusalem (Gal 2:1-10; cf. Acts 11:27-30; 12:25). Some (I agree) think Paul's collection was a two-decades-long fundraising mission alongside the establishment and instruction of his churches,[9] while others think it more likely he was involved in two different fundraisers, one early, in conjunction with Antioch (Gal 2:1-10), and the other a more spontaneous expression of church unity beginning with his third missionary journey.[10] Regardless, the collection receives special mention in 1 Corinthians 16:1-4, is behind every line in 2 Corinthians 8–9, and then appears again in Romans 15—all written about the same time.

How did Paul *understand* this collection? These funds were a visible sign of the unity of the church (Gal 2:10; Rom 15:26-27). In a Roman world where social status and connections were zippered tight by benefaction and reciprocity, Paul was personally obligated to Jerusalem as the mother church and as the nexus of Israel's story, and to the Jerusalem leaders for affirming his mission (Gal 2:1-10). Also, in a Roman Empire where economic benevolence for the poor was far from common, and in a Jewish world where caring for the poor was common legislation, Paul's collection was Torah observance to the core. Most noticeably, in 2 Corinthians 8:13-15, Paul speaks of the collection as embodied economic justice and equality (*isotes*). One must then see in the collection more than unity, reciprocity, and compassion: Paul believed Christians were to develop a culture of economic generosity within the fellowship of believers in order to create economic justice for all believers, and once again we need to be especially cognizant of the Weak's probable economic challenges.

Romans 15, when compared with the letters to Corinth, strikes *a new tone of worship* for the collection. To be sure, as with what he said to Corinth, the collection's roots dig themselves deeply into God's gracious gift of redemption (2 Cor 8:9; 9:8). That is, God's gift prompts reciprocal giving to others. But this theological-social sense of reciprocity spills over in Romans 15 into depicting the collection as *worship*. Thus, in verses 15-16, Paul says, "because of the *grace* given me by God to be a *minister* of Christ Jesus to the Gentiles in the *priestly service* of the gospel of God, so that *the offering* of the Gentiles may be *acceptable, sanctified by the Holy Spirit*." Perhaps the gentiles themselves are the sacrifice, but there are solid reasons to think that he has in mind not the gentiles themselves but their funds. Notice how Paul speaks of this in verse 27: "for if the Gentiles have come to share in their spiritual blessings, they ought also to be of service to them in material things." That is, their material gift is an offering to the poor of Jerusalem. Even more, they are *obligated to Jerusalem* (surely good news to the Weak, surely a stiff reminder to the Strong) because of Israel's covenantal priority and God's utter faithfulness to Israel (1:16; 2:9, 17-24, 28-29; 3:12; 9–11).

Christoformity is a God orientation where the grace of God-in-Christ given to a person prompts Body-of-Christ orientation in generosity, especially toward the poor. As the collection for the saints was designed to express gratitude by the gentiles to the rootstock of Israel, and thus to the saints in Jerusalem, so a third mark of Christoformity in the Body of Christ is peace and unity.

PEACE AND UNITY

Anyone who dwells on the social realities of the house churches in Rome, especially on the tension between the Strong and the Weak, will not be surprised by Paul's theme of peace and unity. The various commands and prohibitions of Romans 12:9-21 revolve around peace and unity. Paul wants peace between the Roman house churches and Rome (13:1-7), and nearly every verse in 14:1–15:13 is somehow connected to both Weak and Strong learning to live in unity with one another. The collection is about unity of the Roman Christians with Jerusalem's (15:22-29), and, just before the curtain falls on this letter, Paul strikes out with surprisingly strong language about dissensions:

> I urge you, brothers and sisters, to keep an eye on those who cause dissensions and offenses, in opposition to the teaching that you have learned; avoid them. For such people do not serve our Lord Christ, but their own appetites, and by smooth talk and flattery they deceive the hearts of the simple-minded. For while your obedience is known to all, so that I rejoice over you, I want you to be wise in what is good and guileless in what is evil. The God of peace will shortly crush Satan under your feet. The grace of our Lord Jesus Christ be with you. (16:17-20)

The condescending judgments of the Strong and the reactive judgments of the Weak in the Roman churches are divisive, and the terms Paul uses are strong: "dissensions and offenses," from *dichostasia* and *skandala*. One must think of house church fractures and factions and fissures cracking up the fellowship. One must also think of the genius of the Pauline mission to knock down dividing lines and the message of the gift of redemption available to Jewish and gentile believers, the Weak and the Strong.

Those fracturing the fellowship "do not serve our Lord Christ" (16:18). So they are to know this: "The God of peace will shortly crush Satan under your feet" (16:20). Which is to say, the dissensions and offenses created by the judges in their midst are diabolical! God wants the Strong and the Weak to crush that diabolical work. How will they crush Satan? The answer is the first word (in English) in chapter 14: "Welcome." Three times in our passage—14:1, 14:3, 15:7—Paul urges them to welcome one another. Table fellowship symbolizes welcome, but "Welcome" is expressed in praying for and with one another, knowledge of one another's names and life and family, material availability to one another, standing with and for one another, and helping one another in Christoformity. To welcome is to cease being the Judges and to become a sibling. To welcome is to create space for peace and unity.

TOLERANCE

There is probably no better or worse word for Paul's instructions in Romans 14:1–15:13 than *tolerance*. Paul puts special weight on the Power and Privilege of the Strong carrying the responsibility and potential for taking the first step toward peace, unity, and reconciliation. Both 14:1 and 15:1 bear this out. We begin there.

What stands tall in Paul's movement into tolerance is his *working conclusion*. In 14:14, Paul says, "I know and am persuaded in the Lord Jesus that nothing is unclean in itself." The Weak surely did not agree, but they aren't writing the letter. Paul is, and that's where he begins. He immediately concedes ground: "but it is unclean for anyone [like the Weak] who thinks it unclean." The Weak deserve respect for their decisions (he's telling the Strong; cf. 14:1, 2, 22-23; 15:13). The working conclusion shifts only slightly in 14:17: "For the kingdom of God is not food and drink but righteousness and peace and joy in the Holy Spirit." What was to regulate access to the Strong's household dining room in Rome was the will of God-in-Christ (righteousness), the reconciliation of Jew and gentile (peace), and inner satisfaction that this is the way of Christ for the people of God (joy). All in the Holy Spirit! "Kingdom of God" in the New Testament is more than the redemptive dynamic unleashed by Christ in the new era but a social matrix of God as king, God's rule by way of redemption and governance, God's people, God's will, and God's space embodied by this people. As food and drink consumed embody church unity, so kingdom is embodied in these virtues for the kingdom to be what it is.[11] In other words, the kingdom wants to become a social reality called "church." To sum this up: Paul's working conclusion is that the kingdom of God's arrival suspends food as a dividing line.

"Nice idea," I say to myself when reading Romans 14–15, "but what does this actually look like?" There are a few guidelines in Paul's theology of tolerance. Before we get to the first, we should observe a *lack of interest in freedom*. One might argue that tolerance implies freedom, and one would have to agree at least in part. The other part, however, can't be ignored. If the theme of the Christian life in Galatians is freedom (Gal 5:1), that is most noticeably *not* the issue for the Roman house churches. The *eleuther-* word group ("freedom") is not in Paul's view in these chapters.[12] What is in view?

His first guideline is *to avoid stumbling blocks* (14:13b, 15, 20-21). In Rome this would mean, to take an obvious example, the Strong insisting the Weak eat pork from the market. The impact of the insistence is a Weak person failing in his or her faith. Paul is not worried that Christians will disagree, for he has already affirmed diversity of viewpoints when he said some eat and some don't, some observe days and others don't (14:3, 5-6). His worry is the destruction of the Weak person's faith! Here are Paul's terms in a graduated incline of seriousness as the passage moves onward: "stumbling block," "hindrance," "injured" (or grieved), "ruin," and "destroy." When insistence destroys the faith of the Weak, the Insister is the one who is wrong. The second guideline for the Strong, which has already been discussed above (on 13:8-10), is *love*. If the Strong insist on the Weak eating food offered to idols, Phoebe, now looking them in the eyes, says, "you are no longer walking in love" (14:15). The third guideline for the Strong concerns the *public*: "Do not let your good [the Strong eating of all foods] be spoken of as evil," or, as I would render it for this context, "be blasphemed" (14:16). The fourth guideline for the Strong is *pursuing peace and mutual upbuilding* (14:19). The fifth guideline is perhaps the most pastoral of all: *the Strong are to respect the Weak's faith condition* (14:22-23). Phoebe turns her eyes toward the Strong in the room: "The faith that you have, have as your own conviction before God" (14:22a). She gives them one more line: a blessing for those whose approval of food does not result in condemning themselves by forcing others to conform. Turning to the Weak in verse 23, she pastorally offers them another way: not to eat if they have doubts (14:23a). Faith in the sense of personal conviction and conscience comes to the fore: whatever is not based on that kind of faith is sin. The churches of Rome are to be places not of coercion but of tolerance of genuine differences between the Weak and the Strong.

Body life, generosity, peace and unity, and tolerance. Now a sixth—and the sixth is the one that matters most. Paul's biggest and best question for the Strong as well as for the Weak is this one: With whom did you dine last night? He'll press it further: Are you the Strong dining with the Weak or not? Yes or no? That's the question, and *the whole book rides on that question as the heart of lived theology*. His sixth point is *welcome*.

WELCOMING TO THE TABLE

The central action of Christian ethics for Paul in Romans is welcome, the foundation is the grace of God in Christ, and the true end of that act of welcoming is the glory of God. *How* the Strong or the Weak were to get to the act of welcome is not spelled out in detail. Reading Romans backwards will get us there, for it shows that Romans 1–4 and 5–8 offer what amounts to two alternatives, one proposed by the Weak and one proposed by Paul, whose proposal stands against both the Strong and the Weak! But that's getting ahead of ourselves. For now we have to look at the theme of welcome.

The instruction to welcome is found at 14:1 and 15:7, and it lurks in 15:1 in other terms ("put up with" means "to shoulder the differences and decisions of the Weak"):

> Welcome those who are weak in faith, but not for the
> purpose of quarreling over opinions. (14:1)
> We who are strong ought to put up with the failings of the weak,
> and not to please ourselves. (15:1)
> Welcome one another, therefore, just as Christ has welcomed you,
> for the glory of God. (15:7)

This welcoming is about eating with one another. It is about invitations to those unlike us to our home and our table and our prayers and our food, and it is about doing this as siblings, not rivals and enemies. In Romans 15:7-13, Paul provides a rationale for a theology of the Strong and the Weak welcoming one another. Four moves are then made in this passage: there is an exhortation (15:7), then a christological foundation for welcoming both Jews (15:8) and gentiles (15:9), followed both by a series of citations from the Old Testament about including gentiles (15:10-12) and by a benediction (15:13). We turn now to each in turn.

The *exhortation* (15:7). Welcome is the lived theology when division is the problem. The Strong's primary act of Christoformity will be to welcome the Weak to the table without argument and without coercion (14:1). But Paul is an equal-opportunity critic, for in this passage the welcome is something for both Strong and Weak. If one reads 15:8-12 without pausing, it becomes clear that Christ himself is to glorify God among the gentiles, and, *because the Roman believers are to become Christoformed*, they, too, will welcome one another as an expression of glorifying God. This theme of God's glory turns on the Strong and the Weak division: rather than focusing on themselves, Paul wants them to turn their focus on God and God's glory (15:1-2, 6).

Welcome *embodies Christoformity* because the (Jewish) Messiah both welcomed and became a "servant" for both Jews and gentiles (15:8-9). This is the Christological foundation for the Christian ethic at work in Paul's exhortation to the Romans. The order matters to Paul: God worked first with the Jews and then with the gentiles—that is, God's covenant is made with Israel and through them also to the gentiles. This glorious expansion of the people of God is anchored in the "truth of God" and the "promises given to the patriarchs."

First-century Bible readers like Paul either had the Bible committed to memory or in conversation with others could come up with texts that mattered, and in this instance Paul *turns to the Bible* to deepen his argument for welcoming one another. Here, Phoebe must be especially looking at the Weak to remind them of what their Bible says. Paul combines the Greek translations of Psalm 18:49 with Deuteronomy 32:43, with Psalm 117:1, and then finally with Isaiah 11:10. There appears to be a subtle move in these quotations, but it hinges on knowing *Who* is speaking in the first use of the Old Testament: "Therefore *I* will confess you among the Gentiles." If the "I" is Christ himself,[13] then perhaps the first three citations are spoken by Christ to the churches of Rome! And it appears Christ is the one speaking: in verse 8, we read, "Christ . . . might confirm," and Christ continues into verse 9 with "might glorify." If this is the case, then Christ is speaking in the quotation in verse 9. That is, it is Christ who will confess God among the gentiles (15:9), then perhaps also (I only suggest) it is Christ who exhorts the gentiles to rejoice "with his people" (Israel, the Weak, 15:10), and then it is also Christ who exhorts the gentiles to "praise the Lord" (15:11). The fourth citation from the Old Testament, then, is a commentary by Paul on Jesus as the ruler of the gentiles, too! This theme of the praise of the gentiles, which is present in each citation from the Old Testament, reveals the doxological orientation of the Pauline mission and anticipates how he understands the collection for the saints (15:15-16, 25-27).

We have not wandered from the concrete expression of lived theology here that crystallizes into the theme of welcoming one another as siblings. As Christ has welcomed the Strong and the Weak, so the Strong and the Weak are to welcome one another. And as Christ welcomed them, so too it was Christ speaking through the Scriptures to announce that the work of God in the world expanded from Israel into the gentiles to bring them all into one family, the Body of Christ. Paul's focus here is not on Jews in general but on Jewish believers in Jesus as Messiah, and it is they who are to see in these Scriptures a summons to welcome the Strong to the table as siblings.

Rom
Wake Up! 13:11

8

CHRISTOFORMITY
IS PUBLIC ORIENTATION

(12:14–13:10)

The lived theology the believers in Rome practiced in the Body of Christ was to filter its way out into their relationships and orientation toward the Roman Empire. For the Strong, a public face would have been perhaps a more comfortable task; for the Weak, especially if they had been expelled from Rome, the challenge would have been far more difficult. They may well have resented the public orientation Paul teaches.

Love First

It begins with love, the central core of Pauline ethics. His direct statements about the empire in Romans 13:1-7 are preceded and followed by statements about love. Thus, "Let love be genuine" in 12:9 means "cease hypocritical pretenses about loving one another and welcome one another to the table." Then, after addressing the temptation to zealotry, Paul says, "Owe no one anything, except to love one another; for the one who loves another has fulfilled the law... [all the commandments] are summed up in this word, 'Love your neighbor as yourself.' Love does no wrong to a neighbor; therefore, love is the fulfilling of the law" (13:8-10). With the Weak and the Strong's tension clearly in view, he gives the grounding test for all behaviors: "If your brother or sister is being injured by what you eat, you are no longer walking in love" (14:15). This love is generated by the Spirit (15:30). Every step into the public is a step toward loving one's neighbor.

Public Ethics

Peter informs his readers about how to relate to the public (1 Pet 2:11–3:12), and Romans 12–16 appears to be the Pauline version of such instruction. In particular, Paul asks the Jesus movement in Rome to face Rome in 12:14–13:10. To understand this section, we need to set the context, and, in so doing, I will contend the focus is especially on the Weak because it was the Weak who had experienced the rough hand of Claudius.

Expulsion and Taxation

Behind the Letter to the Romans was an event on the Roman calendar that went largely unnoticed except to Jews and Christians, an event discussed briefly earlier. By way of reminder, in AD 49, Emperor Claudius expelled Jews from Rome over what a contemporary called the "Chrestus" affair, and surely he meant the "Christ" affair. The expulsion is mentioned in Acts 18:2 ("because Claudius had ordered all Jews to leave Rome"). There are reasons to think the problems arose because of conversions to Christianity that were occurring among high-status Romans. Behind Romans is yet another issue for Jews and Christians: the burden of taxes. Roman historian Tacitus tells us that "there were persistent public complaints against the companies farming indirect taxes from the government." So, he continues, "Nero [the date is not clear] contemplated a noble gift to the human race: he would abolish every indirect tax. But the senators . . . restrained his impulse." (These indirect taxes were on goods entering and leaving Rome.) What was the result? Some adjustment: "Nero's advisers agreed that tax-collectors' acquisitiveness must be restrained."[1] Suetonius confirms that Nero mitigated taxation.[2] When Paul urges the Christians of Rome to pay taxes (Rom 13:6-7), he probably has this irritation with taxation in mind. That irritation was especially severe for the Weak. Temptations to protest or revolt were all the more inviting.

Reading Romans 13:1-7 in Context

The chapter divisions in our Bibles range from the useful to the mistaken. The chapter break at 13:1 prevents many from reading our passage well: the actual passage runs from 12:14 through 13:10. Snipping off the distinctive Christian ethic (12:14-21 and 13:8-10) and reading 13:1-7 apart from the distinctive ethic of those two passages cuts off the hands and the feet of this text. Romans 12:3-8 and 12:9-13 describe how Christians are to relate *to one another*, while in Romans 12:14 Paul turns most especially to how Roman believers were to relate *to non-Christians*, and that section extends all the way to 13:10. Hence, the famous passage about the "church and state" (13:1-7) comes in the middle of a discussion of how Christians, with a focused attention on the Weak, are to relate to outsiders in a distinctively Christian

way, and the verses before (12:14-21) and after (13:8-10) are to shape 13:1-7.
Here is a basic outline:

Beginning: Bless, empathize, pursue peace (12:14-21)
Middle: Be subject to governing authorities (13:1-7)
End: Love your neighbor (13:8-10)

Beginning and End

We can begin with the strategies at work in the beginning and the end.[3] The
beginning (12:14-21) has strategies for how to manage life in Rome with
Nero on the throne, and the overwhelming impression gained from this
passage is that at least some of the Roman believers were tempted to revolt by
resisting taxation. First, they are to *bless* their opponents (cf. 1 Cor 4:12), and
this blessing echoes Jesus (Luke 6:27-28) and carries with it the redemptive
power of God's blessings (Num 6:24-26). Second, they are *to empathize with*
both ends of the happiness scale: rejoice with those who rejoice and weep
with those who weep (12:15). Third, they are to *pursue peace* (12:18-21). The
end of this larger passage has a fourth strategy that encapsulates the first
three strategies: *love of neighbor* (13:8-10). To be sure, they are to love "one
another" as Christians, but Paul's love is not restrictive: he opens the door to
"another / the Other" and the "neighbor." Loving one's neighbor is found in
the New Testament most often when love is to be shown to outsiders (Matt
5:43; Luke 10:29, 36; Jas 2:8). Here, Paul also has in mind those outside
the Christian house churches. Four strategies for the Roman believers, now
especially sensitive to their Jewish connections and the increasing weight of
taxation on a disenfranchised people, are mentioned: blessing their enemies;
sympathizing and empathizing; peacemaking; and especially loving one
another and loving one's enemies into neighbors. The temptation of revenge is
countered with the strategy of love. Romans 13:1-7, then, is not a theoretical
discussion of church and state but a pastoral aside in an exhortation of learning how to love when the odds are stacked against you. No one in the house
churches of Rome felt the sting of Paul's words more deeply than the Weak.

Middle (13:1-7)

To bless, to empathize, and to pursue peace by loving others entails being
"subject to the governing authorities" (13:1). Rome, formed as it was on a
mixed history of theoretical politics of Athens, became a veritable machine
of empire building, efficiency, power, provision, construction, and expansion

through military might and political maneuvering. Rome was sustained by a wide range of "governing authorities." Stay in line or get crushed was the message. For gentile believers, especially those who grew up in Rome, Paul's counsel of subjection was ho-hum, for there were no other options. For the Weak, Paul's approach of subjection grated against their history of oppression. No one heard these words theoretically; everyone heard "subject to the governing authorities" from their own experience. When a white Republican repeats these words in the United States, an African, Asian, or Latin American hears oppression. One person's subjection is another's oppression. One woman's pragmatics is another woman's silencing. One person's strategy for mission is another person's impossibility in life.

Two readings of this passage dominate Christian discussion. The first is a *conservative* approach that affirms divine providence in governments, including Rome in the early reign of Nero, but often this conservative approach attempts to *contextualize* the passage. That is, our passage is about Nero's early years, about a marginal number of Christians (perhaps one hundred), and about the Strong learning to embrace the Weak. It is not about twenty-first-century American political engagement, or Hitler's Germany or Stalin's Soviets, or Afghani or North Korean or Iranian or Iraqi leaders oppressing Christians. The conservative contextualizers continue: Paul is exhorting the hotheads of Rome not to turn to resistance or revolution out of enthusiasm over Jesus as Lord, the kingdom's presence, or the Spirit's power to overcome. Or perhaps Paul is simply offering a cooler-headed, pragmatic, and psychologically subtle approach to difficult days for the churches in Rome. Or perhaps Paul has mission uppermost in his mind: if we get out of hand, he is saying, the churches will be extinguished, what we have gained will be eradicated, and the Lord will be shamed in public—so stay out of trouble, keep your heads down, be good citizens (cf. 1 Pet 2:10-17). But many conservative approaches fail to read our passage in light of what precedes and what follows.

Others, taking a second approach, think Paul's words are at least suggestive of *revolution.* Though words like "subject to the governing authorities" can give an impression of endorsing all governments, the New Testament itself and Paul's life do not confirm such an approach.[4] Inherent to the Bible's story and to Judaism's story is a routine respect for government as part of God's own providential sovereignty over all creation and all authorities.[5] Yes, Jews were nonetheless unafraid of withering critique of paganism's idolatries and authorities, and, therefore, they lived out the necessity of subverting false gods and unjust rulers. This at times was accompanied by a refusal to obey pagan leaders when they required disobedience to the Torah. That refusal was punctuated with memories of suffering for obeying God. For Paul, inherent to this very common Jewish story is a denial of the zealotry option and instead the explicit conscious intention to strike back with the blessings of love and peacemaking. This is one instance of Christoformity. One can see this larger posture toward pagan authorities in the New Testament from Jesus (Matt 4; 21:21) to Revelation. In the Old Testament, read Daniel.

Subjection, we contend, expresses Paul's four strategies of blessing, empathizing, peacemaking, and love. Of these four, peacemaking is to the fore. One might instead call the *subjection* of 13:1-7 a fifth strategy. The zealotry temptation of the Weak is why Paul appeals to the strategy of *nonvengeance as the Christoform way of life*. In such a context, subjection and the divine ordering of government can be both affirmed *and* not sanctioned. There are too many times when the divine ordering of government is corrupted by evil people. Rulers, Paul is saying, are designed by God to be God's servants (13:4) and so are to do good and to establish justice (13:2-5). Which is not to say they always do. Paul says it is the God of the Bible, not the Roman gods and emperors, who ordains government. Above the Roman "governing authorities," then, are not the gods of Rome but the God of the crucified, raised, and ruling Messiah—King Jesus.

Paying taxes, like subjection to the governing authorities, is a second expression of the fifth strategy. Here, Paul asks the Weak—some of whom, as recently arrived emigrants, were suffering under increased burdens of taxation—to baptize their economic condition into Christoformity and to pay taxes[6] for the sake of the gospel and the safety of the churches in Rome. The suggestion, then, is that Paul's strategy is pragmatic but in an entirely new Christoform key. Some of these believers know the way of violence and retaliation; they have seen it work for liberation in the days of the Maccabees. But Paul knows the way of the cross: the followers of Jesus in Rome are to pay taxes and submit to those dedicated authorities as a way of blessing, peacemaking, and loving one's enemies into neighbors.

PUBLIC BENEVOLENCE

Anyone familiar with how the Roman Empire worked—and one could say such is still alive in many ways in our world—knows that reciprocal benevolence is the game many play. That is, the wealthy give, and, in giving, relations are established, expectations formed, and obligations set. The idea of a purely altruistic gift is not how the world works. It is Kantian and not Roman. Giving created social bonds that created reciprocal benevolence, and thus a culture of connections was formed. Gifts created a boundaried, private, mutual-exchange society.

In the midst of our Paul telling the Weak and the Strong how to relate to Rome, we read these lines:

> For rulers are not a terror to good conduct, but to bad. Do you wish to have no fear of the authority? Then do what is good, and you will receive its approval. (Rom 13:3)

Several comments are in order if we want to understand what lived theology looked like in Paul's vision for the Roman churches. There is in this verse a tacit recognition that the ultimate benefactor, the Roman emperor (Nero at the time), has created a culture of benevolence and reciprocation, of patronage and service. As the Benevolent One, the emperor can punish evildoers, or he can *praise and give glory* to those who *donate goods to him and to the public*. Those italicized words are my paraphrase of the cited words above: "do what is good, and you will receive its approval." The terms "good conduct" (*agatho ergo*), "do what is good" (*to agathon poiei*), and "approval" (*epainon*) are all drawn from the social custom of public benevolence that elicits public honor for the donor. These are terms found also for the same kind of public benevolence in 1 Peter (e.g., 2:15, 20; 3:16, 17; 4:19). The language Paul uses for paying taxes (Rom 13:6-7) morphs into public benevolence and public recognition for donors.

If we add these together, I believe we get at least a suggestion, and probably more, that Paul expected the believers in Rome to do what they could for the common good. The context of zealotry leads us to think that Paul is urging the Weak of Rome to consider how they might contribute to the common good rather than resist the empire burdens of taxation. Christoformity subverts public rebellion and turns it toward generosity. The way of Rome could be turned on its head by "striking back" with love, civility, and benevolence.

To summarize lived theology: the central idea is Christoformity, and it is formed by an embodied God orientation, a Body-of-Christ orientation, and a public orientation. The fundamental core to Christoformity is that because you are in Christ, you are not to act according to Privilege and Power but instead to love God by offering your entire body daily to God, to live as siblings with all other Christians by welcoming one another and eating at the table with each other and indwelling one another, and to love your Roman neighbor as yourself with civility and intentional acts of benevolence. That, for Paul, is lived theology for the Roman Christians. That lived theology gave rise to Romans 1–11. Turned around, Romans 1–11 are designed to form the lived theology of Romans 12–16.

9

Read 13:11-14 aloud

KNOW THE TIME IS NOW

(13:11-14) *wake up!*

Humans have innate skills at deciding what is right and what is wrong, and no doubt the Strong had their ways of knowing, just as the Weak had their ways. The clunker in the conversation is that we differ sometimes so dramatically that we either quarrel with one another or must conclude that each person must make up her or his own mind about each moral decision—which of course is fine until you conclude something that impacts me, which is what was happening in Rome among the house churches. The Bible is filled with moral decisions and judgments. How are moral claims made? What Paul says in the paragraph of 13:11-14 is fundamental to understanding Romans, and Romans is fundamental to understanding it.

The ethics of the New Testament comes to expression from several standpoints: sometimes, it is revealed by God or in the incarnation of God in Christ (an ethic from above); at other times, it is formed through the gifts of wisdom (an ethic from below); while at other times, it is an ethic rooted in the final kingdom (an ethic from beyond). In other words—law, wisdom, prophecy. The prophetic ethic from beyond is varied: sometimes, a warrant for an ethical behavior is a threat on the basis of future divine judgment, while, other times, it is the reward of future redemption. The New Testament operates with another form of eschatological ethics—namely, in the incursion of God into our human reality. Sometimes, time almost stops and calls us to stand still to look at the new revelation in a way that reconfigures everything we have ever known.

Our paragraph, one might say, seems steadily to march forwards until the last lines: the incursion of Christ means the believers in Rome can no longer live as they once did. Everything has changed. Christian morality, then, is more than knowing the judgment is coming. Eschatology takes shape only when one comprehends who Christ is and what he has accomplished.

51

Only then does time—the past, the present, and the future—make sense. Put differently, Christology creates a new kind of eschatological ethics for a new time in history.

There are always two themes in eschatological ethics: the time is at hand (imminency and immanency), and, therefore, here's how to live (ethics). Paul moves through both of these themes in Romans 13:11-14: "you know what time it is," and "it is now the moment to wake from sleep," and "salvation is nearer to us now than when we became believers," and "the night is far gone, the day is near." Christian eschatology—which has been captured by wildly unimportant speculations like the time of the rapture and the marks of the beast and identifying the antichrist—is shaped by four epochs: the created design for all creation broken by sin and redeemed by God through covenant; the unleashing of redemption in Christ and the Spirit in the church; the war against evil and the defeat and elimination of it; and, finally, the permanent establishment of justice, peace, love, and wisdom in the kingdom. Redemption in the New Testament is neither now nor future. It is both now and future. We live in epoch two now, and those in epoch two are always looking for the arrival of epochs three and four. Those in epoch two not looking forwards to epochs three and four are stuck in worldliness and failing to see the Spirit-prompted power of hope.

The second theme in eschatological ethics—how to live—brings to the surface specific behaviors that Paul knows are needed for the house churches in Rome. He uses a commonplace set of images: taking off (old clothing, worldliness) and putting on (new clothing, righteousness). A common approach to moral vision depicted morality in terms of light and darkness (cf. 1 Thess 5:4-7): "lay aside the works of darkness," which to the Galatians was "works of the flesh" (Gal 5:19); and, instead of the "fruit of the Spirit" (Gal 5:22) in Romans 13:12, Paul has "put on the armor [or weapons] of light," an early taste of what will become the famous armor of Ephesians 6:10-17. Paul sees the Christian life as a battle of the evils of darkness against the weapons of love and justice and peace. Paul is against common worldliness—that is, "reveling and darkness . . . debauchery and licentiousness . . . quarreling and jealousy" (Rom 13:13-14). These are the notorious sins of Rome's notorious sinners and were known as night behaviors, but alongside such night nonsense was the growing issue of hooliganism (in Rome and elsewhere).[1] To peer into their parties, one needs merely to read Petronius' *Satyricon*, or visit a university after 10 p.m. on the weekend! The churches of Rome are to have none of them, and we perhaps need to be reminded that quarrels and jealousies in verse 13 are just as sinful as debaucheries.

It is only at the end of this paragraph that all becomes clear. Living in the light means Christoformity, so they are urged to "put on the Lord Jesus Christ." As Paul said in Galatians 3:27, the baptized "have clothed yourselves with Christ." Only at the end of our passage does the eschatological ethic from beyond find its ontological source in an ethic from above: the only way to live in the light is union with Christ (see 1 Cor 15:53-54; Col 3:9-10). Union with Christ embraces the fullness of Paul's redemptive and eschatological ethic: the Lord Jesus Christ is God incarnate, and lived and taught and did deeds of wonder, and was resisted and imprisoned and crucified, but he was raised and ascended and rules and will come again. Hence, to be in union with Christ is to be connected to the whole of Christ: to put on Christ is Christoformity.

The problem at Rome is that believers, Weak and Strong—or at least some of the believers—are in the stupor of sleep (13:11). This means that either they are unaware of the imminence of the return of Christ (cf. 1 Thess 5:4) or they, knowing what time it is, are slumbering like sloths after daytime has arrived. It is time for them to become morally consistent with the gospel by acting in sobriety, faith, love, and hope.

II
A Narrative Leading to Peace
Romans 9–11

10

WHERE WE'VE BEEN, WHERE WE ARE, WHERE WE'RE HEADED

(9–11)

My friend Kermit Zarley played on the PGA Tour and then the Senior Tour (now called the Champions Tour). Out of curiosity, I once asked him how far he hit a lob wedge. His posture became more erect, and he began asking me questions: Are we at sea level? What's the temperature? (I think he asked about humidity, but I don't remember exactly now.) How much wind is there? Uphill? Downhill? Flat? By the time he was done asking me questions and I was done giving him answers, I knew we played two different games. He was a pro, and I was, well, a better than average hack. To know how to hit a lob wedge well, you have to know the whole context, and each circumstance needs to be taken into consideration. Not just how far one has hit it in the past. read 12

Reading Romans is the same way. To read Romans 1–11 well, one must know the context, and that context is mostly portrayed in Romans 12–16. Each circumstance deserves careful consideration before we can understand the letter. To know that context gives the reader of the rest of Romans a better chance of reading it well, which means reading toward seeing peace in the heart of the empire as the central thrust of the letter. I cannot begin to count the number of commentaries or academic studies I have read on Romans 1–11 that never bring up the Weak and the Strong or anything from the last chapters of Romans, and thus they too easily miss the importance of peace in the empire. Romans is too often read as if it were theoretical theology. It's not. Romans is a pastoral theology front to back or, in our case, back to front, and its deepest concern is Peace, not Privilege, not Power.

RECAPITULATION OF CONTEXT

The Christians of Rome encountered Romans in the face and voice of Phoebe, which means Phoebe was the embodied presence of Paul as she performed the letter before the various house churches and then fielded questions. We cannot think of Romans being read in one sitting without both ennui and consternation settling into the audience. Nor can we ignore the social realities. We have concluded that the churches were in the poorer sections of Rome—the Trastevere, near and east of the Aventine Hill, and along the Appian Way, and probably farther north, along Mars Field. The original converts to the Christian faith in Rome were among Jews of the synagogues in Rome, and, as Claudius increasingly established himself as loyal to the Roman traditions and so expanded citizenship, he became increasingly wary of religious traditions less amenable to the ways of Rome. So he expelled (probably) Jewish followers of Jesus from Rome in AD 49. When the tide turned back in their favor, and then especially under Nero, the issue for the returning Jews and Jewish believers became taxes. It was to their advantage that Nero created the belief that he would relieve some of the taxes—hence, the concern with taxes in Romans 13:6-7. Of more concern to the Jewish Jesus-following returnees was that the social structure of the churches was no longer the same: the gentile believers were not only socially higher in status but had reshaped the culture in ways less favorable to the messianic Jewish believers. A non-Torah observance culture had formed. Tensions arose, and Paul drills down into them in 14:1–15:13 and labels the parties "Strong" and "Weak," terms that were as much about status and power and privilege as about religious practice. Peace in the heart of the empire was his biggest desire.

By way of reminder, the Weak are Jewish believers who are in the stream of God's election, who know the Torah, who practice the Torah and still probably attend synagogue, but who sit in judgment on gentiles, especially the Strong in the Christian community in Rome, even though they have no status or privilege or power; the Weak were tempted to resist taxes paid to Rome on the basis of the Jewish zealotry tradition. The Strong, then, are predominately gentiles who believe in Jesus as Messiah or king, who do not observe Torah as the will of God for them, and who have condescending and despising attitudes probably toward Jews but especially to Jewish believers in Jesus, and all of this is wrapped up in the superior higher status of the Strong in Rome. Paul and Jewish believers who embrace the nonnecessity of Torah observance are among the Strong. The Strong then are as known for their position on observance of Torah as they are for their status and ethnicity. These two groups are divided against one another.

But Paul's mission was to establish mission churches that expanded Israel's privileged location in God's redemptive plan by including gentiles. Tensions on top of tensions arose in the blending of diverse families in this new family of God. For Paul, Christoformity was the only way Jewish and gentile believers could live in peace, love, and reconciliation. His dominant image for the churches—that is, Israel expanded—was family and sibling language: they were not just Jews and gentiles but brothers and sisters in Christ.[1] Families are shaped by love for one another, so Paul's major ethical vision for his mission churches is love (12:9; 13:10; 14:15; 15:30), the kind of love that would lead to peace in the heart of the empire.

They are also shaped by the story they tell. The story Paul told was not the story his converts grew up hearing unless they were Jewish. His Greek and Roman converts grew up on Homer or Virgil, on Hesiod or Thucydides or Herodotus or Livy, on Plato and Aristotle or on Cicero or Seneca. They knew about Romulus and Remus, about Julius Caesar and then the emperors, not about Abraham and Moses and David and the prophets. They knew Rome and Athens and Carthage, not Jerusalem and Capernaum; they knew Octavian, not David and Goliath; and they knew the laws that found their way into Justinian's *Digest*, not the laws of Moses and their halakhic innovations. If the story matters, then Paul's converts would need a fresh education in the story of Israel and the story of the Messiah and the story of the church, one not unlike the story that becomes Luke–Acts.

The importance and need for a fresh story led Paul to tell the story of Israel graciously, surprisingly, sovereignly expanding into the church in Romans 9–11. Story forms both identity and community, and the story Paul tells is one that forms a narrative for peace. It was surely the case with Israel as it was with the earliest churches, but their stories were not identical. In reading Romans backwards as a hermeneutical tool that keeps the pastoral and ecclesial situation close at hand, we contend that Paul's narrative in Romans 9–11 both articulates and legitimates the lived theology of Christoformity of 12–16. The story Paul tells is the symbolic universe he wants the Strong and the Weak to inhabit together. Reading Romans backwards stands alongside Paul's reading of Israel's history backwards—that is, reading Israel's history in light of what happens to the people of God in Christ. The revelation of God in Christ reconfigured the story of Israel for Paul.

SPECIFICS GIVE THE BIG PICTURE

I begin with some specifics that add up to give the basics of the story Paul tells in these three chapters, but I begin with a tongue-in-cheek proviso. It has become a chess match at times to discover some unnoticed Old Testament echo or allusion in a Pauline text and then to exploit its context to find some echoes of echoes, and, before long, one is reading a New Testament text in light of some obscure Old Testament text with surprising results. Some verses in Paul sound like some verses in the Old Testament the way some English sermons sound like Shakespeare, *but only because they have words that just happen to be identical or similar.* I'm not saying Paul doesn't have huge chunks of the Bible in his head or that at times he's not reverberating with biblical language, but I will focus in part 2 on what is clear and will not appeal to what might be an echo or an allusion.

9:6 - 11

Names

(the Jews)

The names of those mentioned in these three chapters are known very well by the Weak faction in Rome. Here, they are as they appear in 9:6–10:4: Abraham and Sarah, Isaac and Rebecca, Jacob and Esau, Moses, Pharaoh, Hosea, Isaiah, Christ. In chapter 11, Paul brings up Elijah and David. In other words, Paul brings up major *persons* in the history of Israel, persons who are turning points in the shape of that history. Not one word is said about the personal salvation of any of these persons. What is said pertains to God's choice of them as conduits of the divine plan for history. Salvation, of course, cannot be ignored here, and it does pop above the surface for our attention from 9:30 through 11:10, but the more central theme is the plan of God in history: "Who will be next in the line to the Messiah?" and "Who is the people of God?" are the questions, not "Who personally gets saved?"[2]

Comparing Narratives

The reconfigured story of God's way with Israel that Paul tells in these chapters deserves to be compared to other stories told by Jewish storytellers:[3] the story, for instance, of Deuteronomy 28–30, which focuses on *God's covenant with Israel* and its blessing for Torah obedience and its discipline for Torah disobedience, the latter of which leads to exile and, upon repentance, return to the Land with a new heart—all in a reminder of God's utter faithfulness to the covenant; or the narrative now found Sirach 44–51, a eulogy of Israel's *heroes* of obedience and courage that finds its telos in the high priest of Sirach's time, Simon; or the briefer but potent narrative about *zeal* for the Lord, as written up briefly in 1 Maccabees 2:51-64.[4] Two New Testament narratives deserve consideration: the story told by Stephen of Israel's history through the lens of its leaders and the *temple* (Acts 7) and the narrative about *faith* among Israelites in Hebrews

11. These stories overlap in some ways with Romans 9–11 (Deuteronomy and 1 Maccabees 2) and in other ways go their own direction. There is not an emphasis on heroes or faith, as in Sirach and Hebrews 11. From these narratives, we need to conclude that each author learned to tell the story from his or her own angle. There was not *one story for Israel* but a collection of people and events that could be shaped by the belief of the narrator in order to form a story appropriate to the need of the narrator. This is what I mean by "reconfigure." Paul reconfigures the same old people and events into a narrative telling the story he needs for his mission and the Weak and the Strong in Rome.

Events

In addition to turning-point persons and the overall narrative shape of Romans 9–11, Paul traces his narrative through *events* formed in the relationship of YHWH and Israel, again events known especially to the Weak. In fact, there is a list in Romans 9:4-5, which I will provide now with added italics that highlight what also comes to Paul's mind in the rest of the three chapters. Paul's list is not in chronological order though the string of events finds its telos in Christ. Here are the events from Romans 9:4-5, and additional events are in italics: "They are Israelites, and to them belong the adoption, the glory, the covenants, the giving of the law, the worship, and the promises; to them belong the patriarchs, and from them, according to the flesh, comes the Messiah. . . ." We can add then the *Egyptian sojourn and slavery; the golden calf episode; the prophets Moses, Elijah, David, Hosea, and Isaiah; Sodom and Gomorrah; the exile and return; various themes about the northern kingdom;* and *a focus on gentile belief in the gospel* along with *Israel's belief and unbelief.* And into this narrative, *Paul inserts himself and his gospel agent. Never far away are the Strong and the Weak. Never far away is his plotting of peace in the heart of the empire.*

What is the theme of Paul's story from Abraham to the Messiah and the gospel agents of Paul into the mission churches? Clearly, it is about God's faithfulness to his covenant promises to Abraham. The theme is not how to get saved, or even who is saved, but God's covenant faithfulness. Paul reconfigures Israel's story to form a narrative about God's surprising faithfulness in the missionary movement to include gentiles into the one family of God, Israel. That inclusive narrative promotes peace among the Strong and the Weak.

Citations

Along with the persons and events, we need to notice which texts from Israel's Scriptures that Paul explicitly quotes. (We leave aside echoes and allusions.)[5]

Romans 9 is more chronological, while Romans 10–11 is more argumentative by appealing randomly from various Old Testament texts.

In Romans 9, we encounter Genesis three times, then Malachi, Exodus twice, Isaiah, Hosea, then back to Isaiah four times. In Romans 10, we find Paul turning to Leviticus, then twice to Deuteronomy, then he springs ahead to Isaiah and Joel and then back to Isaiah, ahead to Nahum, back again to Isaiah, then to Psalms and back to Deuteronomy, and then one more dip into Isaiah. In Romans 11, we first meet 1 Samuel and Psalms, then back to 1 Kings twice, back yet further to Deuteronomy and at the same time Isaiah, back to Psalms, yet again two more times to Isaiah, and closure with Job.[6]

All in all, a pretty impressive display of Bible knowledge! One cannot sit down with a reference edition of the Bible that notifies readers of Old Testament texts and not be thoroughly impressed both with Paul's grasp of his Greek Bible and with the depth to which he goes to demonstrate his points from it. If we ask a simple question—*Is this aimed at the Weak or the Strong?*—it would be hard to deny that it had to be Jewish readers/auditors (that is, the Weak) who would grasp most completely this story of person, events, and texts. Most of this would be lost on gentile readers unless they were themselves very familiar with the Bible. Also, Paul *explicitly* stating at 11:13 that he is now speaking to gentiles lends credence to the view that 9:1–11:12 was for the Weak in the Roman house churches and that 11:13 and on was for the Strong. (More of that later.) If so, Phoebe must have fielded numerous questions and even explained Old Testament texts as she read the text of Romans aloud. These three chapters were a long evening discussion.

The Questions

But there is one more set of specifics in these chapters that helps us grasp the big picture: the questions Paul asks. Over and over, Paul moves his argument forwards, or at least stands still pounding away at one point, by asking questions. The questions are so numerous that we must stand stunned at the battering approach Paul exhibits in these chapters. One must wonder how those in the house churches responded to so many intense questions. To anticipate a conclusion to be drawn shortly, the bulk of these questions (through 11:10) are shaped toward the Weak of Rome, who are pressing home their elective privilege, God's revealed will in the Torah, and the necessity for the gentile converts to observe that Torah. Here are the questions according to the NRSV:

(1) What then are we to say?

(2) Is there injustice on God's part? (9:14)

(3) You will say to me then, "Why then does he still find fault? For who can resist his will?"

(4) But who indeed are you, a human being, to argue with God?

(5) Will what is molded say to the one who molds it, "Why have you made me like this?"

(6) Has the potter no right over the clay, to make out of the same lump one object for special use and another for ordinary use?

(7) What if God, desiring to show his wrath and to make known his power, has endured with much patience the objects of wrath that are made for destruction;

(8) and what if he has done so in order to make known the riches of his glory for the objects of mercy, which he has prepared beforehand for glory—including us whom he has called, not from the Jews only but also from the Gentiles? (9:19-24)

(9) What then are we to say? (9:30)

(10) Why not? (9:32)

(11) But what does it say? (10:8)

(12) But how are they to call on one in whom they have not believed?

(13) And how are they to believe in one of whom they have never heard?

(14) And how are they to hear without someone to proclaim him? And how are they to proclaim him unless they are sent? (10:14-15)

(15) But I ask, have they not heard? (10:18)

(16) Again I ask, did Israel not understand? (10:19)

(17) I ask, then, has God rejected his people? (11:1)

(18) Do you not know what the scripture says of Elijah, how he pleads with God against Israel? (11:2)

(19) But what is the divine reply to him? (11:4)

(20) What then? (11:7)

(21) So I ask, have they stumbled so as to fall? (11:11)

This ends his interrogation of the Weak, and it lets up at 11:12 until he comes later in chapter 11 to three reassuring questions drawn from Isaiah 40:13 and probably Job 41:11:

(1) "For who has known the mind of the Lord?

(2) "Or who has been his counselor?

(3) "Or who has given a gift to him, to receive a gift in return?" (11:34-35)

In this battering ram of questions, which forms his interrogation of the Weak, we hear the tone, the pastoral concerns, and the theology of Paul. He creates a narrative of Israel's history that establishes Israel's election as well as God's surprising moves, and he creates this narrative so he can include the Messiah, who includes gentiles in God's plan. Conclusion aside, this accumulation of twenty-one questions for the Weak makes the listener uncomfortable and gasp for air, and the whole discourse must be read as aggressive rhetoric designed to make his argument compelling. No one wants to be battered with this many questions. The Weak of Rome encountered this letter not on a computer screen but in a home with Phoebe reading the letter aloud, and they were probably hearing these questions for the first time. As part of a performed letter, each question demands that the auditor give an answer, and probably they did so aloud, and it is not until the auditor has answered the question that Phoebe would have moved on. If she didn't perform the letter in this manner, she didn't give the letter the impact it could have had. This kind of intensity points us to the audience and to Paul's deep concern to persuade the Weak to his viewpoint. My conclusion is that Paul demands and expects more of the Strong but is harsher with the Weak. His concern is disruption and division in Rome.

These five topics—persons, narrative comparisons, events, texts, questions—matter not only for reading Romans well but also for the pastoral theology at work in Romans (and today). How so? What Paul is getting at in the narrative at work in these chapters is twofold: God is faithful, and God's plans are not straightforward chronology. That is, God can be faithful when specific individuals in Israel are not faithful; God can skip and hop left or right. Yet, God is faithful because God continues to work through Israel for the world's redemption. Put differently, God's faithfulness means God shifts from one person to another according to his own plan, but, through it all, *God remains faithful to the covenant with Abraham.* The issue in this letter, especially once we learn to read Romans backwards, is that the Weak assert their privileged position in God's redemptive history while the Strong assert their dominance in the history and social status of Rome. The Weak have this question: "Is not Israel the elect people of God?" The Strong have another one: "Is it not the case that God has moved from Israel to the gentiles in salvation through the cosmic Lord Jesus?"

Now to the pastoral point: to the Weak, Paul announces here that God's inclusion of gentiles and even shifting to their dominance in the people of God because of the unbelief of Israel is not a sign of God's unfaithfulness to the covenant promises. Rather, *the divine move through the Messiah to Paul and the gentile mission is consistent with other divine shifts in history, and these shifts anticipate the basis for peace among the Strong and the Weak.* Thus, the unbelief of Israel is nothing new in the history of God's dealings with Israel. There has always only been a remnant of faithful. To the Strong, Paul announces that their present choice as God's agents of redemption in the world is both the sign of God's grace and faithfulness to the covenant with Abraham and, at the same time, no guarantee that the gentiles will always be the central agents of God's redemption. Pastorally, this means the entire narrative of Romans 9–11 is not about who gets saved in the deeply personal sense but *about who the gospel agents are in God's redemptive plans.* It's about *where we are in the plan of God for cosmic redemption.* The chapter—seen in the persons, narrative comparisons, events, texts, and questions—centers around corporate and not individual predestination. A classic soteriological reading of Romans has often wandered into discussions about predestination and personal salvation but, in so doing, has often missed the context of Rome entirely.

11

TO THE WEAK

(9:1–11:10)

Many read Romans as theoretical theology, with Romans 9–11 treated most theoretically of all. Briefly again, 11:13 is a starting clue. What it tells us is that Paul turns at that point to the gentile auditors, and that means the Strong. Prior to that, Paul has been speaking to the Weak in Rome. The "Weak," by way of reminder, refers not to all Jewish believers but to a particular group as outlined above. The themes pertinent to the Weak and to the Strong lead to or are occasioned by the lived theology of Romans 12–16. The white-hot thrust and parry of Romans 9–11 are designed to deconstruct ideas that divided the house churches in Rome and promote sibling relations of peace among them.

There are six themes in Romans 9–11 that I want to mention here, and then I will provide an approach to sorting the big themes of these chapters: mercy and wrath, gentiles and remnant, righteousness rooted in law or faith, divinely chosen remnant as well as the hardened, the failure of both Jews and gentiles, and the correlations of Israel's hardening and gentile inclusion along with gentile fullness and Israel's eschatological redemption.[1] Paul provides a vital set of clues for our reading of these chapters, and we will discover similar clues obtain not only for Romans 9–11 but also for chapters 1–8, where 1–4 focus (as I hope to show) on the Weak and 5–8 focus on the Strong.

The clues are the explicit statements about audience and the concentration or lack of concentration of scriptural citations. Why, we have to ask, does Paul say, "Now I am speaking to you Gentiles" (11:13)? If we read 11:11-12 as connected to 11:13, we discover that, at 11:11, Paul turns to speak to the gentiles, to the Strong in the Roman house churches, and, in so doing, he reveals he has been speaking to the Weak from 9:1 through 11:10. To support this, I offer this: the battering ram of persons, comparative narratives, events, texts, and questions are far more appropriate for a Scripture-soaked audience—that is, Jewish Bible readers—than for gentile converts.[2] That

concentration of familiarity with Israel's story and the lack of scriptural citations in the rest of chapter 11, though not wholly absent, grabs the reader's or
auditor's attention. The combination of 11:13 with the narrative scripted in
chapters 9 and 10 leads me to conclude that 9:1 through 11:10 is addressed
to the Weak while 11:11 through 11:36 is addressed to the Strong. Phoebe
would have looked at the Weak until 11:10 and then turned her gaze on the
Strong through the rest of the chapter. She would have altered her voice, too,
when quoting various Scriptures.

THE REDEMPTIVE-HISTORICAL PRIVILEGE
OF ELECTION (9:1-5)

Paul's address to the Weak, and, yes, his plan for peace among the Jesus followers in Rome, begins with *the privilege of Israel's election.* The most important
elements of this elective privilege are found in 9:1-5. Paul's sorrow for his
people is rooted in their election (9:1-3; 10:1-3), and he knows the Weak in the
Roman house churches are the beneficiaries of this same election. The terms
he uses evoke various elements of the story of Israel and God's redemptive
plan in history. They are "Israelites," a term of covenant mercy (9:4, 6, 27, 31;
10:19, 21; 11:1, 2, 7, 25, 26), and not simply "Jews" (2:17, 28-29; 3:29). Paul
sums up Israel's relation to YHWH with his own category, adoption. One
may well think of Exodus 4:22 or Hosea 11:1, but one has to pass through the
Father theme of Jesus (Luke 11:2-4) and into Pauline adoption theology to see
what Paul is getting at: Israel becomes God's own family by grace (Rom 8:15,
23). Adoption is followed by "glory"—that is, by eschatological redemption
and status in Christ (8:18-25). Debate chases after his term "covenants": Is
it the old and the new? Is it Abrahamic, Mosaic, Davidic, along with perhaps
the expectation of the new in Jeremiah? Inasmuch as Paul has his mind on
the Weak, there is no reason to exclude the new and no reason not to include
the various covenants God made with Israel.

Inherent to the covenants God made with Israel was the Torah. This bare
statement evokes what Paul has said (and we will examine in a later chapter)
about Israel's and—as will be argued—the Weak's elective privilege in having
the Torah (2:1-29). But Torah is a double-edged sword for Paul: it reveals God's
will, and it accuses the Torah breaker, Jew or gentile; it also is the direction of the
Spirit's transforming work (cf. 7:23; 8:2). What Paul has in mind in Romans 9:4
is the privilege of God's mercy (esp. 2:17-20; 3:2). To speak of "worship" surely
points the Weak to the temple of Jerusalem (NIV adds "temple" to worship).
Next comes "promises," which points the Weak to remember the original

Abrahamic promise (Gen 12) and its many reiterations, but here it is not in contrast with Torah (cf. Rom 4:13-22; Gal 3–4). Romans 15:8 makes it clear that Paul is thinking here of the "promises given to the patriarchs." Which is why in Romans 9:5 he turns to the patriarchs as part of Israel's merciful privilege, to whom were promised a land, a numerous people, and God's protection (e.g., Gen 17:8; 26:3; 28:13-14). Paul skips noticeably from the patriarchs all the way to Jesus, God's Messiah (9:5b), the physical ("flesh") descendant of Abraham, Isaac, Jacob, and Joseph. Paul's language—"Messiah, who is over all, God blessed forever" (NRSV)—draws the Messiah into deity. The NIV's rendering is more precise than the NRSV's: "Messiah, who is God over all, forever praised!"

To the Weak, Paul says this: you are privileged by your election through Abraham to be the ancestors of the Messiah and now part of messianic Israel. Peace in the empire is not jeopardized by their elective privilege.

God's Surprising Elections (9:6–10:4)

What happens next? From 9:6 to 10:4 (or beyond), Paul trots out one example after another of God's surprising elections. These elections demonstrate that God's plan is not uniform, not predictable, and that individual Israelites dare not assume they are next in the redemptive-historical line of God's plans. The point is twofold: first, Israel's election and history come to their fulfillment (*telos*) in the Messiah (9:5; 10:4), and more importantly, second, the election of gentiles as part of Israel (11:11-24) is consistent with God's surprising elective moments in the story. Shifting from Israel of the flesh to the Messiah and including both Jewish and gentile believers in the Messiah as the redemptive-historical line is yet another example of God's surprising election. Israel—and Paul's eye is on the Weak, who want to impose Torah on gentile converts—can no longer claim *exclusive* elective privilege (11:29). Rather, they now *share* elective privilege with gentile believers in the Messiah. This narrative from 9:6 through 10:4, with implications drawn out in 10:5-21, is aimed at the Weak because they are confused that the Strong in Rome are themselves claiming elective privilege. Paul thus both states that Israel, the Weak, remains the elect and presses the Weak to see that they are now sharing election with gentile believers. They are not shoved aside by gentiles, but neither can they shove gentiles to an inferior location in the plan of God. Thus, gentile and Jewish believers are siblings in one family.

The opening line of 9:6 provides the clue to what Paul is doing rhetorically in these three chapters: "It is not as though the word of God had failed."

This follows 9:5 because the Weak believe Paul's gospel of gentile inclusion entails the failure of Israel's election. Right away, then, he makes his point clear: "For not all Israelites truly belong to Israel" (9:6b). In fact, he continues, "not all of Abraham's children are his true descendants" (9:7). Which is to say, Abrahamic flesh is not necessarily elect. That privilege belonged to Isaac, not Ishmael. (Again, this says nothing about who gets saved.) He makes his point doubly clear in 9:8: "it is not the children of the flesh who are the children of God, but the children of the promise are counted as descendants." The same surprising move-by-God occurs with Isaac's wife, Rebecca: it would be Jacob, not Esau (9:10-13). This surprising, sovereign election by God is evident, too, with Moses in the golden calf and exodus events (9:14-18). God reveals intimate mercy to Moses, using the words of Exodus 33:19 on the mountain to make his point, and God elects to use Pharaoh to release the children of Israel from bondage. Hence, from Joseph in Egypt, we come to Moses and out of Egypt to the land, all along God making surprising choices.

Only those who know their prophets will see this, but Paul moves to the prophets (see above for the listing of texts) at 9:20 and 9:25-26 and 9:27-28 and 9:29: Hosea and Isaiah, the exile and the return. From these prophets, what Paul finds are not individual names but bold claims about God's surprising moves. Paul presses upon the Weak with a battery of questions, each proving God's sovereignty to move through history as God chooses. He quotes from Isaiah 29:16 in Romans 9:20, but this simply crystallizes the theme of God's sovereignty (9:19-24). Who do you think you are? Can't God do what God wants? What if? What if? What if God is doing this all, Paul interrogates, "to make known the riches of his glory," not just for the Weak but for the gentiles (Strong) (9:23-24)? His answer breaks through the surface of calm waters. The answer—God has all along promised to make that surprising move to include gentiles in the one family of God—finds support in Hosea and Isaiah. From Hosea: the "not my people" have become "my people" (Hos 2:25 LXX, then 2:1 LXX). From Isaiah: "only a remnant" of the innumerable Israelites will be saved; only a remnant will usher in the next chapter in Israel's history (Isa 10:22-23; 28:22; 1:9; and perhaps Dan 5:28).

This provokes the Weak's assumed question, summarized like this: How can Israel, which has been God's people and has been striving for the kingdom of God all along, be excluded while gentiles, who truth be told have lived in sin all along, are the ones upon whom God's favor now rests? This is the question asked by the Weak, and it alone makes sense of this passage's sharp turns and sudden uphill climbs and twists into hairpin downhill spins. From the opening of chapter 9, Paul has his aim set on the Messiah as the climactic moment in redemptive history. The Messiah (9:30–10:4) proves both God's faithfulness to the covenant and expands that covenant to include the gentiles (the Strong in Rome) without diminishing the election of Israel (the Weak).

On any reading of these chapters, God remains faithful to the covenant with Abraham and Israel. The promises to them are sure; the covenants inviolable. As 2 Maccabees expresses it, "Therefore he never withdraws his mercy from us. Although he disciplines us with calamities, he does not forsake his own people" (6:16). That is Paul's theology, too. The Weak need to see this without ignoring the obvious surprising turns of God. They need to make room at the table for the gentiles as those who *now share elective privilege*.

Before we sketch other themes in 9:6–10:4, here is a brief comment on 10:4 as the fitting completion of the story of Israel. To repeat, God is faithful to Israel as God's elective people; God's redemptive history all along had as its aim a Messiah to rule over God's creation and an expansion of the people of God to include gentiles; God's direction of the course of history includes one surprise after another. However, God's faithfulness is to be matched by Israel's faithfulness. Israel fails to meet the demands of covenant faithfulness (9:30–10:3), but the Messiah did not fail. The Messiah is the telos of the demand of the covenant faithfulness. All righteousness now must be connected to the Messiah's righteousness (10:4).

One surprise after another. To the Weak, Paul says, "God has worked in history from one person to another, from event to another, and all of it led to the Messiah as the faithful Israelite. Expanding Israel to include gentiles is one more example of the way God has always worked." But the question of the Weak is this: Do those gentile believers, the Strong, need also to observe the Torah? Or do they need to become proselytes to Judaism in order to be complete Christians? These questions are taken head-on in our chapters. I want to fill this in a bit more: the issue in Romans 1–11 is *how to transform the minds of both the Strong the Weak so they will live as siblings.* The solution of the Weak is Torah; for the Strong, the solution is no Torah. Romans 9–11 is part of Paul's patented answer to the moral transformation of both groups in Rome. The solution for peace is not Torah; the solution is righteousness by faith and transformation by the Spirit. But that, too, gets us one or two steps ahead of ourselves.

By Faith (9:30–10:21)

At the end of chapter 9 (9:30-33), a theme emerges that lays blame on Israelites, and therefore the Weak, in a way that sets up what Paul says about the

Messiah (10:1-4) and that then becomes a major theme in chapter 10. Namely, *righteousness comes by faith and not by the law or the works of the law.* Nothing could be more Pauline, one might say. Yes, of course, but what is often taken as Pauline needs to be set in the context of Paul's narrative more accurately. At the heart of this "by faith, not by law" is the Strong-Weak controversy and the idea that the way forwards in the Roman house churches is not by way of imposing Torah but by allegiance to King Jesus and to life in the Spirit. (Again, there will be more of that in Romans 1 through 8.)

Hints of a theme to come were dropped at 9:12 and 9:16, when Paul said not by works but by God's call, which in 9:16 varies to "it depends not on human will or exertion, but on God who shows mercy." Our focus here is on the human element of this equation: not works, not will, not exertion. The most surprising turn in Israel's story, no matter how many hints there were in the Old Testament, was the sudden incursion of gentile believers in the Messiah. What made the surprise intensely worrisome was the corresponding lack of belief among Paul's contemporaries. One would have thought when the Messiah came that the entire Jewish nation, or at least most of it, would immediately swing to the Messiah's side. But, no.

The Three-in-One Problem (9:30–10:4)

If one factor is God's sovereign surprises, the other is human response. Remember, at this point in Romans 9–11, Phoebe's still got her eyes set on the Weak. What does she tell them? Over the next chapter, she will press home a three-in-one problem: (1) Israel, works, Torah as boundary markers; (2) faith and Messiah; and (3) gentiles and faith. These three elements are behind the divisions among the Weak and the Strong, and they need resolution to bring peace. Paul starts with the first. The telling, striving footrace expressions in 9:30-33, which are repeated a few times for emphasis, answer why Israel did not win right-standing with God. Paul's answer is, "Because they did not strive for it on the basis of faith, but as if it were based on works." That is, their basis was not trusting but striving, and trusting is aimed at Christ while striving is aimed at Torah. The footrace metaphor can be read too simplistically if the whole of our section (9:33–10:21) does not shape the expression. It is customary today to understand works as boundary markers that distinguished Jews from gentiles, and, whatever one thinks of the meaning of "works of the law," there can be no debate that Jewish observance of the Torah created divisions. We observed that in our section on the Strong and the Weak. That is, "works" evokes the common practices of food laws, Sabbath, and circumcision as singular expressions of life under Torah. These were observances that gave Jews and Jewish believers in Jesus status and worth and honor in their cultural circles. Paul subverts that kind of status making, as he also contends in Romans 1–8 that the path to moral transformation and ecclesial welcoming is not through Torah but through grace, faith, and love.

Even more, there is wisdom in reading works as boundary markers *because of what follows* in Romans. Paul turns immediately from "faith not works," not to human pride and human efforts, but to the Messiah. The Messiah, to echo E. P. Sanders, reveals the gospel, and that gospel reveals the inadequacy of the Torah as the path of redemption, transformation, and ecclesial welcome. The move to Messiah, I repeat, is an interesting move logically. If our Reformation impulses turn on our desire to connect faith-not-works to desires of self-justification, Paul turns to Christology. "They," and here he means Torah-observant Israel, "stumbled over the stumbling stone" (9:32), and this is propped up with a quotation from Isaiah 28:16 (also 8:14): God's plan is to place in Zion the Messiah-Stumbling-Stone, and that Messiah will be the source of both stumbling and faith (Rom 9:33). This twinning of faith-not-works with Messiah brings to the surface the precise point Paul is making: Israel's stumbling-by-works is a Messiah-stumbling, and the reason for that stumbling is explained in 10:1-3 in these important terms: zeal that is not enlightened, ignorance of God's way of accomplishing righteousness, and self-oriented right-making before God. Which is to say: they have not seen that Jesus Messiah was "the end of the law" so that right-standing with God could be "for everyone," not just Israel and not with an inkling of privilege in the faith community for the Weak. They get this right-standing by faith (10:4). So works must be twinned with rejecting the Messiah, and faith twinned with the Messiah as the end of the Torah.

But a third element must be added: gentiles *have accomplished* right-standing by the proper response. They believed in the Messiah, they swore allegiance to King Jesus, and so they did not stumble over the Messiah. In other words, their status with God is based not on their elective privilege or their observances but on what God has accomplished for them—righteousness—in Christ and in Christ alone. Faith alone, Christ alone. This is not so much about Israel's failure to be obedient, as Paul's own life makes clear (Phil 3:3-11), as it is about Israel's combination of not recognizing the Messiah and instead protecting their status. The only way to comprehend what Paul says here is to *embrace the radical revelation of God in Christ as the new creation starting point.* What made Israel unfaithful, then, was not just some acts of disobedience to the Torah but God's revelation of righteousness in the Messiah and their rejecting that Messiah. Unfaithfulness now has a new Christocentric definition.

Israel and works, the Messiah, and gentiles and faith. These are the three-in-one problem Paul is resolving with his aim of peace in the heart of the empire. John Barclay gets this so right that I have to quote him: "Thus, the foil to Paul's theology is not a human self-righteousness that attempts to earn salvation, but the natural assumption that when God acts in saving benevolence, he distributes his gifts to those we consider fitting or worthy."[3] It is not elective privilege and status but God's grace. To repeat, it is too easy to say the problem is self-righteousness, which is stated in a muted form in 9:30-32. Paul's starting point is not Israel's failure to observe the Torah but Israel's stumbling in their zealous race for righteousness, and the stone of stumbling is their failure to see Jesus as the Messiah. That failure turns their previous and present Torah obedience into irrelevancy, their zeal into irrelevant zeal, and their righteousness into irrelevant righteousness and status. If Israel continues to insist on their privilege in history, they will fail; if they turn to the Messiah as the locus of redemption, they will rediscover their privilege along with gentiles. In fact, Paul's sketch of history in Romans 9:1-29 has shown that God has always acted on the basis of grace and that God *has never shaped history on the basis of merit or status*. What seems to be a polemic against Judaism is far more a polemic against the Weak's insistence on the Strong observing Torah. If we read Romans in light of its context, thus reading it backwards, the polemic with the Weak is what comes to the fore, not a diatribe with Judaism per se.

We must not lose our way by wandering off into abstract theological systems of salvation. Rather, Phoebe is here looking at the Weak, the Jewish believers, who are sitting in judgment on the gentile believers, the Strong, for their disregard of precisely those elements of the Torah that provided the Weak with a sense of (yes, biblically based) elective privilege in God's plan. Not only that: their belief is that the Strong can grow into mature morality only if they observe the Torah. Paul thus critiques here the Weak's inherited disposition to think their status from Torah observance grants them privilege. Phoebe, then, is offering at the same time comforting words to the Strong. They've got this one right, and she wants them to know Paul is on their side. Peace in the churches will come, but it will not come by Torah; it will come through faith to Spirit.

New Covenant Renewal (10:5-13)

Now that, and only because, Christ has come, Paul perceives that Moses himself was concerned about correlating right-standing with God and status based on Torah-observance. Righteousness that "comes from the law" (10:5), which is what he sees Israel doing in holding on to privilege and rejecting the Messiah, finds support in Paul's Bible in Leviticus 18:5 (Rom 10:5). But Paul then turns to a creative reading of Deuteronomy 30:12-14 (Rom 10:6-8) that reshapes (but does not contradict) what he says about Leviticus 18:5. The new-covenant commandment God was giving Israel, Moses said, "is not too hard for you" (Deut 30:11): you don't need to go search for it in heaven or across the sea (30:12-13).

This is one of the trickier passages in all of Pauline literature. I have found the most compelling reading to be that of Matthew Bates, and I will rehearse his approach now.[4] Bates thinks there are a number of speakers going back and forth in Romans 10:6-9, and knowing who they are throws light on what Paul is saying. There are three: Paul, a presumptuous person, and a character whom he calls Righteousness by Faith. Bates' presumptuous person, who I am tempted to see as a representative of the Weak (the Judge of Rom 2), asks in Romans 10:6 by reworking Deuteronomy 30:12, "Who will ascend to heaven?" Which implies "so we can perform the commandment?" Paul interrupts this presumptuous (Weak) person and reinterprets: "This is about Christ's descent to earth." The presumptuous (Weak) answers right back with "Who will descend into the abyss?" Which implies getting the Torah so we can perform it. Again Paul interrupts with "This is about Christ's resurrection."

At this point Bates has what is called an imagined character, Righteousness by Faith, say, "You must not say such things in your heart!" (Rom 10:6 citing Deut 9:4); "Don't you know that the utterance is near you? It is in your mouth and in your heart" (Rom 10:8 citing Deut 30:14). Again interrupting, Paul affirms this character's words: Yes, "if you confess with your lips that Jesus is Lord and believe in your heart that God raised him from the dead, you will be saved" (Rom 10:9). This makes sense of the back-and-forth as well as the substance of what Paul believes. Paul here is reading Moses in light of Christ and the new covenant renewal anticipated in Deuteronomy 30.What Paul does with Deuteronomy 30 is bold. How so? He makes it about Christ—that's the bold part—as the one who fulfills the new covenant expectation for those circumcised in the heart (Deut 30:6). The Law (of Lev 18:5, cited in Rom 10:5), Deuteronomy told him, would be doable under the new covenant, which Paul knows occurs in Christ through the Spirit. Paul reads Deuteronomy 30:12-13 as a reference to the new covenant grace of God fully present now in Christ's life, death, and resurrection, and then he reads 30:14 ("the word is near you") to refer to new covenant in-the-heart right-standing on the basis of confessing faith. Thus, thus, thus: Leviticus 18:5 and Deuteronomy 30:12-14 are combined to teach covenant obedience for those with right-standing by faith and fulfillment of God's Torah. Bold, counterintuitive, and very Pauline (and no one but Paul).

We are now back to the three-in-one problem: Israel and works, Messiah-as-Stumbling-Stone or Object-of-Faith, and gentiles with faith. Faith is defined as confessing Jesus as Lord and believing God raised him from the dead. (If you read the use of "lips" and "heart" in Deut 30:14, you will see once again Paul's Christ-shaped reading of Moses.)

Salvation is by faith, not works; and that means it's time for the gentiles-and-faith theme again: "For there is no distinction" and "Everyone" (Rom 10:12, 13). The Weak can't count on their elective privilege; they must see the surprising moves of God to establish righteousness in Christ, and that righteousness comes by way of faith, not Torah. It means the Strong are their (equal) siblings.

THEREFORE, MISSIONS (10:13-21)

The three-in-one problem has been resolved once one confesses Jesus as Lord and affirms his resurrection: redemption is not by works or the status or privilege of Israel's election; the Messiah is Jesus; and faith, which shows up in these gentile believers (the Strong), is all that is needed. This leads to a series of questions and responses, and Paul moves swiftly, leaving readers and surely many in the Roman house churches wondering what just happened.

The citation in Romans 10:13 of Joel 2:32 ("Everyone who calls on the name of the Lord shall be saved") is a hinge that completes the previous section and opens the next section. The people of God, again and again, is composed of those who believe, Jews and gentiles, who, in believing in the Messiah, become siblings. The two sides of this hinge are the sufficiency of faith and the need to tell the world of this Messiah's redemption. Therefore, let's get some missionaries preaching the gospel to all! Romans 10:13-15 is a chain of connections:

[Everyone who *calls* on the name of the Lord will be saved ...]
But how are they to *call* on one in whom they have not *believed*?
And how are they to *believe* in one of whom they have never *heard*?
And how are they to *hear* without someone to *proclaim* him?
And how are they to *proclaim* him unless they are *sent*?
As it is written, "How beautiful are the feet of those [*sent*] who bring good news!"
(This citation from Isaiah assumes "sent" in "those who bring good news," but Isaiah does not use the term "sent.")

Paul's ambition is that both Jews and gentiles will embrace the world's true ruler, Jesus. Those who are missionaries of this message are Paul's best friends.

Reading Romans backwards makes us sensitive to what seems to us to be sudden erratic logical shifts in Paul's rhetoric. His eyes are on the Weak, not on some theoretical argument. So, he returns back to Israel, to works and to rejecting the Messiah: "But not all have obeyed" (Rom 10:16). Right through the end of Romans 10, Paul is riffing on this three-in-one problem, and at this point he turns to the back-and-forth of citing Scriptures and making short comments. Israel has an unsurprising or surprising history of hearing the message, comprehending the message (10:18, pulling from Psalm 19:4), but rejecting it (10:21, pulling from Isa 65:2). And the prophets foretold all of this. In fact, God would use gentile acceptance of the same message to provoke Israel to jealousy (Rom 10:19-20, pulling from Deut 32:21 and Isa 65:1).

Paul has now explained that God's ways in history are often surprising in their sovereignty but that there are human correlations as well. Phoebe is concerned still with the Weak in Rome, and she's not done looking at them until we get through the next paragraph in chapter 11 of Romans. To the Weak, Paul explains the human correlation of God's surprising sovereignty: the Weak want right-standing with God by maintaining status through works of the Torah. The Strong, however, are finding right-standing with God solely through Christ on the basis of faith, and in the middle of it all is Jesus as the Messiah. Once one embraces him as the Messiah, the whole of Israel's story takes on a new configuration: no longer by Torah but by faith in the Messiah.

The Weak, however, do not back down from one very solid conviction—God made a covenant with Israel, God promised to be faithful, and that leaves the Weak in Rome with a question: Has God rejected Israel in this surprising move to include gentiles in the Messiah? Underneath that question is the conviction that God's Torah is God's will, and the Strong (gentiles) become siblings only by adoption observance of Torah.

THE REMNANT REMAIN (11:1-10)

One question haunts the Weak: Is God being faithful to Israel? If faith, not works, upgrades gentiles before God to the level of Israel, has Israel lost its privilege in the plan of God? Put bluntly, has (not) God rejected Israel? That's what Paul asks and what Phoebe reads with her eyes on the Weak, in Romans 11:1. These sorts of questions, which dominate Romans 9:6 through 11:10, are questions Paul has heard in every synagogue and in every house church he has founded from Damascus to Illyricum. These are then not fashioned on the spot but reused in anticipation of what he knows the Weak of Rome will be asking. Deservedly so!

The big question is here: has God rejected his people (11:1)? With his deft rehearsal of the long section on God's surprising moves in history (9:6-29) behind him, Paul now answers the questions with two examples and three basic terms—which will be discussed below.

Two Examples

First example: *himself.* "I myself am an Israelite" is his opening answer to the question the Weak ask. He is the embodiment of Israel's privileges (9:1-5). He's an Israelite, from the covenant king himself, Abraham, and he knows his tribe: Benjamin (cf. Phil 3:4-6). So, God has not rejected Israel in that Paul embodies God's faithfulness to Israel. There's much to extract here and beyond the limits of this format, but Paul sees himself as an example of Jewish belief in the Messiah, a challenge to fellow Jews to join him in the Messiah, and a model to imitate when it comes to fellowship with the Strong and the Weak (cf. Rom 14:2, 14, 20; 15:1).

Second example: *Elijah* (11:2b-4). It is fashionable today to make much of what is not said from the Old Testament and to draw out what many think is assumed. The method is rooted in a conviction that someone like Paul knew his Bible, which he did, and that his audiences would have picked up at least some of what he assumed. This seems reasonable. In this case, Elijah is a paradigmatic prophet; it was believed by some Jews that at the end of history Elijah would return and thus the paradigmatic Elijah has eschatological over-tones. Yes, these could be Pauline assumptions. What is not an assumption and what is on the surface of our text is that Elijah, like the Weak in Rome, is wondering about God's faithfulness to his covenant with Israel. The words used by Elijah tell us this much: "Lord, they have killed your prophets, they have demolished your altars; I alone am left, and they are seeking my life" (Rom 11:3; quoting 1 Kgs 19:10). This, Paul tells us, is Elijah's *plea* (Rom 11:2b) and not only a plea: "he pleads with God *against* Israel." God's answers to Elijah are Paul's answer to the Weak: you are not alone; there are seven thousand faithful (11:4)!

Does Paul see himself as an Elijah figure? Does not the order of the examples guide us there? First Paul; then Elijah. Elijah pleading and Paul pleading (9:1-3; 10:1). It seems so, but there's more: Paul embodies God's covenant with Israel; he embodies the Jewish believer in the Messiah, and hence he is now connected with the Weak; but he also pushes further and embodies the praxis of the Strong in his faith. It seems reasonable then to think that

Elijah serves as a warning to the Weak that they, too, may be pleading and may be complaining that God is not faithful, and the words of YHWH to Elijah become, in the message of Paul, words to the Weak.

Three Terms

Election is the first term: God is faithful to Israel by electing Israelites. This election is not based on worth or status—that is, it is not based on elective privilege or works of the Torah. It is about "whom he foreknew" (11:2) and "the elect" (11:7). This term "foreknew" must be tied to the term "elect" in this context and not diminished by saying God elected on the basis of foreknowledge of who would believe, for that is all but saying God elects on the basis of works. As Romans 8:29 makes clear, foreknowledge, predestination, and election are tied into a bundle of divine direction toward glory. God knows in advance—so I take it to mean—that not all will believe, not all will prove faithful, not all will be obedient. Nonetheless, God will remain faithful to Israel *somehow and in surprising ways,* the most surprising of which surely is Jesus as Messiah, who brings gentiles into the family of God. Those who do believe, those who are faithful, and those who are obedient are those whom he foreknew and who are the elect.

What it means to be elect leads to the second term, remnant (11:5). Paul uses this term to capture his two examples: he himself is part of the remnant of faithful Israel, and so too were Elijah and the seven thousand. Election leads to remnant, and both are the result of grace (11:5-6), the third term. "Grace" here means it is the work of God (priority), is abundant in sufficiency and efficacy in redemption (superabundance), and is incongruous with a person's status and Torah observance (incongruity).[5] Incongruity along with priority are the emphases in this context. What is clear for Paul is that it is not grace if it is based on works (11:6b). Works establish a person's status and worth; grace disestablishes the honor code of the Weak and levels all humans to recipients of God's benevolence. God acts to redeem out of his singular pleasure and benevolence, and he acts upon those Israelites whom he chooses to effect his redemptive plan in history. His choice of Paul and Elijah is not based on their merit or their status in Torah observance; his choice has its own reasons, and humans are not privy to God's freedom. What his election by grace establishes in this passage is that God both remains faithful to his covenant promises and does not reject Israel.

The Weak, like biblical theologians today, want proof from the Bible; Paul has been asked for that proof on many occasions. So before they can raise a hand, Paul quotes Deuteronomy 29:4, Isaiah 29:10, and then Psalm 69:22-23.

Each establishes a similar point: God's surprising moves both awaken faith and judge the disobedient with hardening. In this new set of terms, faith or works (cf. 9:30-33) become a divine work. Paul can explain the rejection of the Messiah by his fellow Jews in no other way, and this explanation derives from exasperation in his gentile mission experience: those who, like him, believe are the elect, while those who turn from Jesus as the Messiah are hardened. Yet, Paul will soon be telling the Strong that hardening is not the final word (11:25-32).

Conclusion

Paul's words shaped for the Weak in Rome are all designed as both comfort and warning: comfort to know they are the elect, the remnant, recipients of grace, and those who know the faithfulness of God to his covenant with Israel. The warning is that they are to believe and remain faithful, for God's ways are surprisingly sovereign—which was a major theme for Paul in speaking to the Weak: he wanted them to know that God's surprising work in the Messiah to include gentiles (that is, the Strong) is just another example of God's ways of shaping history. He wants them to know that salvation is by faith and not by works so any attempt on their part to press gentile believers to adopt the Torah *has nothing to do with right-standing before God and cannot lead to peace in the heart of the empire*. He wants them to know that it is God's grace that creates right-standing and the human response is not works but faith. Because it is by faith and not by works, gentiles are as welcome in the faith community as much as the Weak, and that means the Weak have to learn to welcome the Strong, to eat with them and let them eat their *traif*, and to embrace as siblings all those who believe in Christ. Oddly enough, in Paul's mind, this theology of God's surprising grace and election does not disprivilege the Weak, nor does it wipe out or replace God's covenant with them. Rather, it proves it, and it expands it. Which is precisely Paul's next move, yet another illustration of God's surprising ways.

Read

12

TO THE STRONG

(11:11-36)

Phoebe at this moment in the performance of Romans fixes her eyes on the Strong—high-status gentile believers in Jesus who sat loose with respect to Torah observance and who expected the Weak to abandon their Torah observance to be fully equal siblings in the house churches. At Romans 11:13, Paul makes it clear he's speaking to the Strong, but, because what he says here requires 11:11-12, we must include those verses too. Five integrated themes emerge.

JEALOUSY

The Messiah was a "stumbling block" (11:9; cf. 9:33) for Israel, but the apostle discerns on the basis of his mission experience a divine intention: "so as to make them jealous" (11:11). Paul learned this from Moses (10:19, from Deut 32:21) and adopted it as a personal strategy: "Inasmuch then as I am an apostle to the Gentiles, I glorify my ministry in order to make my own people jealous, and thus save some of them" (Rom 11:13-14). He preaches to gentiles and converts them to Jesus, Israel's Messiah, who for them is the cosmic Lord, and this he believes provokes or will provoke his contemporaries to jealousy.

The word "jealousy" in English is about preservation, protection, and zeal for one's honor and status in society. The term "envy" is about desiring what another has. Paul is writing in Greek with a bucket of Hebrew history loaded into his lexicon, so we need to be careful what we see in this term "jealousy." To begin with, God is named "Jealous" at times in Israel's story (Exod 20:5; 34:14; Deut 5:9; 32:16, 21; Josh 24:19), and divine jealousy is God's response to idolatry, disobedience, and unfaithfulness while it also prompts God's judgment on the disobedient. At work in Israel's history is the zeal of God's people to protect God's honor by acting in judgment against sin,

which is in essence the story of Phinehas (Numb 25:11-13; Ps 106:29-31),[1]
Elijah (1 Kgs 19:10, 14), Jehu (2 Kgs 10:16-17, 30), and the Maccabees. Hence,
we cannot be surprised that in the book of Acts, the leaders of Jerusalem act
in "zeal" or "jealousy" at the Jesus movement's success (Acts 5:17) or that
the Jewish leaders in Pisidian Antioch or Thessalonica do the same (13:45;
17:5). The Weak of Rome, if our reading of 13:1-7 is accepted, belonged to
this zealotry tradition. But what does Paul have in mind in our text? In 2
Corinthians 11:2, we find an answer: "I feel a divine jealousy for you, for I
promised you in marriage to one husband, to present you as a chaste virgin
to Christ." So, this is what Paul has in mind: he wants fellow Jews to repent
from their rejection of the Messiah, to embrace Jesus as God's Messiah, and
to be zealous to protect God's honor by obeying the gospel.

Paul's logic progresses in stages drawn very much out of his mission experience of rejection: in response to his gospel preaching, Israel rejects Jesus
as Messiah and so stumbles over him;[2] Israel's stumbling prompts gentile
belief in Jesus; gentile faith provokes the zeal of Israelites; this zeal/jealousy
prompts Israelites to repent and turn in faith in Jesus as Messiah; and finally
God's faithfulness to the covenant with Israel is established.

It is at least worth wondering if Paul thinks his collection for the poor
saints in Jerusalem—that is, the funds he will take to Jerusalem with his
retinue of gentile believers—is in part designed to provoke nonbelieving
Jews in Jerusalem to jealousy and to embrace the Messiah. The suggestion
emerges from considering the importance of the collection at this time in
Paul's mission and its presence in Romans 15:25-29. One word does more
than make this suggestive: in Romans 15:29, Paul, in speaking of the collection, sees it as the "fullness of the blessings of Christ"; and in Romans 11:12, I
translate "how much will their fullness be!"; and in 11:25, a consistent translation spots again the "fullness of the gentiles." Perhaps then the collection
is connected to the jealousy theme.

When one knows where one stands or, to switch metaphors, when one
knows what to look for, one can look as Paul does at the current state of unbelief in Israel and explain it in light of the Messiah's work as the fulfillment of
the Abrahamic promise and covenant. In other words, Paul knows that both
gentile belief and Jewish unbelief do not erase divine fidelity to redeem Israel.

CORRELATION

Inside this theme of jealousy is another theme, what I call "correlation." Israel's rejection means gentile inclusion, and gentile inclusion means eventual

Israelite fullness—peace now by including gentiles, and peace later by including all Israel. Here's how Paul puts it to the Strong (talking about them and unfaithful Israel in the third person): "But through their stumbling salvation has come to the Gentiles" (11:11). Even more: "Now if their stumbling means riches for the world, and if their defeat means riches for Gentiles, how much more will their full inclusion mean!" (11:12). The correlation expands in 11:15: "For if their rejection is the reconciliation of the world, what will their acceptance be but life from the dead!"

Two images are used to clarify the correlation to the Strong: holy dough and branches. Romans 11:16 says, "If the part of the dough offered as first fruits is holy, then the whole batch is holy." Then he turns to trees: "and if the root is holy, then the branches also are holy." Which leads to extensive exploration of the tree-and-branches image in which he makes clear to the Strong that they have been grafted onto an existing tree: "But if some of the branches were broken off, and you, a wild olive shoot, were grafted in their place to share the rich root of the olive tree" (11:17). Pruning entails grafting, and grafting entails a full tree, including all Israel (11:23-24). The weightiest correlation, one that hints at the warning to come, comes after Paul has explored the tree and branches and pruning and grafting: "And so all Israel will be saved" (11:26a). The correlation turns more graphic in 11:28, and the Strong now become second person: "As regards the gospel they are enemies of God for *your* sake." One final time: "Just as *you* were once disobedient to God but have now received mercy because of their disobedience, so they have now been disobedient in order that, by the mercy shown to *you*, they too may now receive mercy" (11:30-31).

Paul knows this because he knows Jesus is Israel's Messiah, because he knows God is faithful to his covenant with Israel, because he knows gentiles, the Strong, are now coming into the people of God as a provocation of Israelites learning to believe in Jesus—and, since he knows all these things, he knows the correlations add up to both God's faithfulness and Israel's redemption. Like a ball of yarn chopped with a strong whack from a sharp knife, there are loose ends here jutting out in all directions, but the identity of the object remains clear. Some of these loose ends will find clarity as we proceed through the next three themes.

EXPANSION AND WARNING

These terms are glued tightly. Paul wants the Strong to know both that they are grafted onto the tree stock of Israel and that their ingrafting can be undone just as Israel's has been. Paul's image is not completely clear, but sorting out the precise details is neither possible nor necessary. It is possible the "root" (11:17) is the grace and calling of God, the Abrahamic covenant relation of Israel with YHWH, or even (less likely) the Messiah. Israel, it must be noticed, is not the root but the branches, and therefore one must find something for the "root" that is not Israelites. The grace of God's covenant seems best to me.

Israel's location in the rootstock is shaped by its faithfulness, and unfaithfulness can lead to the discipline or "severity" (11:22) of Israel's God. Again, no surprise here, and seeing this judgment against some of the branches is very common in the history of divine discipline (Deut 28). Paul goes out of his way in this passage to point out Israel's unfaithfulness three different times: "because of their unbelief" (11:20), "if they do not persist in their unbelief" (11:23), and thus we circle back to 11:17 to see "broken off" as the result of their unbelief. He has been using stumbling and rejection for what he now calls unbelief.

Their stubborn unbelief and stumbling over the Messiah led to divine discipline, which, in turn, created space on the rootstock for gentile believers to be grafted in. The Strong, then, need to see that formerly they were "wild olive" branches (11:17) but have been divinely nurtured into the rootstock of God's grace and now "share the rich root" with believing Jews. This little term, "share," in 11:17 can be passed over too easily: the Greek term is *sunkoinonos*, and that is one of Paul's favorite terms for ecclesial relations of the siblings in Christ. Ah, this completely resolves so much of the tension between the Weak and the Strong in Rome. As we will see, the Strong only *share* a place in God's grace with others; they are not the tree, the root, or all the branches.

In passing, God remains faithful to the covenant because the gentiles are not a start-all-over or a brand-new thing. Rather, they are simply and elegantly cut into the one grace of God that created Israel in the first place (and, as we will see, does not replace Israel). This has colossal implications for articulating the relationship of Israel and the church, but for now all that can be said is that Israel is not abandoned but expanded. Messiah people—and in Rome and elsewhere increasingly composed of gentile believers—are Israel people. Israel is not supplanted or replaced by the church. Rather, Israel is expanded to include gentiles even if in the process the pruning of Israel's God snips off some branches formerly comprised of Israelites—again, a nod to the Weak and Strong fellowship exhortation of Romans 14–15.

We are now ready for the rhetorical turning by Paul, a turning that becomes a warning. Disobedience, which has led to some pruning of Israelites, is as much a possibility for the Strong gentile believers as well. It is here that Paul's words to the Strong become most obvious: they are arrogant. He uses two terms: boast (11:18) and proud (11:20). They add up to arrogance and condescension toward the Weak in the churches of Rome. Here we are to see echoes of what we saw in Romans 14–15: high-status gentile believers who run over their fellow Jewish believers, who coerce them to eat what they consider disobedient to eat, who do not respect their calendrical observances, and who do not think circumcision is of any use to anyone. This is the arrogance Paul turns against. The alternative is not silence or passive-aggressive tolerance. Rather, the alternative is embrace, is respect, and all done by way of serving one another.

Their boasting leads Paul to explicit warning: "For if God did not spare the natural branches, perhaps he will not spare you" (11:21). The logic is from greater to lesser, and, in so using this logic, Paul betrays a theme that will pop up shortly: Israel is the original people of God; God made covenant with Israel; and if God can snip off the unfaithful of his covenant people, he can surely do it with the gentile believers.

The revelation of their sinful boasting and the warning of potential pruning leads Pastor Paul to explicit behavior that will prevent the pruning of gentile believers from the rootstock of God's grace. If unbelief led to the pruning of Israelites, then the gentiles need to guard themselves from a similar habit of turning from faith to unfaithfulness. The Strong are informed that they stand in the rootstock "only through faith" (11:20) and that they must persevere: "provided you continue in his kindness" (11:22). The Strong, to speak in other terms, need to be more humble about their privileged location in the people of God and to use their status and power in Rome for the good of others, especially the Weak.

After all, God can easily remove them and regraft into the rootstock of God's grace the Israelites who have been removed—thus: "And even those of Israel, if they do not persist in unbelief, will be grafted in, for God has the power to graft them in again" (11:23). Paul uses a fortiori logic: "How much more will these natural branches [Israel] be grafted back into their own olive tree" (11:24).

Loose ends can be ignored because Paul seems to have turned much inside out or upside down. Israel's rejection, so he is about to argue, is only temporary, and Israel's future is redemption!

TEMPORARY UNBELIEF

One loose end tied up is that the unbelief of Israel will not last. Hints of rejection of the Messiah turning into embrace of the Messiah have already surfaced in the jealousy theme, in the correlation theme, and in the expansion-warning theme, so the Strong would not have been completely taken aback when Phoebe informed them that Israel's unbelief and rejection were temporary. So when, in 11:12, Paul speaks of "their full inclusion," it may have jarred some readers, for he had been connecting Israel with stumbling and defeat. Then, in 11:14, he speaks of jealousy and saving some of his fellow Jews, and he adds their "acceptance" (11:15). In his root and branch and grafting image, he speaks again of Israel as grafted back (11:23-24). Israel is now unbelieving (11:28-32), but this is not the last word about Israel.

This means a temporary hardening, a temporary rejection, and a temporary unbelief are woven into the narrative that Paul is sketching for the Strong, all in an effort to press upon them their obligation to be faithful. This hardening, he says, lasts "until the full number of Gentiles has come in" (11:25). Then "all Israel will be saved" (11:26), and that salvation will occur through the Messiah redeemer (11:26, drawing from Isa 59:20-21). The correlation theme yet again: "Just as you were once disobedient to God but have now received mercy because of their disobedience, so they have now been disobedient in order that, by the mercy shown to you, they too may now receive mercy" (11:30-31).

Undergirding this return to faith by Israel is the faithfulness and grace of Israel's God. The "gifts and calling," which is the root of the tree, of Israel's God "are irrevocable" (11:29). The God of Israel is love, grace, and mercy (11:29-32). God will be faithful "for the sake of their ancestors" (11:28). In a curling move, Paul states that the former gentile disobedience is now matched by Israel's disobedience, but there is a divine intent here: "so that he may be merciful to all" (11:32). Disobedience by all humans creates the opportunity for the God of grace to show his love in all its priority, superabundance, and incongruity.

Paul's pain, then, is not interminable. It is not the final word. The final word of God in his relationship with Israel is grace, mercy, and redemption. For Paul, it is at times unfathomable and incomprehensible, but he finds here a resolution to his pain: Israel's unbelief is not final. The inscrutability of God's surprising ways with Israel and the gentiles, with the Weak and the Strong, elicits a Job-like eruption of praise about God's "depth" and how his judgments are "unsearchable" (11:33-36).

ISRAEL'S REDEMPTIVE FUTURE

If Israel's rejection of the Messiah is due to a divine but temporary hardening, one of God's surprising moves shifts from Israel in the flesh to Israel expanded, and, if the unbelief is temporary, Israel's future is final acceptance and belief. Again, this is anticipated and then stated plainly. The anticipations, as already mentioned, include 11:12 ("their full inclusion"), 11:14 ("thus save some"), 11:15 ("acceptance"), and 11:23-24 (grafting back in). It is not entirely clear what "the holy dough" means, but it seems to me that the "dough offered as first fruits" is at least the ancestors of Israel, and, since it is made holy by the gifts and calling of God, then the "whole batch" (Israel) is holy (11:16). He switches metaphors to make the same point: "if the root [gifts and calling of God's grace] is holy, then the branches [Israel] also are holy" (11:16).

All of this leads to the astounding comment in 11:26: "And so all Israel will be saved." How to read this? Israel, which almost uniformly means Israel-in-the-flesh in Pauline letters, has a few options, and they need to be stated to keep the discussion honest: ethnic Israel (that is, all of Abraham's flesh descendants through Isaac); Israel in the flesh plus Abraham's faith descendants; Israel expanded to include gentiles (that is, Abraham's faith descendants but only faith descendants—that is, the Jewish remnant plus gentile believers in Jesus); or Israel as a metaphor for church, which means the church has in some way reframed Israel (and some appeal to Gal 6:16).

The instinct of Bible readers must be Israel-in-the-flesh because the term is so often used that way from Moses to Paul. It is impossible, I contend therefore, to opt instinctually for the fourth option. One can't wipe out fleshly Israel that swiftly. The term "Israel" is used by the apostle, and his use must be respected.[3] An immediate observation of Paul's own usage is his expansion or reduction of Israel-in-the-flesh to become Israel-by-faith. Thus, Romans 9:6 states that "not all who are descended from Israel [in the flesh] are Israel [by faith]." Israel's fleshly numbers may be great, but there remains only a remnant (9:27), and that remnant is Israel-by-faith, who are foreknown to God (11:2). Yet, Paul also uses "Israel" for Israel-in-the-flesh (9:31; 10:19, 21; 11:7; 1 Cor 10:18; 2 Cor 3:7, 13; Eph 2:12; Phil 3:5). Israel-in-the-flesh has been hardened temporarily (Rom 11:25), but in the future "all Israel will be saved" (11:26). Which Israel—in the flesh or in faith—is it?

The decision is rendered by examining the rejection-belief theme. One can speak of full inclusion and salvation, but one can speak of that redemption only if one speaks at the same time of a jealousy that provokes Israel to respond in faith. Thus, "acceptance" (11:15) and remaining in the rootstock requires faith and continuing in that faith (11:20, 22). Hence, Israel is grafted back into the rootstock and therefore redeemed and saved "if they do not persist in unbelief" (11:23). Furthermore, that redemption comes only by way of the "Deliverer," a saving agent who comes into Paul's letter by quoting from Isaiah 59:20-21.[4] In Pauline theology, this is Jesus Messiah, whom God sends for redemption. It is entirely likely that Paul is referring here to a future event, and most likely he is thinking in terms of the parousia. The future redemption Paul has in mind is a redemption through Jesus as Israel's Messiah.

REVIEW

The word "all" now carries all the weight. How can it be "all" Israel if only those Israelites who turn from their rejection and turn to Jesus as Messiah are redeemed? "All" here must mean, as I would argue for Galatians 6:16, Israel-in-the-flesh, who is also Israel-by-faith-in-the-Messiah. This Israel-by-faith joins with gentile believers—the Strong and the Weak now in one family of God, the church. Call it what you want; Paul does not think redemption can be had outside the grace and calling of God in Christ.

WEAK & STRONG

CONCLUSION

To the Weak, Paul says God is faithful to the Abrahamic covenant. God is faithful in surprising ways, including Jesus as the Messiah. God is faithful, too, in raising up in each moment in Israel's history a remnant that remains faithful. God is faithful, too, in including gentiles who turn for redemption to Israel's Messiah—which means: the gentile Strong are siblings of the Weak.

To the Strong, Paul says God is faithful to Israel both in including gentiles and in promising a future redemption for Israel. The Strong cannot become arrogant and think they alone are privileged because their God, who is the God of Israel, is faithful to the covenant. In fact, God's calling of Israel is irrevocable. That irrevocability, however, takes surprising turns, including the Messiah and including gentile inclusion and including a future turning of Israelites to Jesus as Messiah. Since God is faithful to Israel, the Strong are to embrace the Weak as siblings in Christ.

III
A Torah That Disrupts Peace

Romans 1–4

13 GARY

THE OPENING TO THE LETTER

(1:1-17)

Starting at the end, we now come to the beginning, to what is considered by many to be the "theological" or "theoretical" portions of Romans—namely, chapters 1 through 8. One can make a case for three or four parts to Romans: either Romans 1–8, 9–11, and 12–16 or Romans 1–4, 5–8, 9–11, and 12–16. Either way, Romans 1–4 and 5–8 work in tandem. Hence, I begin with Romans 1–4.

In our commitment to reading Romans as pastoral theology, as a letter to specific house churches in Rome for specific issues facing those churches in Rome, we need to keep that situation before us. Thus, we recall the situation about the Weak and the Strong.

THE CONTEXT, BY WAY OF REMINDER

Because it is too easy to turn Romans into theoretical theology written by a theologian to theologians, and because time has shown that the soteriological readings of Romans minimize and even ignore the ecclesial, pastoral context of Romans, I detail three important elements of that context now: the Weak and the Strong, Phoebe, and lived theology.

Wk & Str

The Weak and the Strong

What we said about the Weak at the end of our discussion of Romans 12–16 can now be supplemented after reading Romans 9–11, and the italics are the additional elements: The *Weak* are Jewish believers who are in the stream of God's election *and need to be affirmed in their election*, but who have questions about the faithfulness of God to that election and who need to embrace the surprising moves of God throughout Israel's history; the Weak know the Torah, practice the Torah, but sit in judgment on gentiles, especially the Strong

91

in the Christian community in Rome, even though they have no status or privilege or power; furthermore, the Weak are tempted to resist paying taxes to Rome on the basis of the Jewish zealotry tradition. In addition, *the Weak need to apply "faith in Christ" more radically to themselves, so discovering that they are a new example of the "remnant" of Israel, and they need to see that the sufficiency of faith means that gentile believers in Christ are siblings so they see that Torah observance is not the way of transformation for either themselves or the Strong in Rome.*

The Strong, by way of reminder, are predominately gentiles who believe in Jesus as Messiah or king, who do not observe Torah as the will of God for them, and who have condescending and despising attitudes, probably toward Jews, but especially toward Jewish believers in Jesus, and all of this is wrapped up in the superior higher status of the Strong in Rome. Paul and Jewish believers who embrace the nonnecessity of Torah observance are among the Strong. The Strong then are as known for their position on observance of Torah and for their status as they are for ethnicity. (We will learn more about the Strong as we read through Romans 1–8, especially as we read Romans 5–8.)

Phoebe

Phoebe, we remind ourselves, is the reader, and her female voice speaks for the apostle who commissioned her to communicate this letter in Rome. She is Paul's presence in each setting where she reads this letter; she is the one who will go "off script" if consternation is found on faces and who will know what to emphasize in each sentence. She will know whom to face when addressing specific groups—Strong and Weak—which is important. How long does it take to read Romans aloud? How long does it take to perform Romans when folks can interrupt with questions or wait until the end to probe what Paul meant? Hours. Phoebe's task was to perform this letter in each of the house churches in Rome, and most think there were at least five such house settings. Perhaps more. Think of Phoebe reading this letter daily for a week with conversations shifting from one house church to another. While she may have had the only copy of Romans in Rome, it is at least likely that some may have spent mornings or late nights making at least one copy for the churches of Rome.

Lived Theology

Lived theology was muted but present throughout Romans 9–11. How so? The heightened level of Paul's remonstrations with the Weak in 9:1–11:10

emerges from his desire to see them cease judgment of the Strong and express fellowship of equality at the table, and the warning of 11:11-36 reveals Paul's concern for the faithfulness of the Strong to the gospel teachings. Which are? To summarize the lived theology of Romans 12–16, we have settled on one central term: Christoformity. Christoformity comes to fruition in an embodied God orientation, in a Body-of-Christ orientation, and in a public orientation. The fundamental core of Christoformity is "because you are in Christ, you are not to act according to Privilege and Power, to elective status and to history, but instead you are to love your neighbor by offering your entire body daily to God, to live as siblings with all other Christians by welcoming one another and eating at the table with each other and indwelling one another, and you are to love your Roman neighbor as yourself with civility and intentional acts of benevolence. Only in this way can Peace be found in Rome." That is lived theology for Paul for the Roman Christians, and that is why Romans 1–8 says what it does. Unless and until Romans 1–8 is shaped to speak to Christoform peace, it is misunderstood. We begin with Romans 1:1-7.

THE OPENING TO THE LETTER

Paul describes himself in terms that were probably most important to his self-identity. He is a *slave* of Jesus Christ, a term that simultaneously degrades Paul's status in the Flesh, especially Roman-empire Flesh, and upgrades his status because he is connected to the world's true ruler. His second descriptor is that he's an *apostle,* which here functions as a near equivalent to "slave." He's called and sent out on mission by Jesus himself, which echoes the story of Acts 9, 22, and 26, and he is "set apart for the gospel of God." Paul wants the Roman house churches to see him as a slave of the Messiah who was commissioned by the Lord Jesus.

THE GOSPEL AND OBEDIENCE OF FAITH

Paul slides from self-description into mission description in both slave and apostle, but his gentile mission becomes the focus of Romans 1:1-4 with the term "gospel." Gospel is the announced message of Jesus and the apostles, and Paul defines it here as a message "concerning his Son, who was descended from David according to the flesh and was declared to be Son of God with power according to the spirit of holiness by resurrection from the dead, Jesus Christ our Lord" (1:3-4). Nearly identical terms are used in 2 Timothy 2:8: "Remember Jesus Christ, raised from the dead, a descendant

of David—that is my gospel." If one ties Romans 1:3-4 and 2 Timothy 2:8 to
1 Corinthians 15:1-8, the gospel is defined as the public announcement about
Jesus ("concerning his Son"), the long-awaited Davidic messianic King. This
Jesus fulfills Israel's story/Scripture ("he promised beforehand through his
prophets in the holy scriptures"), he lived and died and was raised, and that
resurrection effectively declares him as the world's true Lord ("declared to
be Son of God"). At work in this declaration is "with power" and "according
to the spirit of holiness" (1:4). Snapping Death is the aim of the redemption
in Christ, while "spirit of holiness" is a Semitism meaning (probably) "Holy
Spirit."[1] Paul says nearly the same thing in 1:9: "by announcing the gospel
of [about] his Son." The word "Son" in this context is a near synonym to
"Messiah/Christ"—which is to say, it means "King" (2 Sam 7:14). The gospel
that Paul preaches, with its Jewish terms and categories, appeals to the Weak
and challenges the Strong to come to terms with their grafting into Israel's
stock. At the same time, it subverts any claims to Power and Privilege outside
the realm of Jesus' kingship.

It needs to be noted that the word "Messiah" (Christ) would not reso-
nate with the Strong or those who had come to faith out of the gentile world.
Messiah connects with the Weak in spades, but one has to wonder if Paul's
words—"Jesus Christ our Lord"—are not an umbrella for the whole church
at Rome. That is, Jesus is "Messiah" for the Weak and "Lord" for the Strong.

This gospel statement (Rom 1:3-4) is the apostolic tradition (1 Cor
15:1-8). Yet, Paul expands that bare-bones gospel tradition. This can be put
into schematic form with twelve features,[2] beginning with the core gospel
tradition: Jesus' preexistence (1:3), human descendance from David, death
for sins, burial, being among the dead ones, resurrection, initial appearances,
and his installation as Son of God at the throne of God. Onto this core gospel
tradition Paul adds Jesus' subsequent appearance to others (1 Cor 15:6-7),
an appearance to Paul (15:8), Paul's commission as apostle (15:7-11; Rom
1:5), and Paul's mission to the gentiles (1 Cor 15:11; Rom 1:5-6). The core
gospel *about* Jesus thus becomes the expanded gospel tradition about Jesus
for the gentiles through Paul's mission. The moment one adds "gentile mission"
to the gospel, the Strong and the Weak stand at attention. Both the core and
the expanded gospel tradition are fundamentally derived from Israel's story.[3]

The gospel "concerning his Son"—that is, the gospel whose content is
Jesus the person—is a performative utterance: the announcement is redemptive. Paul's call into the mission to gentiles meant redemption was expanded.
The purpose of Paul's mission, which must be connected especially to Romans
14–15, is "to bring about the obedience of faith among all the Gentiles."

Though for some any connection of "faith" to "obedience" is jarring, for Paul grace creates faith and faith creates obedience. Paul will finish this letter on this very note: "what Christ has accomplished through me *to win obedience from the Gentiles*" (15:18), "according to my gospel ... now disclosed ... to all the Gentiles, according to the command of the eternal God, *to bring about the obedience of faith*" (16:25-26). The problem in Rome among both the Strong and the Weak is disobedience in the midst of this obedience (16:19), and that disobedience resulted in schisms and tensions. Disobedience leads to division; obedience promotes peace. In the middle of Romans, Paul also focused on this gospel-based obedience (6:12, 16, 17). The purpose of Romans is *lived theology*, or, in terms of 1:7, to be "saints" (holy ones). For Paul, the "obedience of faith" in 1:5 is about the Strong disavowing their power to welcome and empower the Weak (14:1; 15:1), just as it is about the Weak ceasing to think their elective privilege demands that the Strong assume Torah observance (14:10). One might say then that "obedience of faith" is another version of Christoformity or the vital organs of peace.

Paul's mission is to the gentiles, and the Roman house churches to whom this letter is addressed appear to be predominantly gentile: "including yourselves" (1:6) goes with "among all the Gentiles" (1:5). Debate today rages over the demographics of the Roman house churches: Mostly Jewish believers? Mostly gentile believers? In discussing the long section from Romans 1:18 through 4:25, I will attempt to answer that question.

THANKSGIVING

Paul's thanksgivings often look to the past, the present, and the future as they also anticipate themes in the letter itself.[4] I will draw attention to a few themes in this thanksgiving.

Personal Language

This abundance of personal language in Romans 1:8-17 communicates Paul's mission and heart to the Romans—a congregation known to Paul—in order to invite them to welcome his letter. The personal language is found in "I": I thank, I serve, I remember, I may somehow at least succeed in coming to you, I am longing to see you so that I may share, I want you to know ... that I have often intended to come to you[5] ... in order that I may reap some harvest among you, I am debtor, I am not ashamed of the gospel. Add to these "my God" and "my spirit" and "my witness" and "my prayers" and "my faith" and "my eagerness." Paul is flanked in his "I" statements both by God and by the

Romans. God is on his side (1:9) and is guiding him (1:10), and Paul offers
affirmation of the believers in Rome. In these affirmations, he seems to have
both the Weak and the Strong in mind when he says, "because your faith
is proclaimed throughout the world" (1:8) and "that we may be mutually
encouraged by each other's faith." This mutuality is not quite as effusive as
what we encountered in 15:14 ("I myself feel confident about you"), but it is
a public affirmation heard rolling off the tongue of Phoebe. His hope is to
"share with you some spiritual gift to strengthen you" (1:11) or, in other words,
to "reap some harvest among you" (1:13). All in all, it is a personal affective
introduction of Paul to the Romans.

Mission

His mission comes to the fore yet again: "I am a debtor both to the Greeks
and to barbarians, both to the wise and to the foolish" (1:14). Noticeably,
he uses "Greeks," not "gentiles," and he speaks in terms of social status, not
simply ethnicities. As status does not matter to God, so status cannot matter
for Paul. His mission is next explained as his eagerness to preach the gospel
in Rome (1:15). Again, we go back to what we read in Romans 15, where
Paul outlined a map of his plans (probably) to circle the Mediterranean with
gospel preaching (15:19-21).

Why Proclaim the Gospel to Rome?

We have every reason to believe Paul thinks the church people in Rome are
believers. He says they are "called to belong to Jesus Christ" (1:6), and his letter
is for "God's beloved" and those "called to be saints" (1:7). His prayer is as Jesus-
shaped as it can be: "Grace to you and peace from God our Father," and from "the
Lord Jesus Christ" (1:7). *Why then does he say in 1:15 that he wants "to proclaim the
gospel to you also who are in Rome"?* For Paul, the "gospel" is more than a message
designed to precipitate conversions to Jesus. His gospel preaching is not just to
gain converts but is instead the *entirety of his message*. We have sketched Paul's
big vision and soon we will draw attention as well in Romans 5–8 to that vision:
the aim of redemption is transformation of humans into *Christoformity* so peace
can invade the heart of the empire. Hence, his desire to preach the gospel to them
is a desire for a lived theology called the "obedience of faith."

Not Ashamed

Paul's most famous "I" statement is that he is *"not ashamed"* of the gospel
(1:16-17). In Romans 14–15, two groups in Rome help explain this surprising

"not ashamed." The Weak might wonder if Paul's gospel can create moral transformation into holy living for the Strong, and Romans 6 could well reflect the Weak's attitude to the Strong or, even more, the Strong's own terms (more on that later). In addition to speaking to the Weak, the "not ashamed" expression throws shade on those who had status and Privilege and Power. To be connected to Jesus was to be connected to the one crucified, and that was shameful to status-conscious Romans. To call Jesus Messiah and Lord was in their worldview ludicrous. Roman Flesh yearned for status and operated with military power. Paul subverts Roman Flesh. In fact, Paul's so-called shamefulness connected him with a new privilege: he became the apostle of the crucified Lord. What the world calls dishonorable, Paul calls honorable. What it classifies as shameful, he classifies as status giving. And what the world calls powerlessness, Paul calls the power of God for salvation! In other words, the "ashamed" in Romans 1:16-17 is a reprise of Paul's famous words in 1 Corinthians 1:23, 24: "Christ crucified, a stumbling block to Jews and foolishness to Gentiles," who is "the power of God and the wisdom of God." Paul subverts the worldliness of the Roman empire by believing and preaching the Lordliness of the crucified Jesus. He is not one bit ashamed of that gospel. That gospel, furthermore, is taking root in Rome in small house churches, among the poor, and among the low of status, and this kind of Christoformity subverts Roman Flesh and empire ideology.

Gospel Themes

This Lordliness-of-Jesus gospel, this Son-of-God gospel, strikes major gospel themes in Romans 1:16-17: the gospel is God's power unleashed for salvation/rescue, redemption is experienced by faith, it is for both Jews and gentiles, and, in theodicy fashion, it manifests God's own righteousness. A word now about each.

First, the gospel saves. This gospel—outlined in 1 Corinthians 15:1-8 (or 15:1-28), preached in the sermons in Acts, and restated in the same terms in 2 Timothy 2:8—announces that Jesus is the Son of God, that he is a Davidic fulfillment, and that this gospel is demonstrated by his resurrection. This announcement unleashes, through the Spirit, God's "power" and brings "salvation" (1:16)—which is to say that it is not the gospel that saves but God revealed in the Christ who entered into our condition, died for us, and was raised for our justification (4:25; 5:12-21; cf. Phil 2:6-11; Col 1:15-20). Salvation in Paul's theology is about assuming the condition of the unworthy,[6] unraveling and forgiving that condition, rescuing the unworthy and enslaved, and making them and creation itself into the kingdom's new

Spirit-generated creation—all so they can be conformed to the image of the Son himself (8:31-39). Such persons then reciprocate the gift of salvation with a life of loving welcome of others and holiness in all of life; in effect, they become embodied sacrifices (12:1-2), other-oriented, and slaves of God and of righteousness (6:15-23). This process of redemption that finds its completion in the new heavens and new earth is why Paul calls it the "power" of God: power to create new creation.

Second, faith engages us in this redemption. "To believe" or "to have faith" (the two terms have the same Greek root: *pist-*) is not a "work" but a posture of trust and surrender and allegiance. In Romans, the opposite of faith is to practice the works of the Torah, understood essentially as doing the commands of Moses, but with—at least for the Weak—having the divisive edge of covenant election. This edge of Torah observance is found in both Romans 9:11–11:10 and Romans 14–15. Those who read Romans backwards hear a ringing echo of these passages when the word "faith" is mentioned as it is here in Romans 1:16.

Third, the gospel saves Jews and then gentiles. Regardless of who it is, regardless of status (*Dunatoi* or *A-Dunatoi*, Strong or Weak, Powerful or Powerless), regardless of one's measurement with respect to Torah or ethnicity, anyone who turns to God in Christ in faith comes into the ambit of the power of God for redemption. Yet, as Romans 9–11 makes clear over and over, "to the Jew first" means that God's covenant with Abraham/Israel is not super-seded; what God promised to Israel remains firm, and God is faithful to the promise. But Israel is now no longer alone: "and also to the Greek."[7] Romans 11:11-24 argued that gentiles are grafted onto the rootstock of Israel even if some in Israel were cut off. The church of Jews and gentiles then is understood as *expanding* Israel, not erasing Israel. This letter's opening "to the Jew first and also to the Greek" in 1:16 anticipates the full narrative of Romans 9–11 just as that narrative clarifies the language of 1:16.

Fourth, God's own righteousness is revealed. The "righteousness of God" in 1:17 is an attribute of God. God in God's own self *is* the standard of righteousness (ontology), and God utterly conforms to that standard. God, then, is faithful to the promises made from Abraham on, and the *gospel about Jesus as God's Son reveals God's own righteousness.*[8]

Time now to grab the nettle: "Through faith for faith" (*ek pisteos eis pistin*), or more literally "out of faith unto faith." I will sort out various ways of reading this expression, but it does not appear to me that any of these readings are compelling, because each makes sense. This "through faith for faith" could refer to personal growth in faith—Jewish or gentile faith, or a person's growth in faith from one stage to another. Perhaps "through faith for faith" is a pregnant expression for "altogether by faith." Yet, the emphasis in 1:17 is *God's* righteousness, so "through faith" (*from* faith) could refer to God's own faithfulness with "unto faith" pointing to Jews and gentiles embracing the revelation of God in Christ by faith. Or perhaps "through faith for faith" refers to the faithfulness of Jesus ("through faith") that makes possible our allegiance ("for faith") to him. The nettle is many-leaved, for Paul's quotation of Habakkuk 2:4 complicates the discussion.[9] If we read this expression in light of the big themes of Habakkuk 2, we would think of the hopeful trust and obedience of the righteous one waiting for God's redemption.[10] Habakkuk's second chapter contrasts the proud and wealthy with the righteous who live by faith. That chapter in many ways anticipates some of what Paul says about the Weak and the Strong. If one extends this to reading Romans backwards—and this is but an echo of a guess—perhaps he means the Strong's faith ("through faith") and the Weak's need "for faith," just as we can read it vice versa. That is, the Weak are those in Israel's covenant, and now the Strong are being grafted in! Noteworthy, too, is that Paul's mission to the gentiles was emphasized in the verses prior to Romans 1:16-17 (cf. 1:10-15). This lends weight to seeing "from faith unto faith" (1:17) as fulfillment of the Abrahamic promise of Genesis 12:3. Thus, "from faith" points back to Abraham, and "unto faith" to the fulfillment in the church.[11] The ambiguity of the expression itself—"from faith unto faith"—prompts these various readings, and there appears to be nothing that cuts through the ambiguity.

start here for Nov. 4 (1–4

THE RHETORIC OF ROMANS 1–2

Reading Romans 1–4 begins with how we read 1:18-32, and it is customary to think 1:18-32 is about the sinfulness of gentiles, while 2:1–3:8 concerns Jewish sinfulness, and then 3:9-20 points both—that is, all humans—to the way of redemption. Put more traditionally: Paul indicts the gentiles as generic humanity in 1:18-32 and then specifically the Jews in 2:1–3:20. Then he explains redemption in Christ alone in 3:21-26 and so focuses on faith alone instead of works as the proper response to God's grace in Christ (3:27–4:25). One more way of saying this is that he presents bad news (1:18–3:20), the good news (3:21-26), and how to get it (3:27–4:25). This standard reading has a clear agenda: it *universalizes the soteriology of Paul.* It also removes the message from the social context sketched in Romans 12–16.

Who Paul has in mind in Romans 2 may not be as clear as the universalizing approach thinks, but reading Romans backwards sheds light on the sweep from Romans 1:18 through the end of chapter 4. In fact, our approach leads to a more rhetorical reading of Romans 1–4 that unlocks the door to reading the whole of Romans more pastorally.

READING ROMANS 1:18-32 BACKWARDS

Though our outlines are imposed on the text, they are designed to help readers make sense of the text as it is. Romans 1:18-32 is a strong indictment, but just exactly who and why are not as clear. For many, it is an indictment of every human being, or a repeat of Adam's and Eve's sin in Eden, and this universalistic reading fits into a schematic view of Romans 1–4: everyone is condemned (1:18–3:20); everyone needs the Savior (3:21-26); everyone needs to have faith (4:1-25). However, when Romans 1:18-32 is coupled with 2:1-29 or with 2:1–3:26, a more compelling reading becomes possible.

Paul explicitly describes his audience in 1:18-32. This group is marked by sin and suppression of the truth even though God is revealed to them. Knowing God, they did not honor or thank God and became futile and darkened.

They made a claim for wisdom, but they became idol-makers and idolaters. Consequently, God handed them over, and that led to embodied degradation and impurity through uncontrolled desires. This degradation included unnatural[1] same-sex sexual relations, a view derived just as much from Paul's Bible (cf. Lev 18:22; 20:13) as from his perception of what is unnatural. Once again, Paul describes this group's embodied life of sin.

Noticeably, there are no words like "all humanity" or "all creation" or even "all gentiles." We must wait until 3:9 ("all, both Jews and Greeks") or 3:23 ("all") to get anything like that. While summaries like 3:9 and 3:23 are often read back into 1:18-32 with reason, we don't need to rush there quite yet. The emphases of the list above are on those who—knowing the truth or knowing God, *as creatures of God*—choose not to respond to God properly and who choose instead to become *idolaters* with the specific result of *God's consequent surrendering them to their free choices,* which lead to debased desires and manifold sins. Paul brings to the fore the connection of turning from God to God's unleashing sinful behaviors. Theology proper and ethics are inextricably interwoven (1:18, 21, 22, 25, 28, 32). The sins explicitly described in 1:18-32 are not common sins of common sinners, and they are beyond a stretch for describing Jewish sins. Furthermore, Romans 2:14-15 offers an entirely different description of gentiles, one where some are approved by God on the basis of their moral behaviors![2] Thus, 1:18-32 cannot describe all humans or even all gentiles.

A noticeable element in Paul's description is divine judgment, and it recurs in the thrice-repeated "God handed them over" (1:24, 26, 28), each of which is a response to intentional acts of idolatry and sinful behaviors (1:23, 25, 26-27). Notice "they exchanged" (*allasso, metallasso,* 1:23, 25) with "God gave them up" (*paradidomi,* 1:24, 26, 28). At work here is human freedom and divine permission and abandonment that amounts to a depressingly vicious cycle of human diminishment, dehumanization, and destruction. Furthermore, this divine handing-over defines some of what "wrath of God" in 1:18 means—that is, it refers to divine judgment on recalcitrant humans, resulting in divine permission for humans to choose their own moral debasement. As Wisdom of Solomon puts it, "one is punished by the very things by which one sins" (11:16).

To summarize before we take the next step: Romans 1:18-32 describes not typical sins of typical sinners but specific sins of a specific kind of sinner. Paul is not universalizing here. He is setting up the audience of Romans 2. Put differently, talking *about* the gentiles is not the same as talking *to* the gentiles. But before we get to the rhetorical turn of Romans 2, we need to see the context for Romans 1:18-32.

The Stereotype

Romans 1:18-32 is *a biblically rooted judgment on gentile sinfulness.* Thus, Psalm 79:6 reads, "Pour out your anger on the nations." But it is more than biblically rooted. The words in Romans 1 are a *standard Jewish stereotype* of the godless, idolatrous gentiles of the diaspora. Romans 1:18-32 does not describe all humans. There is too much particularity and resonance with other Jewish texts in Paul's descriptions of sinful behaviors and idolatries for this to be about common human sinfulness. Paul has been on a mission among gentiles for two decades, and the language we read in Romans 1 has had some close encounters with the notorious sins of gentiles.[3] So, once again, yes, 1:18-32 is about gentiles, but it is more a Jewish stereotype of a specific sort of gentile.

For support in calling Romans 1:18-32 a stereotype, we need merely to look at the language of Wisdom of Solomon 13–14, which itself emerges from a long biblical tradition of casting deep shadows over paganisms. Two summary statements pull into one bundle the near equivalent of what Paul himself does in Romans 1, most notably in connecting idolatry to moral corruption:

> For the worship of idols not to be named is the beginning and cause and end of every evil. (Wis 14:27)

> But just penalties will overtake them on two counts: because they thought wrongly about God in devoting themselves to idols, and because in deceit they swore unrighteously through contempt for holiness. (14:30; cf. 11:15-16)

Wisdom of Solomon contends, as does Paul, that humans know God and God's ways because they are God's own creation. Knowledge of God, then, is natural to these gentiles. As Wisdom of Solomon puts it,

> For all people who were ignorant of God were foolish by nature; and they were unable from the good things that are seen to know the one who exists, nor did they recognize the artisan while paying heed to his works; but they supposed that either fire or wind or swift air, or the circle of the stars, or turbulent water, or the luminaries of heaven were the gods that rule the world. (13:1-2)

Perhaps most tellingly similar is that Paul's listing of sins and that of the Wisdom of Solomon connect:

Then it was not enough for them to err about the knowledge of God, but though living in great strife due to ignorance, they call such great evils peace. For whether they kill children in their initiations, or celebrate secret mysteries, or hold frenzied revels with strange customs, they no longer keep either their lives or their marriages pure, but they either treacherously kill one another, or grieve one another by adultery, and all is a raging riot of blood and murder, theft and deceit, corruption, faithlessness, tumult, perjury, confusion over what is good, forgetfulness of favors, defiling of souls, sexual perversion, disorder in marriages, adultery, and debauchery. (14:22-26)

This is followed by the line we first quoted above: their sins are rooted in their idolatry (14:27). Not all gentiles live out these sins. *But this is the stereotype of the Jewish prophetic critique and accusation of paganism and its ways.* Jews knew this description; they believed this description; they repeated this description; this was the stereotyped *immoral pagan idolater.* Even the "wrath of God" (Rom 1:18), which is found many times in the Old Testament, has something of an echo in Wisdom of Solomon 14:9-10: "for equally hateful to God are the ungodly and their ungodliness; for what was done will be punished together with the one who did it." He calls this a divine "visitation" (14:11), says a "speedy end has been planned" (14:14), and describes "just penalties" (14:30, 31).

Paul's language is not identical but close enough that it is reasonable to think Paul either is using Wisdom of Solomon or is dependent on the kind of tradition at work in that text. He can contend that these suppressors of truth know God naturally (Rom 1:19-20), he can blame idolatry for all of it (1:23, 25, 28), and he can then specify the sins—the notorious sins of notorious sinners, as it were—as both unnatural same-sex intercourse (1:24, 26-27) and a laundry list of the kinds of sins prophetic accusations pointed out (1:28-31). The sins themselves are divine punishment (Wis 11:16).[4]

The language of Romans 1 is the stereotypical language of Jewish critique of immoral gentile idolaters. A desire to indict all of humanity often becomes the determinative piece of logic, but reading Romans backwards cuts a different pattern on the ice, one that I want to suggest carries us into chapter 2 as we see how this chapter fits rhetorically with chapter 1.

The Rhetorical Turn

The language of the Wisdom of Solomon and Romans 1 is strong, but 1:18-32 is rhetorically shaped to turn the tables in chapter 2 where we meet the Judge. Once again, we are helped by Wisdom of Solomon 13–14: the theme of the larger section in that book (chaps. 11–19) is Israel's election and divine

Talmud ?

favor: "For you tested them as a parent does in warning, but you examined the ungodly as a stern king does in condemnation" (11:10). God loves all and is patient, but his favor rests upon Israel, giving them covenant, promises, and Torah, and judging all people with utter justice. The gentiles are tied into idolatries and sins and deserving of divine judgment, but Israel in God's mercy has learned the way of righteousness. The author of this text, rooting his story in the exodus from Egypt, uses relentlessly strong contrasting images to cast gentiles in dark shadows while the mercy of light and glory shines upon Israel. He glorifies Israel and simultaneously sits in judgment on the gentiles. Wisdom of Solomon, I suggest, sets the tone for how to read Romans 1:18 through Romans 2 (and all the way through chapter 4). What we will see is that Paul has more or less imitated the Wisdom of Solomon in the posture of the Judge. Thus, the Wisdom of Solomon says, "For by the same means by which you punished our enemies you called us to yourself and glorified us" (18:8). Or: "For in everything, O Lord, you have exalted and glorified your people, and you have not neglected to help them at all times and in all places" (19:22). That pride, that sense of election, that sense of privilege is what stands out in the author's relentless critique of the gentiles. That pride, in other words, sets the tone for the Judge of Romans 2 similarly sitting in judgment on the gentiles in 1:18-32.[5] Whoever this Judge is—and I will suggest he is the major representative of the Weak—he becomes the target of Paul's rhetoric as one who is a hypocrite. I suggest that the Judge is either "Amen"-ing or speaking the words of 1:18-32. But Paul puts those words in the Judge's mouth so the Judge's words can be turned against him. The Judge is judged by the Judge's own accusations because the Judge is sinning in similar ways. Here is what Paul says: "You … are doing the very same things" (2:1, 2), and God's patience is being abused (2:4) because of the Judge's hard, impenitent heart (2:5) and self-seeking disobedience of the truth resulting in wickedness and evil (2:8-9). All the while, the Judge is seeking praise and honor (2:29).

Romans 2 shifts noticeably from third person (those in 1:18-32) to second person, signaling not only a shift grammatically but a rhetorical shift throwing weight on the importance of chapter 2. The focus shifts from the stereotyped sinners to the Judge. This is confirmed by everything that happens in Romans 3 and 4, which are questions *the Judge* is asking or answers Paul turns back on the Judge. Three questions are asked: the question about Jewish election, privilege, and priority (3:1-20); the question about boasting (3:27-31); and the biggest question of them all, the question about Abraham and faith (4:1-25). There are no anticipated questions from the gentiles, and hence we cannot see 1:18-32 standing in for the Strong of Romans 14–15. But we have every reason to think chapters 2 through 4 have the Weak in mind, who, like the Judge of 2:1-16, were sitting in judgment on the Strong. Noticeably, the Greek term *krino*, "judge," finds its locations in chapters 2, 3, and 14 (14:3-5, 10, 13, 22). Reading Romans forwards in the traditional manner shows that Paul avoids using the term "Weak" for the Judge. But if in reading forwards we fail to take the whole letter in mind, we will fail to see the pastoral, ecclesial, and rhetorical nature of what happens at 2:1. I contend reading Romans backwards makes that more explicit and suggests that the Judge represents the Weak judges of Romans 14–15.

The diatribe style[6] in 2:1-5[7] and 2:17-24 points us at a concrete audience. Rhetoric was used like this in Greek and Roman schools, and it was how students learned to argue a case. Furthermore, the diatribe style was used for the in-group: the person in the direct address ("You" or the so-called Jew) is in the house churches of Rome. The style then constructs Paul as their teacher and apostle-pastor and the Judge as his opponent. Romans 2 is aimed specifically at an audience in Rome, and there are particular reasons for Paul to buckle down on this audience: namely, the Weak—now defined more narrowly or, perhaps better, reduced to a representative or caricature. The Weak are not simply Jewish believers, nor are they typical Jews; they are Jewish believers who are judgmental toward gentile believers, the Strong. The Weak do not represent stereotypical Jewish election privilege or stereotypical legalism, but instead they *are* Jewish believers in Rome who condemn the Strong of Rome. It is the Christian Judge who claims privilege that concerns Paul, not the ordinary Jew.

To sum up the rhetorical turn as a way of reading Romans 1–2: we may be uncomfortable with Paul's sweeping "Jew" language, but reading Romans backwards presses us to see that *Paul's focus in this letter is not with Jews per se but rather with the Weak*. The Weak are not stand-ins for "Jews," and neither are they a stereotype for a Jew. Rather, as is made clear in Romans 2 and 3, the Weak are limited by Paul to the Judge. The stereotype is real, but it is of a Weak representative sitting in judgment on the Strong because they are not historically the elect and are not observing Torah. Furthermore, the Weak may well be stereotyping the Strong as *idolaters*. They wouldn't be the first or last to overcook a problem group.

Here is a summary to keep the whole of Romans in view and to anticipate what is to come: Paul's polemic in Romans 1–4 with the Judge/Weak arises only because the Weak believe the path to moral transformation for the Strong can be achieved only by adopting and observing the Torah. Romans 1–8 occur then in two blocks: the argument against Torah observance as the path to moral transformation, and an argument in favor of union with Christ and Spirit-indwelling as the true path to moral transformation.

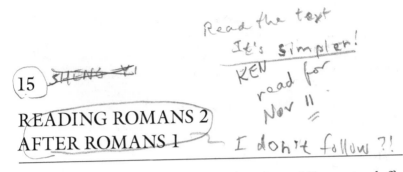

READING ROMANS 2
AFTER ROMANS 1

Paul used Romans 1:18-32 to set up the Judge, who would have entered affirmatively into his rhetoric. That affirmation came to an abrupt end with the opening of Romans 2: "Therefore you have no excuse, whoever you are, when you judge others; for in passing judgment on another you condemn yourself, because you, the judge, are doing the very same things" (2:1). Reading Romans 1 without Romans 2 leads to misreadings sometimes of both chapters. Paul's intent was not so much to cast judgmental eyes on gentiles in general as it was to guide Phoebe's eyes onto the Weak in the person of the Judge and to inform them that they, too, will be judged by God in an impartial judgment. His words are unequivocal: when the Weak sit in judgment on the Strong, they are opening themselves up to the same judgment!

THE AUDIENCE FOR ROMANS 2

The audience of Romans 2:17-29 is almost certainly Jewish believers in Jesus. Just who Paul has in mind in the first half of chapter 2 is a debate today. Some think it is gentile proselyte believers or gentile Judaizing believers trying to persuade other gentile believers to observe Torah. Romans 1:18–2:29, I suggest, points us more directly at the Weak—namely, at Jewish converts to Jesus who in the person of the Judge want to impose Torah on gentile fellow believers (the Strong).[1]

Among the factors that convince me Romans 2:1-16 has the same audience as 2:17-29 is that the judgmental posture toward gentiles expressed in 2:1-16 is found only elsewhere in Romans with the Weak (14:3-5, 10, 13, 22). The language is nearly identical. Further, the confidence in knowing the God of Israel in 2:2 is patently Jewish, and the patience of God in 2:3-4 sounds like God's patience with Israel in 3:25-26. A few other considerations are that the impartial judgment of God is as Jewish as it is gentile in 2:6-16,[2] the theme of partiality pertains to Jewish (not gentile) claims of election (2:11), and the focus of 2:12-16 strikes me as a shocking revelation to Jewish listeners. Finally, "you call yourself a Jew" in 2:17 should be considered in light of rhetorical theories that contend an imagined interlocutor always remains the same in a letter and those same theories also contend such an interlocutor is connected to real people in the audience. These observations have convinced me that Romans 1:18-32 and Romans 2 have the Weak in mind. (I will argue the same for Romans 3–4 below.) Romans 1:18-32, by way of reminder, talks *about* gentiles, not *to* gentiles, and that talking-about-gentiles finds favor with the Judge of 2:1, who is the same as 2:17-29.

Again, the "you who call yourself a Jew" of 2:17 is not every Jew or a representative faithful synagogue Jew but instead the Weak of Romans 14:1–15:13, who in 2:1 becomes the Judge. Furthermore, the Judge's group is not Weak because it is Jewish; it is Weak because it insists on Torah observance for the Strong and sits in judgment on gentiles and therefore the Strong in the churches of Rome, and, if we keep terms in mind, the Weak/Judge blaspheme God's holy name in sinfulness (cf. 2:24 with 14:16). They are Weak, according to Romans 14–15, because they cannot embrace the freedom of the gentile believer from the Torah. The Jew of 2:17 is the Judge of 2:1, and the Judge of 2:1 is the Weak of Romans 14. Paul, then, is not talking about Judaism per se or even Jewish privilege in general; he is talking about a specific audience in Rome—the Weak—and the Weak is a group who knows Torah, believes in Torah, practices Torah, and expects gentile believers to convert the whole way and join them in Torah observance because they know the will of God. They know because they are God's elect, God's remnant, the messianic people of God. Because the gentile believers, the Strong, are not doing the Torah, the Weak judge them as inferior and uncommitted to the fullness of God's revelation in Moses. Yes, Torah observance is a boundary marker, but it is not simply that issue that concerns Paul: it is boundary marking used against the Strong, the gentile believers, that concerns Paul.

SHOCKING RHETORICAL TURNABOUTS

Paul stuns the Weak, first, with what we will soon discover to be his *first turnabout*. He turns the judgmental Weak into a stereotyped character he calls the Judge (2:1). Since the whole chapter has the same audience in mind, we include with 2:1 the words of 2:17-20 to describe the Judge.[3] Because it has been the temptation to universalize everything in Romans and thus to make every statement about Jews to be about all Jews in general, I want to list what Paul says about the Judge. He . . .

(1)   presumes God will judge the gentiles,[4]
(2)   relies on the Torah,
(3)   boasts in its relation with God,
(4)   knows the divine will,
(5)   is instructed in the Torah,
(6)   is a guide to the blind (gentiles) because he is a light in the world's darkness,
(7)   is a corrector of the foolish,
(8)   is a teacher of children, and
(9)   knows the Torah and so teaches others the Torah!

Hubris drips from these Pauline exaggerations of the Judge. His counter is that God is just and on the side of the Weak, who bank on their election (though Romans 9–11 put a dent in a facile claim to that argument), and that means they will survive divine scrutiny. That is what this line in 2:2—"We know that God's judgment on those who do such things is in accordance with truth"—suggests (though whether this is a quotation of the Judge or not is debated). Romans 2:2 could be Paul's words, and "we" could well mean "both you, the Judge, and I, Paul, know." What does he mean by "who do *such things*" in 2:2? He means the specific sins of 1:26-27 and 1:29-31, which surely shocks the Judge's self-perception. Paul's words are relentless. Contradiction and hypocrisy are his themes: "Do you imagine, whoever you are, that when you judge those who do such things and yet do them yourself, you will escape the judgment of God?" (2:3). They, too, are to repent from such sins (2:4). This turning against the Judge (the Weak) is not unlike how Isaiah turns against fellow Israelites (Isa 57:3-13).

A *second rhetorical turnabout* is found in Romans 2:12-16. Divine scrutiny at the end will not say, "Torah people to my right" and "non-Torah people to my left." Judgment will be based on *doing* God's will, and it does not matter if a person knew the Torah or not. God has inscribed the Torah on the heart (1:18-23) of gentiles as well. The judgment will be based then not on historical privilege but upon conformity to the will of God. The Judge's presumption about superior moral status meets a shocking turnabout: they do not know the Torah any more than the gentiles! The Strong, then, are not at the disadvantage the Weak think.[5]

In reading Romans backwards, we gain clarity on what happens in this second rhetorical turnabout. Romans 9–11 wrote Israel's story to explain the Pauline gentile mission. What God was doing all along was preparing Israel to be a light to the nations, and the Messiah was that Light, and the light is now spreading through the Pauline mission throughout the Roman Empire. God is faithful to the covenant; God has made surprising moves all along; God's mercy, not human exertion, is what matters most; inclusion of gentiles is part of God's plan, and it is Paul's mission to preach the gospel to gentiles; Torah has never been the means of redemption, but instead it has always been by faith; Christ is the Torah's terminus; God remains faithful to Israel both in the present remnant and in the future redemption of all Israel; gentile believers, the Strong, have no reason for pride or privilege over the Weak or over God's covenant people, Israel; and Israel remains at the heart of God's covenant and redemption. Those themes must come into play as we read this second turnabout as well. Before we encounter Paul's third rhetorical turnabout, a discussion follows about Paul's piercing words about divine impartiality in this second turnabout.

God's Impartial Judgment

Paul turns to the *criterion* of the judgment—that is, to God's will and human correspondence to that will—and to divine *impartiality*. Election makes Jews first in redemption, but election is not automatic redemption or moral transformation. In fact, Paul turns some themes inside out. While God's universal judgment would catch everyone in its net, it was also believed that Israel had an advantage, if not a big advantage (e.g., Jub. 5:13-19). What matters for Paul, and this too is Judaism to the core, is *lived theology*, and what stuns the Judge as he hears these words is *that it doesn't matter if one is a Jew or a Greek/gentile*. What matters is deeds. The thematic statement is, "For he will repay according to each one's deeds" (2:6), and the conclusion is, "For God shows no partiality" (2:11). What comes between 2:6 and 2:11 fills in the details: "to those who by patiently doing good seek for glory and honor and immortality, he will give eternal life; while for those who are self-seeking and who obey not the truth but wickedness, there will be wrath and fury" (2:7-8). The judgment distinguishes those who *do* evil from those who *do* good (2:9-10). The Torah reveals God's will to God's people, but *doing* God's will is the criterion for divine judgment (2:12-16), and that can be done by gentiles as well as Jews. This is a turnabout for the Judge.

Which all adds up to this: God's judgment is *just and impartial*. God's judgment, as Romans 8 will make clear, will liberate all creation and all God's redeemed people from sins, Sin, Flesh, and Death and will establish Life and righteousness and love and justice, and it alone can bring Peace in the heart of the empire. Judgment in the Christian tradition, not least because of so much medieval art of the last judgment, has been too often understood in purely individualistic categories and only in terms of personal salvation:

Who makes it, and who doesn't? Who goes to hell, and who goes to heaven? Judgment in the Bible is more about evil being vanquished and eliminated and about justice, peace, and love being established and made permanent for eternity. Salvation in an individual finds its important place in that larger framework. Paul was a total adherent of the establishment of God's kingdom both by vanquishing evil and by finally saving God's people in the liberation of all creation. What Paul emphasizes in Romans 2 is the just impartiality of God in that judgment—hence, the emphasis on works.

This judgment by works should not be read as something foreign to the theology of Paul or contradictory to redemption by grace alone. Those who are uncomfortable with what Paul says here have misread Paul. Salvation by grace is consistent with judgment by works and can be found in the Old Testament, Judaism,[6] Jesus, and the apostles.[7] The brother of Jesus, James, teaches the very same thing.[8] Grace that reciprocates with gift in return remains grace. Grace with expectation of gratitude and obedience remains grace. In fact, grace that transforms sinners into saints is the grace of which Paul talks. To be sure, this transforming work is that of the Spirit (Rom 8:1-13), but it is transformation unto obedience and works. I repeat: the vision of Romans 5–8 is a vision of God-wrought Christoformity for all creation. Judgment by works, then, is the mirror image of salvation by grace alone through faith alone. The latter without the former is not the grace of which Paul writes. What Paul says in Romans 2:12-16 we already heard in Romans 14:12: "So then, each of us will be accountable to God." (Somebody quote Dietrich Bonhoeffer!)

With Phoebe's eyes on the Judge, the words ring loud and clear: Jew or Greek, what matters is not election or nonelection; what matters is good and evil. That is, what matters is deeds. Gentiles (hear this, Strong!) who don't even know the Torah may well be doing God's will and not know it is Torah-shaped behavior. Those who do such things will gain eternal life (2:14-15). The Judge who knows the Torah may well not be doing the Torah, and that Torah knowledge and privilege will do him no good in the judgment. God is absolutely fair in judgment. This is God's criterion: "on the day when, according to my gospel, God, through Jesus Christ, will judge the secret thoughts of all" (2:16).

Relativizing Circumcision, the Third Turnabout

Paul relativized aspects of Torah observance in the house churches of Rome (14:1-9, 12, 14-23), and he taught them that Torah observance is permitted but is not demanded for the Strong. What is unacceptable is the Weak demanding

Torah observance and judging the Strong. What Paul says in Romans 14 will have come off as liberal to the Weak and perhaps as a denial of the Torah itself. Some could accuse him of condescension or patronizing, while Paul believed halakhic rules are fine so long as they are a personal decision. The effect of Romans 14 is to relativize Torah observance or halakhic rulings as unnecessary for the lived theology Christoformity.

In alignment with what Paul said in Romans 14, Paul utters *a third rhetorical turnabout*. He relativizes circumcision: circumcision—commanded by God, an expression of faithfulness to God, a sign of contrast with gentiles, the rite of all rites in the Torah and Judaism (Gen 17)—is fine, but it's not enough. Some years before Romans, he wrote these words to the Galatians: "For in Christ Jesus neither circumcision nor uncircumcision counts for anything; the only thing that counts is faith working through love" (5:6). About the time he wrote Romans, he informed the Corinthians with these words: "Circumcision is nothing, and uncircumcision is nothing; but obeying the commandments of God is everything" (1 Cor 7:19). His words have the same impact here in Romans 2. He pushes hard against claims of Torah observance (covenantal nomism) as giving the Weak, the Judge in fact, an advantage, while at the same time he criticizes the same person for disobedience that profanes the very name of God among the gentiles (2:17-24). The hubris here emerges out of divine election and "being in the know," not from meriting God's favor. These are words for the Judge. Then Paul redefines, in Jewish fashion,[9] circumcision and therefore what it means to be a true Jew (2:25-29). The effect here, then, is to relativize circumcision and Jewishness when it comes to the work of God in Christ through the Spirit, but this relativization pertains to life in the mission churches of Paul. What Paul would say to a nonbelieving Jew is not on these pages. Paul's concern is with the Weak and the Strong.

Notice these words: "Circumcision indeed is of value if you obey the law; but if you break the law, your circumcision has become uncircumcision" (2:25). In fact, gentile "uncircumcision [will] be regarded as circumcision" (2:26) if the gentile does God's will. Here, Paul raises an old category from his past: the righteous gentile, the "observant" or moral gentile upon whom God's favor rests.[10] With a complete reversal of roles, Paul says the gentile Strong will turn in judgment on the Judge, the judgmental Weak (2:27). Paul is intent on transforming gentile believers by redefining circumcision: "For a person is not a Jew who is one outwardly, nor is true circumcision something external and physical" (2:28). How so? "Rather, a person is a Jew who is one inwardly, and real circumcision is a matter of the heart—it is spiritual [or, better, Spirit-prompted] and not literal. Such a person receives praise not from others but from God" (2:29). The gentile who believes in Jesus becomes the true Jew for Paul. Circumcision, then, is Flesh; instead of Flesh, Paul turns to the Heart and to the Spirit and to the Inner Person where genuine confession, repentance, faith, and obedience are to be found.

The struggle with sins and Sin, with Flesh, with the Torah, and with Death for Paul was resolved, as we will see in Romans 8, with life in the Spirit. One will not find liberation to love and holiness and peace and justice simply by Torah. The vision for lived theology in Romans 12–16 comes by way of the Spirit. One finds that liberation only through the grace of God in the Spirit. Those who turn to Christ will discover that "the just requirement of the law might be fulfilled in us, who walk not according to the flesh but according to the Spirit" (8:4). Even that requires some fleshing out, and Romans 10:5-11 comes to our aid: to do the Torah for Paul, to do the Torah in the Spirit for Paul, means to believe in Jesus as Messiah, to confess him as Lord and to believe he was raised from the dead. All of Romans 12–16, then, is at work in Jews or gentiles who do the Torah, knowingly or not, and who will be judged by the gospel of Jesus (2:15-16).

Text: Romans 3:3
2-4 questions
(McKnight 16)

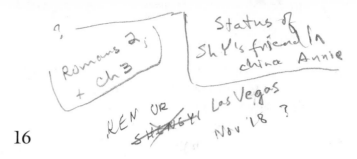
16

THE FIRST QUESTION—ADVANTAGE

(3:1-26)

The history of interpretation of Romans creates a momentum of reading Romans 3–4 as a kind of theological argument that runs back to 1:18 as it sets the stage for redemption in Christ at 3:21-26. Also, this reading tends to turn these chapters into an abstract argument devoid of context. However, Romans 3–4 is framed by questions and responses with occasional forays (as in 3:21-26) into theological explanation. The soteriological reading ignores the framing device that Paul himself is using as it also ignores Romans 14–15. These chapters are far from abstract theology and are instead pastoral theology for the church at Rome. The questions Paul both asks and addresses are questions Paul has heard time and again in his mission, and the questions are those either of Jewish opponents or more likely of fellow Jewish converts to Jesus. The questions of Romans 2–4 are shaped for the Weak in the churches of Rome.

Three principal questions are asked in our chapters: the question about *Jewish privilege and election* in 3:1-20, with a parenthetical elaboration in 3:21-26; the question about *boasting* in 3:27-31, which shifts the first question about privilege into boasting; and the question about *Abraham* in 4:1-25, which again is a variant on the question of privilege in 3:1 (and 3:9 and 3:27).

Inherent to Israel's story and to the identity formation of observant Jews was a sense of election and advantage. Thus, we read in Deuteronomy 32:8-9:

> When the Most High apportioned the nations,
> when he divided humankind,
> he fixed the boundaries of the peoples
> according to the number of the gods;
> the LORD's own portion was his people,
> Jacob his allotted share.

115

It is this election and advantage that every Torah-observant Jew thought
the gentile-mission apostle was calling into question, if not erasing from the
pages of history. When Paul asks the Advantage Question throughout chapters 3 and 4, he is bringing to the surface the question he answered in every
community. He will ask this question in 3:1, 3:9, and 3:27, with attending
questions like it popping up throughout the chapter. This is the question of
Paul's mission life, and his answer moves across a spectrum from "none" to
"highly advantaged." In Paul's Letter to the Romans, especially chapters 9
through 11, Paul says Jews have an inviolable promise and yet they have to
believe and they can be snipped off the rootstock. Here is the framework of
his answer: "Yes, the people of Israel have an advantage, but, no, the advantage
is not always what is thought."

PROBING WITH QUESTIONS

Paul asks the basic question in various ways: "Then what advantage has the
Jew?" This is then followed with its twin question: "Or what is the value of
circumcision?" (3:1). Perhaps the problem is Jewish unfaithfulness. Does God
then become unfaithful too (3:3)? Paul shifts sideways to answer issues about
God's just judgment (3:4-8), but uppermost in his mind still is Israel's privilege. Again: "What then? Are we any better off?" (3:9). Four probes into the
same basic question. If the Weak are sitting in judgment on gentiles, if they are
sinners too, if a Jew is one who is an inward Jew, if Jews have the Torah as a gift
from God, and if God's just and impartial judgment evaluates on the basis of
works whether one is a gentile or a Jew . . . these and other assumptions are at
work behind Paul's move to open Romans 3. The Advantage Question emerges
straight from a commonsensical reading of their Bible! Paul's answer seems to
be coming from outside the Bible. Their question then is justified: is there an
advantage for Jewish believers?

ANSWERS

Paul's answers move on three fronts. First,[1] *they have the Torah.* Jews have
the "oracles of God" (3:2), and "oracles" suggests God's revelation to Israel to
mediate the covenant to the world. This was said at 9:4-5.[2] One can expand
this to say the oracles of God are Israel's Scriptures and they tell the story from
creation to Messiah in Jesus, from the calling of Israel to the inclusion of the
gentiles, and that story is one that reveals Israel's unfaithfulness, God's faithfulness, and their resolution in Jesus as Israel's Messiah (9:1–10:4). Israelites

have been in on the mystery of God's plan all along. Paul therefore concedes Jewish advantage, but, second, he pulls the slack tight. How so? God's judgment of the oracle-possessing Weak is the same as his judgment of the gentile Strong: what matters is works, not elective privilege or Torah possession.

That's fine, the Judge says, but this advantage-but-not-really impugns God. If we read 3:3 through 3:8, we discover Paul responding to the Weak's typical criticisms of his gentile mission. Paul has heard them before, and he has a readymade answer: Israel, not God, has been unfaithful. Hence, Paul starts in 3:3 with Israel's unfaithfulness,[3] and he quickly claims God is unimpeachably faithful. Even more, God's faithfulness is manifested in a just judgment (3:4-8). God is true even if every human is a liar (3:4). Israel's "injustice" (3:5) actually shows God to be just (3:5-6). Suddenly taken away with the notion that Israel's unfaithfulness brings glory to God for God's own faithfulness and justice, Paul pushes into what his opponents often shoved in Paul's face—namely, an ad absurdum: Why not just sin (3:7-8)! Paul's response to such absurdity is that those who live like that deserve "condemnation" (3:8). Here we see what Paul was doing from 3:3 on.

Paul brings criticisms of himself to the surface in 3:7-8:[4] in his gentile mission work, he is accused by Jewish opponents, and probably too by the Weak in Rome, of falsehood, of being a sinner, and of urging evil to produce what is good. How so? Paul teaches that failure to observe the Torah brings both God's holiness and God's faithfulness even sharper into focus. Some claimed that Paul, riding the slippery slope, was then sitting loose with respect to Torah observance. But this is absurd, for Paul knows that human sinfulness can be overcome through the power of God's Spirit and lead to righteousness, love, peace, wisdom, and holiness (8:1-13), *even if not through Torah observance*. Details aside, these are criticisms of Paul's gentile mission, of the conversion of gentiles into the church without Torah observance, and not least his relativizing Torah observance for Jewish believers for full acceptance in Christ (2:25-29; 14:1–15:13). For the Weak of Rome—that is, the Judge—any give on observance was total capitulation.

His third answer—which flows directly from the statement in 3:2 of Jewish advantage, with 3:3-8 as an interruption—is as shocking as anything Paul ever said and surely an offense to the Weak and to any Jews of Rome who overheard Phoebe's reading of Romans. *Yes, Jews have an advantage, but their unfaithfulness nullifies that advantage.* This leads, then, to the same advantage question, but now more intense: "What then [are we to conclude]? Are we any better off [than the gentiles, the Strong]?" (3:9). The answer? "No, not at all." Why? "[F]or we have already charged that all, both Jews and Greeks, are under the power of sin" (3:9). All, he is saying, are trapped under the tyrant called Sin, and this is a theme emerging with force in Romans 5–8.

The Old Testament Texts

At this point (3:10), Paul cites a number of texts, mostly from the Psalms,[5] that speak of *universal* sinfulness, but a closer reading shows these texts are aimed at Israelite sinners and rhetorically at the Judge or the Weak in Rome. When he says "all" are "under the power of sin," Paul can be read as (1) talking universally or (2) making sure the Weak see that they, too, are part of the "all." The context favors the second emphasis, and 3:19 recapitulates what those Old Testament citations proved: "Now we know that whatever the law [those texts] says, it says to *those who are under the law,* so that"—and there the "all" is recapitulated—"every mouth may be silenced." Paul is not waxing theoretical here in 3:10-20. While gentiles are unquestionably sinners (1:18-32), his point is that the Judge and the Weak, too, are inside that same circle of sinners. They will be judged justly by God and are no better off than the gentile Strong believers. Torah observance isn't the path to justification. So, instead of seeing this listing of texts from the Psalms as simple universal indictment, we need to see it as indictment of the posture of the Judge. Notice, too, that in the Psalms' indictment, the primary audience was not gentiles but Israelites. To be sure, some of these texts target gentiles,[6] but others were originally aimed at the unfaithful and wicked in Israel.[7] There is, then, a mixture of texts and original audiences that cannot have given the Judge the comfort of sitting in judgment on gentile sinners, which is precisely what Romans 2 was designed to accomplish. Paul is calling out here not Jewish sinfulness in general but churchly status-mongering and privilege.

Romans 3:19-20 and the Weak

Emphasis on the Weak in the face of the Judge as the intended audience of Romans 3:1-18 is confirmed by the concluding words of this section in 3:19-20. How so? I repeat: Paul concludes by focusing on "those who are under the law"—that is, Israelites, the Jews, the Weak, the Judge. I have argued that Romans 2 had the Judge as the face of the Weak in mind, not because they are Jewish, but (and here I want to refresh our memories on the meaning of "Weak" in Romans) because they are Jewish believers who are in the stream of God's election. They need to be affirmed in their election but have questions about the faithfulness of God to that election and need to embrace the surprising moves of God throughout Israel's history; the Weak know the Torah, practice the Torah, but sit in judgment on gentiles, especially the Strong in the Christian community in Rome, even though they have no status or privilege or power; furthermore, the Weak are tempted to resist paying taxes to Rome on the basis of the Jewish zealotry tradition. In addition, the Weak need to apply "faith in Christ" more radically to themselves, so discovering that they are a new example of the "remnant" of Israel, and they need to see that the sufficiency of faith means that gentile believers in Christ are siblings so they see that Torah observance is not the way of transformation for either themselves or the Strong in Rome. This Weak faction in Rome is embodied in our chapters in the Judge.

Since there is nothing to tip off a change of audience from chapter 2 to chapter 3, and since a change of audience would destroy the logical flow from 2:29 to 3:1, I contend that the same audience is in mind in 3:1-20: the Weak of Romans 14–15. Romans 3:19-20 declares that those under the law (and the Weak heard this with special force) cannot find redemption by Torah observance. What they will find in Torah observance is that they are sinners bound to Sin and the Flesh and Death and therefore are in need of redemption and transformation some other way—which is why 3:21-26 follows, but that's advancing ahead of where we are at this moment.

In Romans 3:19-20, we hear echoes of what Paul told the Galatians, and there it was also in a similar situation of Jewish believers imposing Torah observance on gentile converts. What did Paul tell the Galatians? He told them that no one can be justified/declared right by works of the Torah and that the Torah was given for a limited time (until the Messiah) and for a limited reason (to turn transgressions into sin) (2:15-21; 3:19-26). Here, in Romans 3:19-20, we learn that the Torah presses the Weak into seeing their own sins but that they won't be justified by Torah observance.[8]

The pronouns in 3:1-20 reflect a common rhetorical strategy of Paul: he begins with the third person ("Jews" and "some" and "their"; 3:1-4) but converts that into first person ("our" and "we" and "I"; 3:5-9). This is his way of identifying with fellow Jewish believers in a common experience but also with fellow Jewish believers in Rome, the Weak, whom he is trying to draw out of their judgmentalism against the Strong. After identifying with them, he turns toward third-person rhetoric ("they" and "their") and to "all of us" (3:9b-20). Thus, his moves are from They to We/I and then to All of Us, with emphasis on fellow Jewish believers in the "All of Us."

"Works of the Law"

Every conversation today about Paul's theology extends into late night to figure out the meaning of "works of the law" (NRSV: "deeds prescribed by the law"; NIV: "works of the law").[9] Along with "works of the law," one also has to discuss "covenantal nomism." Several observations are in order: the "law" here is the Torah of Moses and not law as a general idea, and thus "works" refers to embodied actions of Jews that are consistent with the Torah. Thus, "works of the law" describes the faithful Jew's consistent observance of the Torah. Still, there's more at work, since the focus of this expression in Pauline contexts is on singular and identity-shaping laws like Sabbath, food laws, and circumcision, and so it is reasonable to see "works of the law" as acts that are boundary marking and evocative of election and privilege, and that can generate some boasting. In Rome, the Weak, in the face of the Judge, believed gentile converts were incomplete in their conversion until they embraced the fullness of the Torah and observed the whole Torah, especially the singular embodied acts of Sabbath practice, food laws, and circumcision. Which is to say, for the Judge, "works of the law" locates a person in the redeemed people of God and Israel and marks them off from outsiders.

In the history of theology, "works of the law" has been laid into a network, the doctrine of salvation, and in that network it describes proud humans who are merit-seeking before God. It has been argued that "works of the law" describes Jewish self-righteousness and thus that Judaism became a religion in which humans sought salvation by works.[10] However, the substance of Romans 1:18–3:20 is not aimed at universal human attempts to prove one's merit before God, and neither is there emphasis in these verses on gentiles, though they appear in "the whole world" in 3:19.[11] The focus, once again, is on "those who are under the law" in 3:19. In context, then, "works of the law" is far closer to boundary-marking behaviors than to merit-seeking universal human attempts to prove oneself good or honorable enough to survive God's scrutiny. The rhetorical focus is not on Jews but on the Judge who claims redemptive privilege and who judges the Strong.

Theological Elaboration (3:21-26)

The interpretation of a paragraph can overwhelm its original function. One thinks of the Lord's Supper passage in 1 Corinthians 11:23-26 and the brilliant hymn in Philippians 2:6-11, which appear only because Paul had to deal with church conflicts in Corinth and Philippi. Romans 3:21-26 is like these in that it is filled with theological significance but originally (only!) an elaboration of 3:19-20. The move from 3:20 to "But now" in 3:21 is also a move in style: from lively questions and answers with eyes darting to cover all questions to a focused, dense elaboration involving assumptions in hermeneutics, soteriology, theology, and Christology. Once finished with his elaboration, Romans 3:27 picks up right where Paul left off with 3:9-20 and the issue of the Weak, or the Judge, asking questions about God's faithfulness and Israel's privilege by election. In other words, 3:21-26, even if it has had a wonderful life in the construction of Christian soteriology, was originally a part of Paul's pressing home to the Judge that, yes, gentiles are sinners but so are Jews who don't do God's will; that privilege by way of election and possession of the Torah requires that they be obedient to the Torah if they wish to survive divine scrutiny; and that the truest form of Jewishness is circumcision of the heart. Once again, this is an intra-Christian problem, not a Christian vs. Jew problem.

In reading Romans backwards, we are pressed to keep our eyes on the Weak and the Strong—that is, Jewish and gentile *believers*, not Jews and gentiles per se. We are pressed also to keep in mind the Strong's insensitivity to their privilege and the Weak's judgment of the Strong's moral scruples. This passage destroys the "privilege" of both: the Weak are sinners, and the Strong are sinners; both need redemption; that redemption will not come from Torah observance, and status in the church does not come by way of Torah observance or Torah nonobservance; and it does come from God's gift—Christ on the cross, who secures atonement for all who believe, Jew or Greek. So, Paul is saying, "apart from works of the law," to speak not to Jews in general but to the Weak in their particular problems with the Strong in the churches of Rome.

The most important topic in Romans 3:21-26 is *God's righteousness*, which is openly revealed in the cross of Jesus Christ.[12] Righteousness describes an attribute of God and thus became a measurement, standard, or relationship of God being true and faithful to the attribute of righteousness. God is righteous, and his acts and being are therefore righteous. In addition, righteousness at times emphasizes the power of God at work to save/redeem/liberate in the world. Thus, righteousness becomes a gift to those who are unworthy of it. As God's power, righteousness is communicated to believers to render them fit for God's presence. This righteous God makes people relationally right (justifies) as a gift. In other words, God's righteousness is both an attribute of God (God is righteous) and a gift of God. It is God's gracious redemptive power at work to make the world right through forgiving sin and establishing righteousness for all (creation included). The dual side—attribute and gift—is explicit at 3:26 ("he is righteous and . . . justifies," or "he is righteous *in justifying*," where both terms are cognate in Greek: *dikaios* and *dikaioo*). King Jesus is the agent of righteousness and making things right in the world, and he makes things right by death and resurrection (4:25).

Paul opens the theological articulation with: "But now, *apart from the law*" (3:21). If Paul's emphasis has been on the Weak and the Judge—that is, on "those who are under the law"—and if he has emphasized that Torah brings not life but only the knowledge of sin (3:19-20), then it is vital for him to say that God's saving power has been unleashed "apart from the law." This the Weak needed to hear, and perhaps the Strong let out a sigh of relief. Yet, Paul remains true to God's own faithfulness in laying right next to that "apart from the law" the following words: "and is attested by the law and the prophets"! God's saving righteousness is not from the Torah, but it is witnessed or testified to by the Torah and the Prophets. This affirms both shift in discontinuity and consistency in continuity. He wants the Weak to know they aren't justified by following the Torah, but justification's message is found in the Torah and Prophets. Their elective privilege remains, but they must not think it comes by way of Torah observance.

God's saving power of making things right *reconfigures revelation*. The NRSV translates "has been disclosed" (the Greek word is *phaneroo*, "to make manifest, to reveal, to expose, to make clear"). This revelation establishes a new reality ("now")—an apocalyptic, eschatological reality in Christ. This word "disclosed" needs to be tied to two others: Paul's mission to include gentiles as the divine "mystery" (11:25; 16:25) and the term "revelation" (*apocalupsis* and cognates: 1:17, 18; 2:5; 8:18, 19; 16:25). These terms do not indicate absolute newness, nor do they shatter everything that came before. Paul has just spoken words that combine continuity with discontinuity. Rather, this term emphasizes God's *fresh and full grace*. The old has been reconfigured, and that means, "new creation; everything old has passed away; see, everything has become new!" (2 Cor 5:17). That newness, as in our passage, is tied to the "righteousness of God" (5:21).

The revelation is the Pauline *mystery of expanding Israel to include gentiles* (11:25; 16:25). God's righteousness (his making things all right by grace in Christ) is "for all"—that is, for the Weak and the Strong—that is, no one's status counts more than another's. More pointedly, this righteousness "in Jesus Christ" is "for all who believe" (3:22). It is, to repeat the point, "apart from the law [Torah observance]," which means it is not reserved for the Weak or for those in God's covenant with Israel already. It is for those who trust and surrender themselves to Jesus as king in allegiance. This theme of "all" is pushed harder for Paul, and here he aims his words at the Weak in Rome: "For there is no distinction" (3:22). Why? Because, as 1:18–3:20 proved and 5:12 states, "all have sinned and fall short of the glory of God" (3:23), and here God's glory is connected to God's standard of righteousness that is God's own righteousness.

"Apart from the law" in 3:21, even if already anticipated in both Torah and Prophets, leads Paul to two terms: (justified) through *faith* and *by his grace as a gift* (3:24). Again, this takes us right back to "apart from the law." No human being can be justified by observing Torah. Justification—the courtroom scene of God's recreating someone in the right through Christ—is a gift for "all who have sinned" (3:24). That gift is spelled out clearly in two ways: "through the faithfulness of Jesus Christ" (3:22, my translation)[13] and "through the redemption that is in Christ Jesus, whom God put forward as a sacrifice of atonement by his blood, effective through faith" (3:24-25). Two terms are used by Paul: "redemption" (*apolutrosis*) and "sacrifice of atonement" (*hilasterion*), the first drawn from the commercial world and suggesting we are purchased back and liberated at great expense (cross), and the second drawn from the cultic word and suggesting the temple's ark of the covenant covering where mercy was granted (place of atonement, mercy seat, place of mercy) on the Day of Atonement. The second term refers to the place where the sacrificial system effected forgiveness through sacrifices performed by priests.[14] Our focus is not the history of atonement theory. Rather, we see here that God declares sinners right by grace, and it becomes "effective through faith"—that is, through the faithfulness of Christ. Again, the Weak hear this as apart from observing the Torah.

Paul's focus on the Judge, those believers in Rome sitting in judgment on the Strong for not observing Torah, becomes clear once we get to 3:25b-26. Here, Paul emphasizes the patience of Israel's God (Acts 17:30) in putting up with the sinfulness of Israel[15] throughout the course of Israel's history until "faith in Jesus" or, better yet, until "the faithfulness of Jesus." Alongside this emphasis on divine patience is divine faithfulness: "He did this to show his righteousness," and "it was to prove at the present time that he himself is righteous and that he justifies the one who is rooted in the faithfulness of Jesus" (my translation; cf. CEB: "who has faith in Jesus as righteous"). Which is to say, God is faithful (3:4-8; 9-11) because, though he put up with sins in the past,[16] God alone has now put a complete end to sins in the faithful obedient death of Christ. The faithful covenant God is demonstrated faithful in the covenant faithfulness of Jesus.

All those—Weak or Strong—who attach themselves to the faithful Jesus are justified. In reading Romans as the context for each passage, what is eminently noticeable here is the absence of language about Adam (as in 5:12-21). The focus here is not on humans in general but on Israel, Israel's sins, and divine atonement. And it is therefore on the Judge and the Weak in Rome. The point is that the Weak's insistence on Torah observance too easily becomes an insistence on the need for the Strong to observe Torah and to move from Godfearers to proselytes if they want to be morally transformed. Paul's point to the Judge is that transformation cannot be achieved by Torah observance.

17

THE SECOND QUESTION—
BOASTING IN ADVANTAGE

(3:27-31)

Reading Romans backwards sheds light especially on how to read Romans 3 because it puts 3:21-26 back in its original place and brings to the fore the Advantage Question. That question has shaped the entire discussion from 1:18 to 3:20. If someone removed 3:21-26 for an unsuspecting reader, there would be nothing missing when the reader turns to 3:27. The same argument or question is at work: What about Jewish privilege? What about elective privilege? What advantage has the Jew? What advantage does the Weak believer have? These were the sorts of questions at 3:1 and 3:9, and now again with his second question (3:27-31). The only variant is the word "boasting": "What then becomes of boasting?" (3:27). The Boasting Question, which draws out the use of the same term in 2:17 and 2:23, is asked in this passage again in 3:29 in other terms: "Or is God the God of Jews only? Is he not the God of Gentiles also?" That dual question is then turned over to ask this in 3:31: "Do we then overthrow the law by this faith?" The Boasting Question becomes the God-of-Israel-Especially Question, which becomes the Law Question.

These are not identical questions, but they can all be bundled into the Advantage Question. In brief, the Weak represent for Paul the common question he has been hearing throughout his gentile mission. Namely, if the God of Israel is now at work to include gentiles in the one family of God and if the Torah is not required of them, what becomes of God's election of Israel and the privilege or advantage? This question has driven Paul from 3:1 on, and it was provoked by what he said in 1:18–2:29 and especially in 2:1-5, 17-24. Those now asking that question are not Jews in general but the Weak in the house churches of Rome. The one most upset by Paul's words is the Judge, who speaks for the Weak. These are mission questions.

Boasting Reframed

Boasting must be reframed to avoid the very common Christian temptation to turn this into boasting about one's self-righteousness, boasting about what one deserves before God, boasting about meriting eternal redemption. Since Augustine's debates with Pelagius, Christian theologians have framed humans as striving to justify themselves before God on the basis of good works or at least contending they are worthy of justification on the basis of their good behaviors. Boasting thus mirrors self-justification. Boasting, however, had a Greco-Roman context that is not the same as this Augustine-Pelagius framework, a Greco-Roman context that infiltrated the Weak in Rome who had learned the ways of Rome—boasting that the Weak in Rome, in the face of the Judge, had chosen because of covenant election. In that reframed context, boasting was common and expected. How so? The Roman male of privilege and status was expected to pursue the cursus honorum, the life path toward public honor, and it was the path for those who had power and who were of noble birth (1 Cor 1:26), or who had beautiful or swift bodies, or who were generous with their wealth, courageous in battle, or capacious in public speaking. The path to honor was competitive to the core, and what one had accomplished on the path—marked by public appointments to public offices—required boasting. Our Christian avoidance of boasting and even fake humility were not the ways of Rome. One was expected to boast, and because this is so unnatural—or socially frowned upon—in our culture, we need to cite two texts that flash boasting onto the screen.

Leaders create cultures, and the culture of the Roman Empire was created by the emperor. Notice these lines of boasting from Caesar Augustus' famous *Res Gestae Divi Augusti*, "The achievements of the deified Augustus":[1]

Twice I triumphed on horseback and three times in a chariot, twenty-one times I was hailed as victorious general; when the senate voted me more triumphs, I abstained from them all. I put aside in the Capitolium the laurel from the rods of office, paying back the prayers which I undertook in each war. Because of my achievements or those of my deputies, which I successfully accomplished with auspicious omens both by land and by sea, the senate voted fifty-five times that sacrifices ought to be made to the gods. In fact, there were 890 of these days in accordance with senatorial decree. In my triumphs nine kings or children of kings were led in front of my chariot. I was consul for the thirteenth time, when I wrote this, and I was in my thirty-seventh year of tribunician power [AD 14]. (4.1–4)[2]

We may say, "Goody for you, Mr. Arrogance," but that would fail to comprehend the expectation of boasting in that world.

About what did they boast? Roughly contemporary to the first-century church in the Roman Empire is a group of writings called the "progymnasmata," or preliminary exercises in rhetoric. Students, future public leaders in that world, were taught how to praise the noble leaders of their day in what are called "encomia." Hermogenes taught his students what to focus on in these praises, and they both illustrate the cursus honorum and taught students what to strive for in life (I have reformatted and italicized principal terms for ease of reading):

> You will mention also any *marvelous occurrences at birth*, for example, from dreams or signs or things like that.
>
> After this, *nurture*; for example, in the case of Achilles, that he was nurtured on lions' marrow and by Cheiron;
>
> then *upbringing*, how he was trained or how educated.
>
> Of course, the nature of *mind and body* will be examined and each of these divided into several Qualities. You will say about his body that it was beautiful, large, swift, strong; about his mind that it was just, temperate, wise, brave.
>
> After this you will draw on his *pursuits*; for example, what sort of life he led: Was he a philosopher or an orator or a general?
>
> Most important are *deeds*; for deeds are included among pursuits; for example, having chosen a soldier s life, what did he accomplish in it?
>
> As for *externals*, they include relatives, friends, possessions, servants, luck, and the like.
>
> Moreover, from the topic of *time* comes how long he lived, much or little. Each provides the starting point of encomia; for you will praise one who had long life because of that fact and one who did not in that "he had no share of the diseases of old age."
>
> Further, from *the manner of his death* (for example,) how he died fighting for his country; and if there was anything unusual about it, as in the case of Callimachus, because his corpse remained standing. And you will praise him because of who killed him, for example, that Achilles died at the hand of the god Apollo.
>
> You will examine also *events after death*: if they held games in his honor, as for Patroclus (Iliad 23); if there was an oracle about his bones, as with Orestes; if he had famous children, as did Neptolemus. The best source of argument in encomia is derived from comparisons, which you will utilize as the occasion may suggest. (Hermogenes, *Progymnasmata* 15–17)[3]

About one's path to glory one was to boast, and these are the central elements
of boasting in the Roman Empire. This is what made someone honorable;
these are the elements one mapped out on one's path toward honor.

Paul himself knows the sinfulness of boasting in wisdom, might, and
wealth from his Bible (Jer 9:23-24), he can boast if pushed (Phil 3:5-6), and
boasting is at times virtuous when it is of Christ or others (1 Cor 1:31; 15:31;
2 Cor 1:14; 1 Thess 2:19; Phil 3:13).[4] But he also has accused the Weak of
boasting in a negative sense (2:17, 23). It is not only the Roman way of boasting that provokes the Boasting Question. Any reading of Romans or of Galatians or of many texts not in the Bible reveals that election created a sense
of divine sanction of Israel as the apple of God's eye. This sense of elective
privilege also shaped the Weak's boasting, but I contend it was contaminated
by the Roman way in the face of the Judge. Paul's experience in his gentile
mission constantly encountered this question. Paul's own answer, fleshed
out in Romans 9–11, was that God would remain faithful to Israel, Israel
would still be God's people, but gentiles would be grafted onto the vine's
rootstock—and that union with Christ was by faith (not works). Gentiles,
too, could acquire the elective privilege of Israel.

TORAH OF FAITH

The Weak's claim of privilege and primacy in the family of God was a source
of boasting for the Judge, but for Paul it was relativized, or completely shut
down, because status in Christ is determined not by "works" but "by the law
of faith" (Rom 3:27). Paul's special phrase here can't be ignored: he labels
this positive response to grace "the law of faith," which could be translated as
"*the Torah* of faith," including as well "the Torah of the faithfulness of Christ."
It's jarring to combine Torah with faith, but only because too many have
dissociated faith from Torah. The "law [Torah] of Christ" in Galatians 6:2
is a similar expression.[5] But reading Romans as a whole leads us to Romans
7:7-25, where the Torah's work of revealing sin was clarified as a spiritual
work. There, Sin and the Flesh seize control of us. One chapter further along,
Romans 8:2 speaks of the positive sense of the Torah: "the law of the Spirit of
life in Christ Jesus." And back in 2:25-29, we observed that there is an internal vs. an external relation to the Torah. The "Torah of faith" has to be that
internal sense, which—to recall—means some gentiles are actually living
out the Torah of faith. Back also to Romans 9:30-33, we heard of gentiles
who were practicing the Torah by faith.

Paul reminds us that a Torah of faith implies redemption for *all who have faith*—which is what he reminds the Weak of next, with his eye on the Judge, in 3:28: "For *we* hold that a person is justified by faith apart from works prescribed by the law." This "We" sounds like the "We" of Galatians 2:15-21, which pointed to Peter and Paul. Which is to say, it pointed to a Jewish "We." With "We hold," Paul's mind is on the Weak at Rome. He next turns his angle onto the same Weak-believer Advantage Question: "Or is God the God of Jews only?" (3:29). Since he is now speaking of the Torah of faith, he immediately asks the Weak a question about the Strong: "Is he not the God of Gentiles also? Yes, of Gentiles also, since God is one" (3:29-30).[6] Faith can be found among both Jewish believers and gentile believers. He reiterates his point, and his point is one more hammer blow to the Advantage Question: God "will justify the circumcised on the ground of faith and the uncircumcised through that same faith" (3:30). The Torah of *faith* raises believing gentiles to the privilege of Israel but simultaneously strips away some of that privilege.

Ah, but once again the Judge comes back with words of Paul: "Do we then overthrow the law by this faith?" (3:31). That's the question that every Torah-observant Jewish believer asked Paul, and it is a question that will dog him to his death in Rome.[7] It was the question that drove observant Jews in Jerusalem to have him arrested, and it led to Paul's long incarceration and trials (Acts 21–28). Paul's answer, no matter how dogmatic and certain, did not satisfy the Torah observant: "By no means!" He adds a zinger that sounds like Galatians 3: "On the contrary, we uphold the law" (Rom 3:31). Just how his inclusion of gentiles by faith and, in addition, how that inclusion of gentiles required Jews to suspend their boasting of advantage . . . just how these uphold the Torah is not spelled out here, but Romans 2 and 7 are our indications. The law was never given to justify; the law was given to turn sins into Sin and to reveal Israel's culpability. Turning away from the status and advantage of Torah works and turning toward God in Christ through the Spirit *by faith* and by the faithfulness of Christ both was the ultimate form of observing Torah and led through that same Spirit to living out the Torah (8:1-8). For Paul, the story of Israel's fulfillment in Christ turns everything inside out.

18

THE THIRD QUESTION—
ABRAHAM, FAITH, AND ADVANTAGE

(4:1-25)

Another form of the Advantage Question opens chapter 4, and I offer my own translation of 4:1: "What are we to say then?[1] That Abraham, our forefather in the flesh [= Jews], found favor [= righteousness] with God [by works—that is, by the circumcision of Genesis 17 or the Aqedah of Genesis 22]?" This question is the third variant of the same question asked in 3:1, which was itself reframed in 3:9 and then again asked at 3:27. Each question is Paul's, but each is put in the mouth of the Weak, the Judge, in Rome. The three questions of 3:1 and 3:9, 3:27, and 4:1 can be listed, with the reframed third question asked in 4:9 yet again:

(1) Then what advantage has the Jew? Or what is the value of circumcision? (3:1)
What then? Are we any better off? (3:9)
(2) Then what becomes of boasting? (3:27)
(3) What are we to say then? That Abraham, our forefather in the flesh [= Jews], found favor [= righteousness] with God [by works—that is, by the circumcision of Genesis 17 or the Aqedah (binding of Isaac) of Genesis 22]? (4:1)
Is this blessedness, then, pronounced only on the circumcised, or also on the uncircumcised? (4:9)

These are three approaches to the same general Advantage Question. Each carries Paul's argument along, but each must be seen as an instance of the same general question. The Judge in Rome believes that the Weak alone are faithful to Israel's story in their messianic faith *with* Torah observance and that the Strong fail to complete their full conversions. From different angles, Paul presses home the same big points: there is one God; works of the Torah

131

have never justified anyone; Christ was faithful; justification comes by faith; Jews and gentiles are justified in the same way. The *reason* for all of this is the tension between the Weak and the Strong in Rome. The *goal* is reconciliation, unity, peace, and tolerance energized by love. This is not theology for the sake of theology. Rather, this is lived theology in search of theological underpinnings.

ABRAHAM THE PARADIGM AND FATHER

Abraham in Romans 4 is both an exemplary believer and the father of those who believe (whether Weak or Strong). To use other terms, Abraham is both a paradigm and also more than a paradigm. He *is* covenant father of faith and faithfulness in motion. Anything happening in the covenant must go back to and cohere with Abrahamic faith.[2] Abrahamic faith defines the breadth of the new people of God—*anyone, no matter their status*, who has faith like Abraham, the distinguishing feature of this family, is part of the family.

Now a subtle reminder: Abraham was in the Jewish world the paradigm of both faith and *Torah observance* (1 Macc 2:52; Jas 2:21-24). One has to think Paul is cutting a sharp angle into the wind in how he uses Abraham because the Torah-observance element of Abraham is dropped. In Judaism, Abraham's faith was demonstrated in offering his son Isaac (the Aqedah of Gen 22), and it is more than noticeable in what follows in Romans 4 that nothing of the Aqedah explicitly appears. Covenant-by-faith in Genesis 15 precedes circumcision-as-works in Genesis 17, and for Paul everything important happened in Genesis 15. Everything hinges on this chronological argument from Genesis: first comes God's gracious offer of covenant, Abram's faith, and righteousness, and only after those do we encounter works like circumcision and Aqedah. Faith (Gen 15) precedes; works follow. The chronology is "faith then works," not "faith and works," and the chronology proves his point. He has read the Bible in such a way to support the everyone-by-faith mission, and this anchors his lived theology of unity and peace.

Romans 4 moves steadily forwards with each new line developing what is before, but I will cut the chapter into three separable units: the general Torahs of 4:1-8 with their emphasis on "reckon" (4:3, 4, 5, 6, 8), the implication of circumcision following faith in 4:9-12, and then, third, the connection of promise to faith and not circumcision in 4:13-25—with both the circumcision and the promise sections emphasizing faith (4:9, 11, 12, 13, 14, 16, 17, 19, 20, 22, 24) and with 4:23-25 turning more directly toward the implications for Paul and the house churches in Rome. The whole way through the chapter, Paul is midrashing on Genesis 15:5-6 in the context of Genesis 12 (promise), 15 (covenant), 17 (circumcision), and 22 (Aqedah). His text for consideration (Gen 15:6), "Abraham believed God, and it was reckoned to him as righteousness" (Rom 4:3), becomes also his conclusion: "his 'faith was reckoned to him as righteousness'" (4:22).

Two Torahs and Righteousness

The issue, to repeat, is the Advantage Question. The point of contact is Abraham, who by all accounts was the father of the Jewish people (Sir 44:19-21) and who was lauded for this faith-reckoned-as-righteousness (1 Macc 2:52). The Advantage Question is doubled: "What are we to say then? That Abraham, our forefather in the flesh [= Jews], found favor [= righteousness] with God [by works—that is, by the circumcision of Genesis 17]?" But reading Romans backwards prompts us to notice that the Advantage Question is asked by the Weak in Rome. Paul forms his answer into what can be called "Two Torahs": the Torah of works (4:2, 4) and the Torah of faith (4:3, 5, 6-8; the term "Torah of faith" is found in 3:27).

Torah of Works Does Not Lead to Righteousness

The Torah of works entails the ability to boast (4:2), which ties back to 3:27, and it entails the obligation of God to reward the worker (4:4). Works in 4:2, for some readers of Romans and Paul, dances very close to what the new perspective has often held against the "old" (or Augustinian, or Reformation) perspective. That is, in this Torah of works, Paul, so it might seem, lays down the claim that humans want to glory in their achievements and hold God accountable for their moral accomplishment. Yes, but there's more here than this. First, reading Romans backwards (and what we have so far seen from 1:18–3:31) presses upon us to see in Paul's vision not Jews in general or even humans in general but the Weak believers in Rome who are pressing the Strong to become full converts by adopting the whole Torah. Second, behind "wages" is the Greek term *misthos*, which is the exact term used in Genesis 15:1.[3] We need to explain this briefly: YHWH informs Abram not to be afraid because, he says to Abraham, "your reward [*misthos*] shall be very great." It is worth asking what Abram's reward was, and the answer is balled up in a number of terms: a child, a son, an offspring, an heir, and most importantly descendants equivalent to a heaven full of stars. That is, the "reward" is a multitude of descendants who will dwell in the Land and who will become many nations! Once one recognizes that, in Romans 4, Paul is pondering and interpreting Genesis 15 in light of the nation-blessing promise of Genesis 12

as well as keeping an eye on circumcision and the nation-blessing in Genesis 17, then one sees that "works" and "wages" and "something due" are not
theological abstractions about how to get saved. Rather, they are woven into
the faithfulness of God to work through Abraham to the Messiah, who will
become the agent that sends the gospel into the world to include gentiles.
Reward is about the blessing spreading out to the nations. Romans 4:13
defines the "reward" of 4:4 as Abraham "would inherit *the world*," and the
inclusion of both Jews and gentiles is emphasized in 4:11-12 and 4:16-18.
If the *misthos* is the worldwide family of God, then the Weak believers are
being admonished once again to embrace the Strong (and the Strong also to
embrace the Weak) if they want to be true to Abraham, which they sure do!

This nest of Paul pondering Genesis 15 precipitates Paul's turn to boasting and "wages." Again, he is criticizing not Jews or humans in general but
Weak believers in particular. It is they who need to see that they are boasting
in their status and making claims on God for moral transformation through
Torah observance. One might argue that behind the Weak are Jews in general,
but it is hard for me to think that Paul would be carrying on a debate with
non-Christian Jews in Rome. His concern is the Weak-Strong schism. His
concern is the Judge, not humans in general.

Torah of Faith Leads to Righteousness

His second Torah is the Torah of faith, which involves the ultimate verdict
of God ("it was reckoned to him as righteousness" [4:3, 5]) upon those who
are—shocking word to the Judge, for it sounds like 1:18-32—"ungodly"
(4:5). The incongruity of God's grace is obvious if given to the ungodly. This
grace is activated not in the one who observes Torah—that is, who "works"
(4:5)—but in the one who believes (4:3, 5). David's words from Psalm 32:1-2
come next (4:7-8), and they support some of Paul's claims about Abraham.
Instead of righteousness or justification, David has "blessedness"; David has
forgiveness and covering of sins (4:7), and these two terms define blessedness.
Also, they are approximations of righteousness and justification.[4] Paul has
found a text that supports his reading of Genesis 15:6 about Abraham. His
justification occurred by faith and well before any works, and therefore it
was incongruous grace.

Two Torahs then are at work: the Torah of works, which leads to boasting
and to "wages" that give benefit automatically to the Weak, and the Torah of
faith, which leads to divine reckoning as righteousness, which amounts to
forgiveness of sins for both the Strong and the Weak. The point of contact,
once again, is Abraham (with a glance at David). Recall that Paul is arguing

with the Weak who want to impose Torah observance on the Strong if they want to be fully accepted in the expanded Israel. Paul is largely repeating what he said with respect to Peter in Galatians 2:15-21. What follows from his use of Abraham is that the Strong don't have to observe Torah to be in the one family of God.

Paul has two more arguments scratched out on his legal notepad: one about circumcision and one about the promise. Each proves his point about the Two Torahs.

CIRCUMCISION AND RIGHTEOUSNESS

Circumcision was the sign of faithfulness to covenant and Torah. Circumcision was nonnegotiable in Israel's story, and it was also the point of contact with (male) gentile converts. Until they had undergone circumcision, they remained on the periphery of Israel. Paul has already relativized circumcision into a deeper circumcision (2:25-29), but he takes a new step in Romans 4. Remember, Abraham was justified in Genesis 15 by faith, not in Genesis 17 by circumcision.

Paul begins with the word he has used from David: "blessedness," which approximates justification. The third Advantage Question (4:1) is now asked in a slightly different form: "Is this blessedness, then, pronounced only on the circumcised, or also on the uncircumcised?" (4:9). If Abraham's faith led to being reckoned a blessedness-called-righteousness (4:9b), then the question is, "how" or "when" was he reckoned righteous (4:10)? That is, which came first? Faith or circumcision? The answer to "when" was he reckoned righteous is: "before he was circumcised."

Since circumcision is here equated with works, Paul has proven his point: justification has nothing to do with circumcision/works and everything to do with faith. Circumcision is but the "seal of the righteousness that he had by faith" (4:11), and one can at least wonder if the term "seal" does not for Paul evoke baptism in the new covenant community.[5] Paul's gospel is established: faith in Christ, not works of the Torah, leads to the divine blessing of righteousness. Paul knows somehow the divine purpose in all this: "The purpose was to make him the ancestor" (4:11b). Of whom? All who believe as he believed in God. That is, both Jews and gentiles, both Weak and Strong.

PROMISE AND RIGHTEOUSNESS

Paul pulls out one more argument sketched on his notepad: the promise to Abraham, like justification, is given to him not upon being circumcised (=

works) but upon believing. The Torah of faith then proves that the promise
is for those who believe. He states this in clear terms in 4:13,[6] and then he
digresses for a moment in 4:14-15, where he makes the following claims: if
Torah creates the heirs of the promise to Abraham, then the faith and its
promise are nullified; his second claim is that Torah brings not blessedness or
justification but "wrath" (cf. Gal 3:10-14); a third claim, anticipating Romans
5:12-14, says that, without Torah, there is no violation and that, without violation, there is no wrath, which is also a gurgling tremor in Romans 7:7-25.

Paul's Torah of faith bubbles to the surface now at 4:16 in what is the
deeper Torah, the Torah of grace: "For this reason it depends on faith, in
order that the promise may rest on grace." Notice that faith rests on grace,
revealing that Paul perfects the priority of God's loving grace. Since justification is by grace and since grace is prior to faith and apart from works, *all can
know this grace, and therefore all can experience faith and justification.* This is
his argument—better yet, his ultimate aim and conclusion—as found now
in 4:16-17. The promise (and reward), it must be remembered, was, "I have
made you the father of many nations" (4:17, quoting Genesis 17:5). The words
here occur prior to the act of circumcision, thus prior to works, which are
recorded in Genesis 17:9-14. Then the next verse in Romans, 4:18, with its
emphasis on "father of many nations," sends us back to the covenant formed
earlier in Abraham's life (back to Gen 15:5). Thus, the chronology proves his
point: the promise occurs prior to any of the works—before circumcision
and before the Aqedah.

Paul then draws out the kind of faith Abraham had (4:18-22), ignoring
for rhetorical reasons the doubting bits (e.g., Gen 17:17-18). For Paul, the
odds were against Abraham. How so? In "hoping against hope," Abraham
believed that two aged people could bear a child who could generate a tribe
and a nation that would spread to all nations. He was nearly a hundred, and
Sarah was barren (4:19), but Abraham trundled on in faith because he knew
the creator God could do the impossible, which was to be faithful to his own
word and fulfill that covenant promise of abundant blessing to the nations
(4:21). Faith like that led to the divine reckoning of Abraham (4:22).[7]

Paul uses the two Torahs of works and faith to press upon the Weak,
in the face of the Judge, that Torah observance does not lead to the divine
reckoning, to blessedness, and to the promise (4:23-25). Works like circumcision cannot justify but only reveal sin as Sin and Flesh and Death and wrath.
Furthermore, those works of the Torah will not lead to the transformation
needed for the Strong and the Weak to dwell in love and peace as siblings in
Rome. If Abraham believed the impossible, so too the believers in Rome are

to believe that the God who "gives life to the dead"[8] and thus in effect who raised Abraham from the dead (cf. "as good as dead" in 4:19) also raised the faithful Jesus from the dead. Those who believe in that God find a God who rescues them from their "trespasses" and grants them "justification" as a result of the handing over of Jesus to death (cf. "handed over" in Rom 4:25 with Isa 53:6, 12). The Weak, now, have had Paul's full attention for nearly four chapters. Paul will turn to the Strong especially in chapters 5 through 8, but his point has been clear: the Weak are to welcome the Strong because they are all welcomed by God through Christ by faith, not by Torah observance.

IV
A Spirit Creating Peace
Romans 5–8

19

ALL

(5:12-21; 8:1-8)

It is right and good to finish reading Romans with chapters 5 through 8, because these chapters are not only the high point of the letter but the solution to the problems vexing the Weak and Strong relations in Rome's house churches. We are reading against the grain of Paul's letter not because I think most readings are wrong but because reading Romans from 12–16 backwards creates a deeper impression of the church context of the letter. If we read Romans 5–8 after 12–16, something else happens. We begin to ask more directly, *Who does he have in mind in these chapters?* Are these paragraphs directed at specific church groups in Rome? No matter how one reads Romans—backwards or forwards—the reader observes a dramatic lack of citations of the Old Testament in Romans 5–8. Both Romans 1–4 and 9–11 are loaded with citations, while Romans 5–8 are noticeably not. One might easily surface some echoes or allusions in these chapters, but that does nothing to the obviously dense citation method of the other chapters. This illustrates as much as it demonstrates: Romans 5–8 may well have a different audience than 1–4 and most of 9–11.

READING ROMANS 5–8 BACKWARDS

Romans 12–16 articulated the context of this letter and located tensions between the Strong and the Weak. The *Weak* are Jewish believers who are in the stream of God's election and need to be affirmed in their election, but who have questions about the faithfulness of God to that election and who need to embrace the surprising moves of God throughout Israel's history; the Weak know the Torah, practice the Torah, but sit in judgment on gentiles, especially the Strong in the Christian community in Rome, even though they have no status or privilege or power; furthermore, the Weak are tempted to resist paying taxes to Rome on the basis of the Jewish zealotry tradition. In addition, the Weak need to apply "faith in Christ" more radically to themselves, so, discovering that, they are a new example of the "remnant" of Israel, and they need to see that the sufficiency of faith means that gentile believers in Christ are siblings so they see that Torah observance is not the way of transformation for either themselves or the Strong in Rome. Paul presents the Weak as the Judge in Romans 2.

The *Strong* are predominately gentiles who believe in Jesus as Messiah or king, who do not observe Torah as the will of God for them, and who have condescending and despising attitudes probably toward Jews but especially to Jewish believers in Jesus, and all of this is wrapped up in the superior higher status of the Strong in Rome. Paul and Jewish believers who embrace the nonnecessity of Torah observance are at least at times among the Strong. The Strong, then, are as known for their position on observance of Torah and for their status as they are for ethnicity.

This letter was written because of the tension between these two groups, and reading Romans backwards brings that tension into all the chapters.

LOGIC OF ROMANS

The logic of Romans works like this: Romans 12–16 is the context, 9–11 is a narrative approach to the problem of that context, and Romans 1–4 is Paul's rebuttal of the Weak's claim to priority, elective privilege, and approach to how to live as followers of Jesus in Rome. Their claim was that "if everyone would agree with us and follow the Torah, then we'd be one big happy family." Paul's Abraham-rooted gospel of redemption in Christ by grace through faith is what creates the big happy family, not Torah observance. So, Romans 1–4. This means Romans 5–8 *maps Paul's theory of the theological rationale for the lived theology of Romans 12–16.* That is, Romans 5–8 is the solution to the problem of tension between the Strong and the Weak in the Roman house churches.

Paul's aim for the whole letter is lived theology in two directions: *Toward the public*, toward the empire, toward unbelievers, Paul wants the Roman Christians to live an orderly, nonrebellious life by learning to love one's neighbor as oneself. Part of this orderly public life is to live within the laws of Rome (submission) and to pay one's taxes. *Toward one's fellow believers*, toward the opposite faction among the Roman Christians, Paul exhorts all of them to a lived theology marked by open and welcoming table fellowship with one another, by supporting the mission of the church, including Paul's collection for the saints in Jerusalem and his future Spanish mission, by ordering all of life with the principles of Christoformity and unity with one another, and by a life that is oriented simultaneously toward God, toward the Body of Christ, and toward others. They are to do all of this in light of the eschaton (13:11-14). They are, to use the terms of John Barclay, to be "walking miracles."[1] Only in this way can there be peace in the heart of the empire.

To read Romans 5–8 well, one must grasp its comprehensive cosmic vision. The comprehensiveness of this vision is in fact key to understanding each passage in the entire set of chapters. We discover in Romans 5–8 a sketch from Adam to the glorious kingdom, from creation to consummation, from sin and Sin and Flesh and Death to salvation, redemption, rescue, and both present and future transformation of both humans and all creation. Those in Christ are being transformed into Christoformity, a transformation that begins now but that is completed in the eschaton. Our set of chapters opens on the note of peace with God and closes with the sense of being conquerors because of the permanence of God's love for us, and everything in between is aimed at God's commitment of love to his people toward glory.

Each section of these chapters dips into this comprehensive sketch, capitalizes on a theme or two, and moves on. Most important in this comprehensive sketch is the undercurrent that emerges from reading Romans backwards: these chapters are as pastoral and ecclesial as Romans 12–16. Paul will sketch here two lines, one from Adam to Death and one from Christ to Eternal Life. Advocates for each line are the undercurrent of the chapters, and Paul is an advocate for the Christ to Eternal Life line, while his opponent—the Judge of Romans 2:17-29, the leading voice of the Weak in Romans 14–15—is an advocate for (Paul thinks) the line that leads from Adam to Death. At the heart of this undercurrent is how best to do lived theology: Is the lived theology of the gospel to be accomplished through the Torah's prescriptions and life (the Judge, the Weak) or through the grace of the Life in the Spirit (Paul and the Strong)? The answer in this and the next chapter will be Life in the Spirit.

Personal Pronouns

Everything in Romans 5–8 is intertwined, causing the reader to take four steps forwards and two backwards and then eight forwards and then back to where the reader started. Hence, instead of the backtracking and forwards jumping that is typical of sound readings of these chapters, I will proceed by way of synthesis by using Paul's own mode of conversation. There are four modes of conversation in Romans 5–8: sections that are Generic or for All (5:12-21; 8:1-8), You sections (6:11-23; 8:9-15), We sections (5:1-11; 6:1-10; 7:1-6; 8:16-17, 18-39), and one long I section (7:7-25). To map to whom Paul is speaking in each—Weak, Strong, others—requires that we look at each

of the four modes separately. It is not hard to see the Generic mode as more
abstract theology and as theological foundation. It may be harder to discern
who is in mind with We, I, and You. I shall attempt to clarify each below.

I begin with the Generic mode.

ALL

The Generic sections express one part of the comprehensive cosmic vision of
these chapters, and this vision is what keeps the reader on task with Paul as we
travel across this bumpy and twisty path, not always clear where we are and
who's talking to whom. One gets the impression that Paul and his coworkers,
with Phoebe present, are having a very serious discussion, and sometimes Paul
says "I" and other times "We," and he looks at someone and says "You," and the
You in the room wonders if he means him or her or everyone or someone else.
That comprehensive cosmic vision contains a sketch of history from Adam to
Christ, from sin to Death, from Christ to Eternal Life, and from sinfulness now
to transformation now and glorification in the future. That vision is both about
individual humans and all creation. But this is not abstract theology; this vision
has the problem of the Weak and the Strong in view at every moment. The Judge
knows this entire section is the alternative Paul is offering in his mission churches.

Anyone who reads Romans 5–8 from front to back and marks the personal
pronouns can see quite noticeably how Paul moves from "we" to "all" to "we"
to "you" back to "we" and then into "I" before, in chapter 8, "you" and "we."
We begin with the generic All passages because they are the theoretical reflec-
tions on which the We, You, and I passages are based. Romans 5:12-21 has no
personal pronouns until the very last word in the Greek of verse 21 (in English:
"through Jesus Christ *our* Lord"). Paul removes the personal from the passage
as he explains how redemption works. In this passage, we get a clean sketch of
the cosmic vision that shapes how the Strong and the Weak are to live.

ROMANS 5:12-21

There are two ways: one that begins with Adam and one that begins with
Christ. Adam is a tragedy; Christ is redemption from tragedy.[2] Better yet, for
a long while there was one way, the Adam way, and then Christ came and a
second path was created: one that stayed in the Adam way and one that shifted
over to the Christ way. The placards on the Adam way read: Sin and Trespass
and Disobedience, Adam, Sinners, Torah, Judgment and Condemnation,
Death, All. The placards on the Christ way are mirror opposites: Free Gift (or

just Gift) and Grace,[3] Christ, Obedience, Gift of Righteousness, Justification,
Life and Eternal Life, Many/All. These are two Powers at work on humans
and not two elements in each human; this is about cosmology more than
anthropology. The cosmic, however, inhabits the anthropology.

It is perhaps easier to create these two ways, broken into their constituent
parts, in a flow chart toward Death or Eternal Life. I will call this the Two
Ways, to distinguish it from the Personal Way in the We sections.

THE TWO WAYS

The Way of Adam   **The Way of Christ**
Body of Sin   **Body of Christ**
                                  (1) *Grace*

The Determinative Act

(1) *Sin*   (2) Obedience of Christ

Trespass   Reception of Grace

Disobedience

Minds set on Flesh

Status

(2) Sinners   (3) Righteous
Flesh

Means of Knowing God's Will

(3) *Torah*   (4) *Torah*

                               Gift of Righteousness

Divine Decision

(4) Judgment   (5) Justification

Condemnation

Consequence

(5) *Death*   (6) *Life*

                               Eternal Life

Parameters of Divine Decision

(6) Many/All*   (7) Many/All*

*"Many" and "All," echoing Hebrew, are synonyms.

One can get into a twist wondering if Torah might fit also into the Way of Christ, but once we get to 8:4 we will see that the Torah has an important location in the Way of Christ. Most importantly, I have placed Grace at the forefront of the Way of Christ and not as a part of the Way of Adam because, for Paul, grace is Christ.

The Rhetoric

The rhetorical impact of these two lines is to force *everyone* in the Roman house churches to examine themselves with this question: Am I in the Way of Adam or Christ? Those who answer "The Way of Christ" must then infer that *everyone in the Way of Christ becomes siblings* and, therefore, that the divisions between the Strong and the Weak betray their union with one another in Christ. Reading Romans backwards drives us to make this connection, and it drives us to see that peace in the heart of the empire is connected to the Christ line.

The Two Lines Explained

Sirach   p219

Paul uses *Adam*, neglecting Eve entirely, as the origin and exemplar of the line that leads to Death. He is "a type of the one [Christ] who was to come" (5:14).[4] Adam sinned (5:12, 14). That sin brings two consequences: the spread of sin to all, and death as the consequence of sin, as Genesis 3 announced and much Jewish literature affirmed and expanded. (Sir 25:24 narrows it to Eve's sin, and "because of her we all die.") This death is God's judgment and condemnation (5:16, 18). Theoretically, sin needs Torah for the act to become known for what it is, but death's presence from Adam to Moses (5:14) establishes that sin was rampant without Torah. The entrance of the Torah multiplied sin into Sin (5:20). Those in the line of Adam are sinners (5:19).

The counterpart to Adam is the *Second Adam*, though Paul does not use "Second Adam" here. The line of Christ is eschatological, as this is the moment in history when all of history changes for those in Christ. The first word and the operative power in the line of Christ is grace:[5] "But the *free gift* is not like the trespass. For if the many died through the one man's trespass, much more surely have the *grace* of God and the *free gift* in the *grace* of the one man, Jesus Christ, abounded for the many" (5:15). In the grace line of Christ, the weight is entirely on the shoulders of God's initiative and what God does. Christ obeys God (5:18), his obedience abolishes death, and, due to the superabundance of God's grace, those in the Christ line receive the gift of righteousness, justification, life, and eternal life (5:17, 21). In 5:9-10, the gift of righteousness and life are eschatological salvation. Those in the Christ line are "righteous" (5:16-17). God's grace is the expression of God's love for us; even if "love" does not appear in 5:12-21, it appears in the passage immediately before (5:5, 8). Grace here is prior, superabundant, incongruous, and efficacious. There seems to be yet one more grace theme at work in our passage. Because grace here is a power and has causal agency, this grace becomes a circular power: those who experience grace become agents of grace. How so? In 5:19, "many will be made righteous" may well transcend the forensic declaration of justification, but especially in 5:21 Paul says, "grace might also *exercise dominion* through justification leading to eternal life." Exercising dominion is more than the classic sense of acquiring a redemptive status before God. Exercising dominion describes the abounding circular power of God's grace and the—yes, for sure—rule of Christ and his people over all creation. In contradiction to the Body of Sin, we have here the Body of Christ.

Noticeably, there is a kind of identity on the parameters of these lines: the last item in each line is "Many/All." Both many and all sin, are sinners, are judged, and are condemned to death (many: 5:15, 19; all: 5:12, 18), and both many and all are righteous (many: 5:16, 19; all: 5:18). That "many," instead of "all," are considered dead in their sins is as problematic as "all," instead of "many," being justified and granted life (5:18; see too 1 Cor 15:22). At times some have suggested Paul is a universalist—all will be redeemed by Christ—and he certainly can be read that way when we see "so one man's act of righteousness leads to justification and life for all" (5:18), but one cannot hold to universalism in this sense and believe at the same time in the Way of Adam that leads both to divine condemnation (5:16) and to Death.[6]

It must be asked what distinguishes the Adam line from the Christ line, and the answer that pops up quickly is God's grace in Christ. But there is a human conditionality to this Christ line, and that conditionality is faith. Thus, at 5:1, we read, "since we are justified *by faith.*" What is remarkable about our Generic-mode passage is that faith is not even mentioned, and that contrasts noticeably with Romans 4. Seemingly, in Romans 5:12-21, the *entire weight of redemption is laid on Christ as the expression of God's love and grace*. It was his act of obedience (5:18-19) that countered Adam's act of disobedience (5:12-14). So the emphasis must be given to what Christ does for us, not what we have to do. Yet, the requirements of faith emerge from below the surface in Romans 5:17 when we read, "much more surely will *those who receive* the abundance of grace and the free gift of righteousness exercise dominion in life through the one man, Jesus Christ." The correlation for those in Adam to

Christ's obedient act—surely his life, and especially his death, resurrection, ascension—is reception of that act as God's loving grace.

Three more specific items in the two lines are worthy of our more concentrated attention.

Sin, Flesh, Systemic Sin, and Death

The words in italics in the chart above—Grace, Sin, Flesh, Torah, Death, Life, and Eternal Life—transcend abstractions and ideas, and become active agents.[7] The agents on the dark side (Sin, Flesh, Death) emerge out of the human's individual sins, while the agents on the light side emerge from Christ's act of obedience.[8] This much is clear in an obvious sort of way, but these agents not only emerge out of acts of obedience/disobedience. They also become causal agents acting upon the sinner or the redeemed. A recent study explains all this as emergence theory, which points us to two nodes, and I want to use this theory's terms: supervenience and downward causation. *Supervenience* describes the causal basis in human sins that emerge into a genuine reality (Sin, Flesh), and then those emergent realities (Sin, Flesh) act with *downward causation* on the human to establish more and more sins. This illustrates each:

Sin/Flesh   Righteousness/Justice

Acts of Sin   Acts of Righteousness/Justice

The acts of sin at the bottom left become a reality known and experienced as Sin, which becomes the Agent or Tyrant, while the acts of righteousness and justice at the bottom right are experienced as a world in which Righteousness and Justice become themselves active agents, and these active agents—Sin/Flesh and Righteousness/Justice—act downward on humans to activate either acts of sin or acts of righteousness and justice. Humans experience the upper level as a reality. The systemic world of Sin and Flesh and the systemic world of Righteousness and Justice are known to us as realities, not just good ideas.

The relationship of the two levels is cyclical or as a feedback loop. What results from human sinning (Sin, Flesh) is something on the order of a "person" or a "self" and hence "exists in reality." Sin in the upper case, then, is more than a metaphor and personification: Sin is an emergent reality, a Self, a Person. Sin, then, is both personal-individual and corporate-systemic, and as such Sin becomes an agent working against the plan of God for humans. The same can be said about the second column, and thus the two-line diagram above can be seen as dual-direction motion: from sins to Sin and Death, and from Death back to sins, from grace and the obedience of Christ to Life, and from Life back to individual acts of righteousness and justice.

There is more to this. There is no such thing as a pure individual in either of these lines. Each human being *is* who he or she is in relationship to *others* so much so that he or she is constituted as a *self-* or *person-in-relation-with-others*. Much has been said about modernity and individualism as well as about the difference in the ancient world, where one speaks more about corporate personality or person-in-relation. But no human being is an island, no human being is simply or purely a self-outside-relations, no human being acts entirely out of his or her own self. The Ego, or first-person narrative of each of us, comes into reality and consciousness only in relation with others. There is then *a second-person narrative that forms our identity prior to a first-person narrative.* Too much of Romans studies root Paul's anthropology in a first-person narrative for identity formation. That is, "I am an Ego, and as an Ego I relate to other Egos, and I get saved as an Ego and grow as an Ego." But we are both: one needs both the self-in-relation-to-others and the-self-in-relation-to-self. We are, You are, and I am a dual-narrative person.

For Paul, something vital comes to the surface now: the self-in-relation-to-self is both a reality and at the same time a dead reality. The self-in-relation-to-self is a self-in-relation-to-death—which leads to this important conclusion for all readings of Paul: no human is neutral, no Ego is in Eden, no will is faced with the first moment. That is, each human is nurtured multirelationally into the World of Sin, Flesh, and Death. Each person is from birth a self-in-relation-to-Death or a self-in-relation-to-Life, an Adamic Self or an In-Christ-Self. There are no alternatives for Paul's anthropology, which means Paul's anthropology is a cosmology and a Christology at the same time.

Theologically, we can complicate this by adding "self in relation to God" and "self in relation to creation or material reality." Sinning then is never an individual-corporate act with individual-corporate consequences. This perception of a person only in relation with others makes systemic Sin and Flesh (not to ignore "original" sin) far more pervasive in sound theology and gospel mission work. As the mind forms in relation to the brain, so the mind forms in relation to other minds; as sin forms in relation to the individual, so the individual forms sins in relation to other sinful individuals. The implication becomes systemic and corporate. Redemption, then, if it is genuine, must also be corporate and systemic. This brief discussion of Sin as a tyrant and the Self as in-relation explains why Paul's theology is a cosmology; it is not just about individual redemption.

To summarize: The *Adam line* elements (Sin, Flesh, Torah, Death), these intruders from the darkness, are not simply relics of human sins framed as systemic injustices and institutions; they are not simply personifications dressed up as if they are persons; and they are not reducible to some kind of demonic reality. In the world, these items become something real and exercise power as agents with selfhood. The *Christ line*, too, finds something similar: God's grace and the obedience of Christ become agents with causal power as do life and eternal life, and as agents each acts upon humans in the line of Christ. The Strong and the Weak, or at least the tension between them, now has a cosmic explanation: what is at work in the judgment of each other is sin, Sin, Flesh, and Death. What is needed is the grace of God that in Christ's obedience created a new cycle of righteousness, justice, and love.

Romans 5:12

Romans 5:12 has generated a history of theology by itself, a history that made a mistake early when the Vulgate translated *eph' ho* as "in whom." Instead, it needs to be translated with "because all have sinned" (NRSV) or, better yet, "all sinned" (NIV, ESV) or "with the result that all sinned" (CEB).[9] This early mistranslation ("in whom") generated a type of a theology of original sin and original guilt that was narrower than Paul's words here. What he says is that Adam sinned, sin and death entered the world as agents, all die, and all die because all sin/sinned. Paul does not say that all die because all sinned when Adam sinned or in Adam's sin (original guilt). Original sin has its importance in Christian theology, but some of its particulars should not be assumed for Paul, since he does not state them and since that view is so unusual in his Jewish world.[10] He says less because his emphasis is elsewhere: on human culpability for death on the basis of sinning. Paul's words here are not unlike those of 2 Baruch 54:19: "each of us has become our own Adam."[11] Because this is Paul's orientation, we are drawn to the responsibility of each person, Weak or Strong, in learning to love the other in Roman house churches.

Sin and Torah

At about the same time Paul was writing Romans, he told the Corinthians that "the power of sin is the law" (1 Cor 15:56; cf. Rom 4:15). Paul's brief note to the Corinthians complements what he says in Romans 5: sin was prior to the Torah because of Adam sinning before the Torah (5:13-14). In 7:7, Paul will say, "if it had not been for the law I would not have known sin." He turns sin into an active agent in 7:8: "But sin, seizing an opportunity in the commandment, produced in me all kinds of covetousness." *In Paul's theology, Sin as active agent manipulates the Torah into a provocation of sin.*

But in Romans 5:12-14, Paul wants to establish this point apart from the Torah, so he says *sin existed prior to the giving the Torah.* Paul's sudden and interruptive concern in 5:13-14 with the Torah's subsequent-to-sin entrance into the world informs the Weak that sin is bigger than disobedience to the Torah. In other words, these verses, like Galatians 3:15-29, show that the Torah was given at a specific period for a specific reason and only for that specific period. So, this looks like a pushback against the Weak, who, as we have already seen, operated with something like covenantal nomism. They thought the Torah was permanent and needed to reveal sin, but Paul contends sin precedes Torah.

Paul's argument makes all humans guilty of sin, and this pushes against the Strong, or believing gentiles who need to be reminded of their sinfulness apart from their knowing the Torah. Thus, dimensions of this passage are Generic—that is, it is for All in Rome, both the Strong and the Weak. The narrative of Romans 9–11 (a narrative about God's surprising moves throughout Israel's history, about the privilege of Israel as God's covenant people, and about gentiles as grafted into the one people of God but nonetheless responsible for faithfulness) speaks into what Paul says here. All along, from Adam on, God has been at work for the redemption not only for those with the Torah but for those before and without the Torah. Strong or Weak, God's redemption is abundantly effective.

ROMANS 8:1-8

The second passage in the Generic mode—once again absent of I, We (except at 8:4), and You—extends, expands, and clarifies the Two Ways chart above. The Torah was mentioned as an intruder in the first passage (5:13-14, 20) to join forces with Flesh and Sin to capture humans in the journey toward Death. Describing the Torah as captured by Sin was for the Weak at least a jarring idea, if not scandalous, while for the Strong such an idea was welcome and (I presume) obvious. Yet one more surprise in God's unfolding plan in history!

With a glance at the Weak, Phoebe here turns to the Strong. If the Torah multiplied sin and turned it into a cosmic power (Sin), in 8:1-8 we learn that the Torah is the "law of sin and of death" (8:2), that it was "weakened by the Flesh" (8:3) so that it did not bring righteousness, that God "condemned sin in the Flesh" (8:3)—Flesh is the location for Torah observance and the location of Sin—and that he reveals that the "just requirement of the law" can be fulfilled by believers "who walk not according to the Flesh but according to the Spirit" (8:4)! Her words ring out to the Strong: they, after all their worries about how Torah-observant they need to be, are doing God's will by living in the Spirit.

Not only does Paul develop in 8:1-8 what he said in 5:12-21 about Torah, but he develops, too, the theme of Flesh. Again, he ties Flesh to Torah, and that means to Israel and that means to the Weak in Rome and that means to status shaped by elective privilege. To repeat, the Torah was not only captured by Sin but weakened by Flesh (8:3), Flesh has become a hostile-to-God embodied existence and so needs to be condemned (8:3), Flesh is not the embodied existence for successful obedience (8:4), Flesh people have Fleshy minds (8:4), Fleshy minds are headed toward Death (8:6), and Flesh is hostile to God in that it does not submit to God and in fact *cannot submit to God* (8:7), so those in the Flesh "cannot please God" (8:8). To deal with Flesh, Christ had to come in the flesh to destroy the Flesh (8:3). It is easy for readers today to turn Flesh into a term of only anthropology—human mortality in its weaknesses—but there are reasons to think Flesh here is also connected to gentile Flesh, to status and privilege, and to a history of pagan idolatries. It is also connected to Jewish Flesh, to the privilege of Israel's election, to circumcision and boundary markers. That it is tied to Torah makes this all the more likely in our text. Furthermore, Flesh is an emergent reality that acts downward on humans in the line of Adam and Death. Flesh as Flesh then pertains to all humans.

For Paul, Flesh is the old creation era, and Spirit is the new creation era. Flesh and Spirit, then, are terms of history and eschatology, of humanity and redemption, but also of gentiles and Israel according to the Flesh as well as of gentiles and Israel in Christ. Flesh is the story of pagans and Israel until Christ, and Spirit is the story of pagans and Israel expanded in Christ. Yet, Paul's entire pastoral theology operates not so much in such radical extremes: those in the Spirit and in Christ now at times succumb to the Flesh. Paul's lived theology is a theology of the overlapping ages: in Christ but still in this world, longing for the eschaton but living in the here and now. Believers are both dying and living, both dead and alive.

Torah and Flesh, however, are not the last word.

The opening note of noncondemnation in 8:1 is one of the most famous lines in all of Romans: "There is therefore now no condemnation for those who are in Christ Jesus" (cf. 5:18-21). It should be: Messiah Jesus makes people right with God, and in the line of Christ they are transformed into loving people of peace and unity (with a glance at both the Strong and the Weak). Verse 1 works well with verse 3: "no condemnation" occurs because the Father sent the Son "in the likeness of sinful flesh, and to deal with sin." The expression "to deal with sin" (*peri hamartias*) probably comes from Leviticus' sin offering (5:8; 14:19, 31), so the better translation could be "as a sin offering" (NIV) rather than the blander "to deal with sin" (NRSV, CEB).[12] Calling Christ the sin offering brings atonement into the picture. Paul's most pristine atonement theology was expressed about the time of writing this verse in Romans 8, and it is found in 2 Corinthians 5:21: "For our sake he made him to be sin who knew no sin, so that in him we might become the righteousness of God." Christ became what he was not (sin) so that we could become what we are not (the righteousness of God). I call this "identification with us for the sake of incorporation into Christ."[13] This precise formulation in 2 Corinthians is expressed in a number of ways in Romans 5:12-21 and here in chapter 8, with the important addition that "righteousness of God" is not just standing but praxis in the power of the Spirit (cf. 8:3-8). To emphasize the point, notice that Jesus' sin offering has a lived-theology goal: to condemn sins and Sin in the Flesh and to slay Death itself. One could say his lived theology prompted his atonement theory! The enemies of Pauline theology—sin and Sin, Flesh, and Death—are dealt a death blow by Christ's death and resurrection. He not only dies our death, but he conquers the enemy and shuffles us from the Adam line to the Christ line where victory over Sin, Flesh, and Death are found. That is, Romans 8:4: the just requirement of the Torah is realized in those in Christ as they walk in the Spirit. Noticeably, this is an act of God, not of the human will ("be fulfilled" is passive voice). Notice, too, that this resolves the quest of the Weak to "transform" the Strong by Torah observance, and it transforms the Strong who think Torah is a waste of time.

The second verse of Romans 8, "for the law of the Spirit of life in Christ Jesus has set you free from the law of sin and of death," forms a version of another famous passage in this letter—namely, 12:1-2. In the line of Christ, there is the Spirit of God, and where the Spirit of God is there is transformation from people of the Flesh into people of the Spirit who know Eternal Life. That is, new creation happens so they might be people of righteousness, peace, joy, and love. It is more than noticeable that Paul uses the term "law" (or Torah) in 8:2-4 in a way that makes abundantly clear that Paul thinks believers, both Weak and Strong, will accomplish the Torah. The Torah captured by Sin and Flesh is conquered by the Torah of the Spirit in Christ Jesus. Here are Paul's primary terms in 8:2-4: "For the law of the Spirit of life in Christ Jesus has set you free," and "the just requirement of the law might be fulfilled in us." Who? His answer is those "who walk . . . according to the Spirit."

Again, we are face to face with Paul's *lived theology*. The Strong are free from the Torah, but the Strong actually live the Torah—by following it not in the flesh but in the Spirit. It appears that the Generic mode of Romans 5–8 has the positive life of both the Weak and the Strong in mind. But there's an emphasis in Romans 8 on the Strong. Who, after all, is experiencing "condemnation" (8:1, 3) in the Roman house churches? In light of this same term's use by the Judge in 2:1 and the Weak in 14:23, one can reasonably suspect the Strong are the ones who need to be told they are not condemned.

Summary

Our chart about the Two Ways, an ordering that moves from Adam to Death and from Christ to Eternal Life, can now be updated:

The Two Ways

The Way of Adam	The Way of Christ
Body of Sin	**Body of Christ**
Flesh	Spirit
	(1) *Grace*

The Determinative Act

(1) *Sin*	(2) Obedience of Christ
Trespass	Reception of Grace
Disobedience	Sending Son . . . to deal with sin
Mind set on Flesh	
Hostile to God	

Status

(2) Sinners	(3) Righteous / *No condemnation*
Flesh	Through Spirit-prompted observance of Torah

Means of Knowing God's Will

(3) *Torah captured by Sin and the Flesh*	(4) *Torah of Spirit in Christ*
<u>Weakened by the Flesh</u>	Gift of Righteousness
<u>Torah of Sin and Death</u>	<u>Torah of Spirit of Life in Christ</u>
<u>Minds on the Flesh</u>	<u>Minds on the Spirit</u>

Divine Decision

(4) Judgment	(5) Justification
Condemnation	<u>Condemned Sin in the Flesh</u>

Consequence

(5) *Death*	(6) *Life*
	Eternal Life
	<u>Peace</u>

Parameters of Divine Decision

(6) Many/All*	(7) Many/All

*"Many" and "All" are synonyms.

Combined, the two passages under consideration—Romans 5:12-21 and 8:1-8 with new bits now underlined—are not abstract theology or moral philosophy per se, as if now we need to examine Paul's theory of Torah or compare Paul to Qumran or to the Stoics to see where he is like and unlike each. While those comparisons are worthy of attention, what is more important is that this letter is pastoral, ecclesial theology and the Flesh and the Spirit have rhetorical intentions. When we read Romans backwards, something different emerges. Paul's theology is lived theology, and his pastoral concern is the Strong and the Weak in the Roman house churches just as it is how to live in the Roman Empire as followers of Jesus.

The judgments that both the Strong and Weak aim at the other, which abound in Romans 14–15, have been judged by God (8:3) and there is no condemnation left (8:1). Even more, both the Strong and the Weak in their accusations and disunities are operating in the Flesh and not in the Spirit. They are living according to the "law of sin and of death" (8:2). When they live in the Spirit, they become a Body of Christ (12:3-8) and not a Body of

Sin and Death. The Weak cannot observe the Torah because of their flesh; genuine observance occurs only because of the Spirit. The Strong are not living in love because they are controlled by the Flesh, the Flesh of status, but that life of love occurs only because of the Spirit. So, if they live in the Spirit, they will sympathize with one another, they will not sit in judgment on one another, they will welcome one another, and they will live in love of one another.

We turn now from the "All" section in Romans 5–8 to the "We" sections, where we will be able to offer only brief syntheses of Paul's major points, all with an eye on the context of Romans (12–16).

20

YOU AND WE

(6:11-23; 8:9-15; 5:1-11; 6:1-10; 7:1-6; 8:16-17, 18-39)

Paul speaks in four modes in Romans 5–8: All (Generic), You, We, and I. The larger vision of Romans 5–8 seen in the Generic passages sketches a story from Adam and sins and sinfulness to Christ and cosmic redemption—all of which has direct implications for the Strong and the Weak. The You section occurs in the midst of this cosmic liberation that flows into glorification. Glorification is not a state of the ethereal or disembodied soul-worship but rather humans achieving the design of creation as begun with Adam and Eve as *eikons* (images) of God. To be glorified is to be a glowing *eikon* of God in the creation of God accomplishing in an embodied state the purposes of God for all creation.[1]

The You passages, which are to be found at 6:11-23 and 8:9-15, *mirror* the Two Ways found in the All, or Generic, sections. But the You passages' rhetorical force is more direct: at 6:12, we get direct imperatives. Something like: "[You] Do not let sin rule amongst yourselves!" The concentration of "you" and "yourselves" in these passages is noticeably direct even if the terms reiterate the Way of Adam: sins, Sin, Flesh, and Death. The Way of Christ, however, focuses on the gift of the Spirit and the ushering in of life, both as a transformation in the present and as eternal life in the future. Thematically, Romans 6:23 mirrors the Two Ways passages: "For the wages of sin is death, but the free gift of God is eternal life in Christ Jesus our Lord." Sin leads to Death, while the "charism"/gift of God brings Eternal Life in Christ.

The You passages make a singular contribution to the overall vision of these chapters in that they clarify *what kind of sin* Paul has in mind for those whom he addresses—that is, sin exercising dominion (*basileuo*) in the mortal body (*soma*) that obeys the passions (*epithumia*; all in 6:12). Furthermore, the audience (You) are not to offer their "members" (*mele*) to sins and Sin as "instruments of wickedness" (*hopla adikias*, 6:13). He turns this offering of the bodies to these sins into a kind of slavery in 6:15-19, and in this passage he clarifies Sin even more: obedient slaves (to sin) (6:16) as well as impurity (*akatharsia*) and "greater and greater iniquity" (*eis ten anomian*; 6:19). He reminds the You people that they are now "ashamed" of their former life (6:21). To use slavery as an image, particularly an image in which the negative implications of slavery are part of their past and the positive implications now transferred from human masters to God, may well have appealed to the gentile believing slaves and freed of Rome.

These You passages also draw the audience into *moral commitments*: "do not let sin exercise dominion in your mortal bodies" (6:12a), and "no longer present your members to sin" (6:13a). Positively: "present yourselves to God" (6:13b; cf. 12:1-2), or "so now present your members as slaves to righteousness for sanctification" (6:19). If Paul emphasizes powers here—both Sin and Spirit and grace—he does not minimize the necessity of the Roman believers to embody their faith, to carry out a lived theology. This all happens not simply in some spiritual realm but in the body. It happens when the Strong and the Weak welcome one another without quarrels to the table and live with one another as siblings.

Spirit in 8:9-15 appears no fewer than ten times, each of which means the Spirit of God. In the Christ line, then, the Spirit is active, regenerating a person into new creation Life. Such a person is rescued from the Adam line into the Christ line and thus has Life. In the Christ line, they discover righteousness (8:10) and putting to death the deeds of the body (8:13) and assurance of God's grace as children of God (8:15-16) and eternal life (8:16-17). Noticeably, the grace and life those in the Christ line now have turned the Adamite from a life of Sin and Flesh and Death into being alive (6:11), offering oneself to God so the body can become an instrument of righteousness (6:13), becoming slaves to righteousness (6:16, 18, 19) and God (6:22), heart obedience (6:17), which all leads into sanctification (6:19) and eternal life through the resurrection and redemption of mortal bodies (8:11; cf. 8:23). These virtues are gifts of God through the Spirit (8:9-15). Here, then, the comprehensive vision is once again clear: the aim of the Way of Christ is a transformed people who actually fulfill the Torah (8:4) in the power of the Spirit in their bodies (8:11).

To identify the You people, there are two clues: the first of which appears in the connecting lines of 6:14 and 6:15: "*not under law* but under grace." One might think "not under law" means the You are the Weak who have turned to Jesus and are no longer under the Torah. Or perhaps Paul is speaking both to the Weak and to the Strong and shifting back and forth. Again, that's not clear. Here's the second clue that I suggest tips the balance in one direction: in Romans, the Judge (the Weak accusing the Strong) is accused of breaking the Torah (2:17-29). The Judge, in spite of supposed superiority, commits the same sins (2:1-16) as the stereotypical gentile who lives in the Way of Adam (1:18-32). The two mentions of those who are "under the law" are side glances at the Weak who are seeking to get the Strong or gentiles to discover Christoformity by following the Torah. Those "under the law" are the Weak in the face once again of the Judge, not gentile believers. The You passages are aimed at the Weak.

We

The most extensive sections in Romans 5–8 are the We passages: 5:1-11; 6:1-10; 7:1-6; 8:16-17, 18-39. Romans is repetitive either because Paul believed in repetition or because the various sections of Romans, and especially the various units of Romans 5–8, are sets of parallel observations. Hence, to explain Romans is to repeat points made in other contexts. The fundamental lines of thinking were discovered in the "All" passages above, and the You, We, and I sections each in their own way bring to the fore the themes already set out in the All sections. What distinguishes the All sections from the We sections is that the first is a Two Way, more theoretical set of ideas while the We sections form into the Personal Way of redemption.

Once again, the comprehensive vision is the place to start. The story, it will be remembered, is about the lines of Adam and Christ, about sin and obedience, about Death and Life / Eternal Life, and about creation enslaved and creation liberated. It is about how best to live in such a way that we know this redemptive liberation and moral transformation. And how best to live is the point of tension in Rome. The answer for the Weak is More Torah! For Paul, the answer is All Grace and All Spirit! The result, ironically, is the same (8:1-4). Those in Christ who live in the Spirit do all the Torah originally stated and more. The question in Romans is how to get there, and Paul opposes the Judge, who thinks it is through More Torah. The Strong will never become reconciled with the Weak simply by More Torah, and neither will the Weak. The solution is to be found elsewhere. For the Strong, there may be a lack of perception of what genuine lived theology looks like and communicates. They either flout their non-Torah life, or they presume upon grace and forgiveness.

Whichever is their option, the one thing that is obvious is that they are hard-headed when it comes to the scruples of the Weak. They are status driven, insensitive, and coercive in their relations with the Weak. That, too, must be transformed. The Weak say More Torah! But Paul says More Spirit!

There are a few preliminary observations about the We passages. *First,* the We sections like the You sections mirror the Generic sections in terms and lived theology. The difference in the six elements mapped below and the flow charts above is that in the All passages, a human being begins in the left column but is shifted by baptism into the right column. What we see in the We sections, then, is the journey of the transformed believer. *Second,* the We sections and the Generic sections form a network of ideas, a tangled web of terms that clarify one another only in relationship to one another. To proceed verse by verse through the We sections makes for too much redundancy. Hence, I will seek to untangle the web into six separable (but networked) themes. *Third,* the identity of the We deserves careful consideration in our passages. At Romans 7:1, Paul identifies an audience—"those who know the law"—and this is the Weak. Yet, in 7:4, he speaks to the Weak as "You," and in 7:5-6 the You become the "We." (The same happens in 7:7 and 7:14, where We here seems to mean We Jewish believers.) One cannot then simply infer from personal pronouns (You is Weak, We is Strong, etc.) to a specific group in Rome, and, of all the personal pronouns, We is both the least restricted and the most inclusive. Yet, in the We sections of Romans 5–8, "We" is used mostly for the Strong, and a close reading of the passages demonstrates that what Paul says here is for the Strong. He includes himself with We when he agrees.

There are six themes present in the We passages, and I label them the Personal Way: the former condition of all humans; the revelation of God in Christ to rescue humans from sins, Sin, Flesh, and Death; the gift and its benefits that come to humans in Christ; the new condition of life with the gift; the human participation in the gift; and the future in Christ. We will proceed through these themes in order as a way of explaining the We sections, but we need to keep in mind the pastoral, ecclesial context of our passage and that Paul's aim is lived theology, which in a shortened form is Christoformity.

Personal Way

(1) *Former Condition.* Unlike so much of our modern world, Paul is unafraid of naming our problem, and in this the Personal Way rolls off Phoebe's tongue with pointed conviction. In our passage, Paul parades before the Roman believers what their life was like before Christ. He concentrates this theme in one passage (5:6-11). They were "weak" (5:6),[2] and here he means

human frailty before God. They were "ungodly" (5:6), "sinners" (5:8), and "enemies" (5:10), terms that describe in Pauline theology the stereotyped past of gentiles (hence, the Strong are in view). Paul's theology, however, is not restricted to individualistic themes. This former condition of 5:6-11 realizes a cosmic former condition that emerges into personlike realities (Sin, Flesh, Death) that become agents in this world. The cosmic frame appears in the We passages in that creation itself has been captured by Evil, which is the accumulation of sins and Sin and Flesh and Satan and evil spirits. Creation is groaning and longing for liberation. Thus, "creation waits" because "creation was subjected to futility (*mataioteti*)" (8:19-20), and thus all of creation is to be liberated from its bondage and redeemed for new creation (8:21).

In Pauline theology, perhaps the best explanation for this connection of sinners to the cosmic decay and bondage is emergence theory. That is, sins become the causal basis for the emergence not just of human-sin-based sinful patterns in our world but of some kind of Sin-Self or Sin-Person that is aligned with an evil spiritual force. The alliance of Sin with Satan, then, works back on sinners to keep them in sinful behaviors so that Sin and Satan can guide humans to Death. Creation, itself, then has been captured by Satan and Sin in Paul's cosmological soteriology in such a way that if Christ is the Savior, he will need to rescue not only humans from their ways but all of creation— which is what Romans 8:18-39 magnificently announces. God—Father, Son, Spirit—is at work to redeem creation and usher into the cosmic vision God has planned for creation. The solution to their former condition, then, is not Torah observance but Christ, whom Paul can equate with God's gift, grace.

(2) *The Gift of God in Christ to Rescue.* Paul draws on the All passages to explain in this Personal Way how a human moves from the Adam line to the Christ line by appealing a number of times to the gift of God in Christ. Again, there is a concentration of God's gift to us in Christ in Romans 5:6-11, but there is more. I will begin with the two most comprehensive expressions in our chapters. *First*, this is an act of God: God "did not withhold his Son, but gave him up for all of us" (8:32). This act of God emerges from God's love that becomes grace or gift. "God's love has been poured into our hearts" (5:5), and "God proves his love for us" (5:8). The gift is summed up in the death and resurrection in 5:10: "For if while we were enemies, we were reconciled to God through the death of his Son, much more surely, having been reconciled, will we be saved by his life" (cf. 4:25). His death atones by way of identification for incorporation, including the ideas of sacrifice and substitution. His resurrection snaps the powers of Sin, the Flesh, and Death, and it ushers in new creation Life and thereby regenerates the death-directed sinner from

Death to Life. Thus, his death and resurrection rescue the human from the former condition. We see the same in "If God is for us" (8:31) but even more in "Who will separate us from the love of Christ?" (8:35) and that nothing "will be able to separate us from the love of God in Christ Jesus our Lord" (8:39). Grace is God's love in the form of a gift: the prior act of God's love toward us in the death-resurrection of Christ regardless of our status that is superabundant and effective. The reception of this gift triggers gratitude and gift back to God to his glory.

Second, in 8:34, Paul says, "It is Christ Jesus, who died, yes, who was raised, who is at the right hand of God, who indeed intercedes for us." Christ died for us, Christ was raised for us, and—because "raised" entails the ascension to the "right hand of God"—Christ now intercedes for us. Everything has been in the past, in the present, and, as we will see as well, in the future *by Christ alone.* Paul's formula "through" Christ then evokes this fuller perspective (5:1, 11). God's gift of Christ is our redemption. True to Pauline form, redemption as designed to lead us to Christoformity emphasizes the gift of God to us in the cross of Christ. Thus, "Christ died" for the ungodly and for us (5:6, 8, 10); his death is "through his blood" (5:9) and "through his body" (7:4). Even if the cross is clearly more prominent, his comprehensive statement includes the cross, resurrection, and ascension. Paul says in 5:10 that we are saved *by his life,* which is the resurrection.

Here, *third,* we must notice that Romans 8:4 reveals with unmistakable clarity the point of redemption: "so that the just requirement of the law might be fulfilled in us, who walk not according to the flesh but according to the Spirit." Redemption is not so humans can go to heaven when they die but so they can be transformed by God's grace into Christoformity, and that means they become people who choose not their own way but the way of loving God and loving others (Phil 2:6-11). What this means is that the Gift of God, namely Christ, is directional. The lived theology of Romans 12–16, then, is why Romans 5–8 sketches the journey of the human who shifts from the line of Adam to the line of Christ. This will be developed slightly more in the sixth point below.

(3) *The Gift Itself.* In the Personal Way, humans are sinners and alienated by God and are trapped by their own fault in the systemic cycle of sinning and evil, and that becomes Sin and Flesh, and they work back on the humans' own sinning. God's will for humans is not bondage to Sin but liberation from sin, Sin, Flesh, and Satan, and so God sent his Son to deal with Sin, liberate all creation from slavery to Flesh, and usher them into Christoformity. That act of God is all gift.

That gift itself is described by Paul with an abundance of freshly reshaped terms. Here is a listing, and it would consume a conference of specialists to work out which of these terms is most important (if one is) and to rank them in order of importance for Paul, but all that can be done here is to provide the list, a list that by its enumerating becomes all the more impressive:

(1) Grace (5:2; 6:1)
(2) Justification, righteousness (of God), justice (5:1, 9; 8:30, 31, 32, 33, 34)
(3) Peace with God (5:1) and reconciliation (5:10, 11)
(4) Glory, God's glory, sharing in God's glory, boasting in glory (5:2-3; 8:17, 18)
(5) Hope (5:4)
(6) Life (5:10, 17-18, 21; 6:4, 10, 13, 22-23; 7:10; 8:2, 6, 10, 13)
(7) Love (5:8; 8:31-39)
(8) The Spirit (5:5; 7:6)
(9) Saved (5:9 [from wrath], 10 [by life]; 8:24)
(10) Liberation (6:18, 22; 8:2, 21bis)
(11) Belong to one another in the Body of Christ (7:4)
(12) Children of God/Adoption (8:16, 19, 23)
(13) Redemption (8:23 [for our bodies])
(14) Called and predestined from human condition to glory (8:28-30)
(15) Christoformity (8:29)
(16) Christ's intercession (8:34)
(17) Secure relationship (8:31-39)
(18) Conquerors in life (8:37)

God's gift is manifold, superabundant, and out of sync with what the Roman Christians deserve. God's grace, then, is incongruous with who they have been and who they are, whether the social status of the Strong or the elective privilege of the Weak. The gift is redemption in all its fullness: a secure and confident standing before God, relationship with God, power for living in the Spirit and intercession by Christ for them, fellowship with those in Christ, and a moral future that is nothing less than Christoformity. As Christ invaded the world of sin and Sin and Flesh and Death and Satan to rescue the believers of Rome, so on the other side of the rescue they will be conquerors (8:37). Here is one brief observation on which of these is most important: if the most significant terms in the Pauline framing of the former condition are Sin, Flesh, and Death, then the terms that undo each of these become the most prominent terms. I'm inclined here to tip my hat to *liberation* as the beginning point of redemption for Paul, and that means *cosmic, personal liberation unto Christoformity*. But that, as I say, takes more than a statement to establish.

Some of these terms in this section of the Personal Way call for comment, not least justification. The pleasure and the problem of these terms—righteousness, justification, justice—is that they have been examined endlessly in the church, and consequently one knotty turn after another confronts the traveler. It is not possible to explain or defend every turn taken in what follows, but my aim is to sketch an outline by stating eight theses: (a) The *righteousness of God* is an *attribute of God*, by which I mean God is relationally faithful to the covenant and altogether morally and ontologically right and just (Pss 36:6; 71:19; Isa 42:21) in being and the actions of redemption and judgment (Isa 5:16; 10:22). (b) Furthermore, righteousness is *a gift from God*—that is, it is the saving action and power of God that makes humans and creation right (Isa 46:13; 56:1; Mic 6:5; CD 20:20).[3] Romans 1:16-17 puts most of this into a tight bundle of terms: "For I am not ashamed of the gospel; it is the power of God for salvation to everyone who has faith, to the Jew first and also to the Greek. For in it the righteousness of God is revealed through faith for faith; as it is written, 'The one who is righteous will live by faith.'" Notice the terms tightly woven together: gospel, power, salvation, righteousness, faith, Jew, and Greek. (c) *Righteousness*, when descriptive of Israelites, refers to *behaviors* that conform to the will of God as revealed in Torah.[4] (This is not legalism but covenantal nomism.) (d) To be *"righteoused"* (to be *justified*),[5] as the outworking of the righteousness of God, means to be declared right by God; that is, it is forensic (Ps 18:20; Isa 43:9, 26; 45:25). (e) Justification is a gift—that is, it is given to us apart from merit because it is achieved by the death and resurrection of Christ (4:25). (f) In addition, as a gift, *justification liberates* and thus creates a *reciprocation* of obedience and love (6:7). Hence, righteousness is a gift that transforms (cf. 1QS 11:13-14). (g) Justification is the result of the gift/grace of God in Christ *in a Spirit-prompted reality.* Justification happens only in union with Christ. Hence, Mike Bird speaks of "incorporated righteousness," and I myself have framed it as "identification for incorporation,"[6] by which I mean incarnation leads to identification with sinners in order to liberate us from Sin, Flesh, and Death and plant us in the people of God. Christ's identification with us enables us to be united with Christ so that believers receive the fullness of the gift, which leads to our next observation about these terms. (h) This justification-by-union-with-Christ comes *by faith and by faith alone,* not by works of the Torah—which is why righteousness is connected with confession of sin, repentance, and trust in God's mercy (Dan 9:14-19; 1QS 11:12-15). Because the theme of this book is reading Romans backwards, the term "righteousness" or "justification" or "justify," whichever term is at work, always evokes the tension that Paul wants to resolve between the Strong and the Weak. Justification becomes in the hands of Paul a pastoral word leading to reconciliation and peace between siblings in Christ.

Part of the pleasure and the problem of the many terms expressing the gift of God is that each points to the same reality and not to separable realities. The *ordo salutis* so popular a generation ago and beyond, while it brought attention to distinct dimensions of the gift, tended to reify each element—regeneration before justification before sanctification before glorification—and separate one from the other as if they were not overlapping dimensions of the gift of God. If we can agree that the work of Christ can be framed as identification with us in order to incorporate us into life with God in the kingdom of God, then each of the terms becomes a facet of the same reality. Thus, take *adoption* (Rom 8:16, 19, 23). God is the Father, the Son is the Father's gift of redemption, and those who are in union with the Son become both children of God and siblings to one another and learn to live as siblings with one another. Adoption, then, travels from the same location (where we were) to the same location (glorious Christoformity). Take, too, *peace with God and reconciliation* (5:1, 10-11). We were, Paul says, "weak" and "ungodly" (5:6) and "enemies" (5:10), but God in Christ reconciled us and created peace with God—again, the same journey from where we were to where we are headed, with special emphasis in all these terms on the Strong and the Weak of Rome.

These terms are distinguishable as linguistic units and language games. To be reconciled is drawn from the world of relationships, while justification is more drawn from the courtroom and adoption from the world of family, parenting, and relocating a child from one condition into a family. Yet, each of these terms also overlaps, and, more importantly, each of these terms is a linguistic journey from the same location to the same location. The terms transplant humans in the line of Adam into the line of Christ, leading to new creation itself—that is, to Life.

(4) *Life with the Gift.* By all accounts, Paul's *theory* of the Christian life—righteousness, life in the Spirit, obedience, love, peace, unity—conflicts with the *reality* of those in his churches (and his own practice too, truth be told), not least in Rome itself. Hence, Life with the gift for those who have switched from the Adam to the Christ line remains a struggle or battle, and there is an abundance of sinning on the part of the believers in Paul's mission churches. Even more, his theory conflicts with how Paul ends Romans 5: "but where sin increased, grace abounded all the more" (5:20). Some knothead consequently barks out, "If sin prompts grace, let's sin all the more!" Which is where Romans 6 launches its theory of Life with the gift, Life with grace

vs. life with Adam and Death. The Way of Adam, then, is descriptive both of an unredeemed Adamite and of believers—that is, with those who are "somewhat" Adamites.

The Personal Way's life with the grace of redemption starts with *baptism*, and this baptism refers to the watery rite as well as its theological implications. The earliest Jesus movement understood the watery act of baptism as union with Christ ("name of" in Acts 8:15), as connected to forgiveness (Acts 2:38; 22:16; Gal 3:27; 1 Cor 6:11; Titus 3:5; Heb 10:22; 1 Pet 3:21), and as connected to the gift of the Spirit (1 Cor 12:13; again, Acts 2:38). We need not be forced to choose between the physical act of baptism and theological union with Christ, for in fact the latter is impossible without the former. Thus, in their baptism, the believers of Rome were plunged into the death of Jesus and died in his own death. He can refer to believers as, "We are those who have died to sin" (6:2), because they died in baptism (6:3). But death is not the final word of baptism: life is. Thus, it appears that Paul thinks baptism is both a baptism into death and a baptism into new Life by coming out of the grave of the water into new creation Life as Christ rose from the dead (6:4). In 6:6, he says the "old self" (*ho palaios anthropos*) "was crucified" so that the "body of sin might be destroyed, and we might no longer be enslaved to sin." Those who have died to sin, he continues, have "been set free from sin" (6:7). There in a nutshell is Paul's theory of the Christian life, and it is all rooted in the Adam line vs. Christ line in Paul's Generic sections. Hence, beginning the Christian life in baptism, the Adamite embodied a death to sin and an awakening to new creation Life in Christ through the Spirit.

We turn to the Weak and then to the Strong, both of whom are addressed in these chapters. To the *Weak*, Paul turns in 7:1-6, and I concentrate on verse 4: "you have died to the law through the body of Christ." Only Jews can die to the Torah. "While we," and here "we" means Jewish believers in Jesus, "were living in the flesh" of Israel's election, we didn't have automatic righteous living. No, "our sinful passions, aroused by the law, were at work in our members to bear fruit for death" (7:4-5). Hence, in Life with the gift, "we" (Jewish believers, the Weak) "are discharged from the Torah, dead to that which held us captive," and now the Weak have become enslaved "in the new life of the Spirit" (7:6). These words are an amazing development for Torah-observant Jews like Paul and the Weak in Rome. Paul is not against the Torah so much as he is for the Spirit that empowers a life that realizes the Torah and more. Yet, to back up to Romans 6, there are some who think if grace is superabundant, then sinning becomes the opportunity to manifest grace! Paul drops the hammer on this: "By no means!" (6:1-2). His questions in 6:1-4 are rhetorical ploys to get them to agree and see his point. The Strong's inclination to sin in order to magnify grace contradicts the unfulfilled cosmic longing for liberation and justice and reconciliation (8:18-26).

The Strong and the Weak need to know that their only hope of Christoformity is the *Holy Spirit*. God's love has been "poured into [their] hearts through the Holy Spirit" (5:5), who witnesses to them of God's presence (8:16); they are now living "in the new life of the Spirit" (7:6) with the "first fruits of the Spirit" (8:23), they experience the advocacy of the Spirit in their prayers (8:26-27), and they are caught up into the Spirit's (divine) longing for redemption (8:23). Paul here has transferred the focus of transformation. Christoformity be realized not by Torah observance or by reckless freedom but only in the power of the Spirit who makes them holy.

(5) *Human Participation in the Gift.* The gift in the Personal Way remains a gift from beginning to end, and the gift is God's liberation through Christ. The gift is both redemption in the sense of reconciliation but also redemption in the sense of transformation. The Strong and the Weak have participated in this redemption, and there are four operative categories describing this participation: faith, hope, love, and baptismal death.

In our passage, the first operative word is *faith* (5:1; 6:8), in the sense of trust in Christ, allegiance to Messiah Jesus as king or Lord. Faith receives Christ as the gift of redemption. In addition to faith is *hope* (5:2, 4-5; 8:20, 24-25). "Hope" here means confidence, assuredness, even certitude at times, and thus it propels the person to live in light of what one hopes for, which is the full realization of the gift. Hope is unfolded by Paul in Romans 5:3-5 in a unique chain of character development: the hope of "sharing the glory of God," which means full Christoformity, empowers the Weak (paying taxes) and the Strong (moving downward socially) to face suffering as an opportunity for moral growth. This posture of hope toward suffering morphs at the end of chapter 8 into the counter-Roman theme of "more than conquerors" (8:37). Hence, in our passage, faith and hope are indistinguishable as we read, "For in hope we are saved" (8:24). Thus, hope is also indistinguishable from a present form of hope in "patience" (8:25). As Romans 4 makes clear, the premier model of faith-as-hope is Abraham. But one cannot forget to read Romans backwards when it comes to hope. The "God of hope" (15:13) is the one who is redemptively energizing the people of God to expand to include gentiles in a united worship (15:8-12), which begins with "welcome" (15:7).

Next comes *love* (8:28), and human love reciprocates in gratitude to God's own love (5:5, 8; 8:35, 39) and arises in the believer through the Spirit (5:5). To love God is to be ruggedly, affectively committed to God, to be

faith
hope
love

present to God, to be an advocate for God, and to be transformed by God's presence into Christoformity. To participate in the gift, then, is to believe in God, to hope in God, and to love God.

Romans 5–8, however, develops this mature sense of participation in a unique way in 6:1-10 and 7:1-6. How so? Participation in Christ occurs through baptism. He first speaks to the Strong (6:1-10) and then to the Weak (7:1-6). Paul says those who are baptized into Christ have died to sin because in baptism the baptized one identifies with Jesus Christ, *who died to annul death and who was raised to usher in new creation life.* Baptism puts to death sin and the body of sin, thus liberating the baptized from enslavement to Sin and Flesh, and it brings to life righteous living. To the Weak, he uses the analogy of life-under-the-Torah and says the days of the Torah are now over just as the laws about marriage and adultery are over when a person dies (7:1-3). As Paul and Peter themselves had to learn (Gal 2:15-21), Jewish participants in the gift of redemption in Christ have died "through the body of Christ" (a trope for the crucifixion embodied in baptism). Their participation in baptism has several implications, including sibling relations with the Strong (7:4), learning to "bear fruit to God" (7:4), ending their Torah-provoked fleshly life of passions headed toward Death (7:5-6), and a radical liberation into "new life in the Spirit" (7:6).

Participation, whether it is the triad of faith-hope-love or baptism, is a full participation from the moment of faith/baptism to the end of life. The obsession at times in Christianity with the moment of decision runs against the grain of how Paul understands participation in Christ. God's gift creates reciprocation or circularity: the gift creates humans who become givers, or grace promotes grace. God's gift creates what calls participation in the very way of Christ.[7]

If we read Romans backwards, another point rises to the surface: the inclusiveness of redemption recalls the redemption of Israel and then of gentiles in the surprising grace of God and the future redemption of "*all* Israel" (11:26). This leads me to think that "all" and "many" refer to the redemption of both Jews and gentiles, each by faith and none without faith. This takes us also back to Romans 14–15, suggesting that the "all" and "many" refer to both Weak and Strong, and, if both Weak and Strong are redeemed, then they are siblings and are to welcome one another to the table in fellowship.

The We sections seem, then, to focus on the Strong with the exception— and Paul makes that exception clear—in 7:1-6. There are always implications for both the Strong and the Weak in the Personal Way. The critique of the Weak was that the Strong lacked moral transformation; the solution of the

Weak was Torah observance. Paul says, no, the solution is not Torah observance but God's grace in Christ through the Spirit that awakens participation in the way of Christ. This has implications for both the Weak and the Strong. Yet, I think Paul's focus is the Strong. It is the Strong, the high-status Romans, who are most in need of learning what it means to participate in the new creation gift of life in Christ and to be empowered by the Spirit. The language of their former condition is the language of gentiles; the morality aimed at in this Personal Way is designed for those with a gentile past. Here we find the theological roots for what he must tell the Strong in Romans 14–15 about how to live.

In reading Romans forwards, one encounters Romans 7 before Romans 8, and what Paul says through the "I" of that passage creates a wider expanse of redemption in Romans 8. If the "I" of Romans 7:7-25 is not the Strong but the Weak (and the Judge), then the Future of Christ in our next section encompasses redemption both for the Weak and the Strong.

(6) *The Future in Christ.* The future for those who participate in Christ begins now and extends into eternity. Paul uses a few expressions to describe that future in 8:31-39: glory, resurrection, life, heirs with Christ, Christoformity, and experiencing God's love. That future begins now, and that means the whole of Romans 8 can be taken up into the future of the Roman house church believers' future.

The future glory I take to mean full Christoformity. In the eschaton, the believers will "share in the glory of God" (5:2) as Christ himself did with the Father (6:4). The destined end of the believer is "to be conformed to the image of his Son" (8:29), and that means cosmic liberation (8:18-25). The redemptive process itself—foreknowledge to glory—has the same Christoform glory in view (8:28-30). The poetic stretches of 8:31-39 about confidence in God, with their Christocentric (even proto-Trinitarian) and "nothing can separate us from God in Christ" emphases, provide another glimpse of final Christoformity. Eschatological Christoformity then explains what it means to be "heirs, heirs of God and joint heirs with Christ" (8:17), which, as Paul continues to say, means to "be glorified with him." Because Paul ties together this theme of creation, futility, Christ, and future glory as Christoformity, we have every reason to think he sees the future as the realization of the purpose of Eden. Thus, to be joint heirs means creation will be back under the rule of God, and those who are in Christ will rule with Christ over all creation.[8]

What is now is not what will be, for in our passage the final cosmic liberation will happen only when history reaches its goal in the new heavens and new earth. Christ was raised, Paul says, so we will then be raised (6:4-5, 8-10), or we will then experience the "redemption of our bodies" (8:23). Thus, the last word for Paul is "Life" (5:1; 6:4; 8:38), a word that evokes God's gift of Life in Christ, who entered Death to break its shackles and ushered those enslaved into new creation Life for eternity. Eternity for Paul is so at odds with how most Christians talk about heaven that a word must be said: for Paul, "heaven" or eternity or Life is about God's love—being loved by God and loving God—and therefore, through that circular gift, those who are loved by God love one another. An endless commerce of love is the pure plan of God for all creation, including the children of God.

If we read Romans backwards (and not just forwards), we see that the fundamental pleas of Paul in chapters 12 through 16 for unity, for peace, for love, for reconciliation are the mirror opposites of the sins he has in view in the Generic, You, and We sections. Furthermore, a Spirit-prompted life (so clear in the You section) produces the kind of life marked by devotion and slavery to God, which sounds like 12:1-2, as well as obedience, righteousness, and holiness. Hence, for the Weak and the Strong to work for mutual "welcome" is at the heart of what Paul means with sanctification, obedience, and righteousness. Peace in the heart of the empire flows from the Holy Spirit. The terms in the You and We sections are generic moral terms for the concrete lived theology of 12–16. The Strong's former slavery to sin and flesh in the Adam line to death is a way of speaking of violating the conscience, whether that is through arrogance or coercion or disfellowship, of the Weak.

21

I

? not fully understood yet (handwritten)

(7:7-25)

One more time, the comprehensive vision of the All sections—the Two Ways (Adam or Christ)—needs to remain before us. But this time I want to update the Two Ways chart that I have used twice already with some elements from the Personal Way:

THE TWO WAYS

The Way of Adam	The Way of Christ
Body of Sin	**Body of Christ**
Flesh	Spirit
	(1) *Grace*

The Determinative Act

(1) *sins/Sin*	(2) Obedience of Christ
Trespass	Reception of Grace
Disobedience	Sending Son ... to deal with sin
Mind set on Flesh	
Hostile to God	
sin becomes Sin	

Status

(2) Sinners	(3) Righteous / *No condemnation*
Flesh	Through Spirit-prompted observance of Torah

171

Means of Knowing God's Will

(3) *Torah captured by Sin and the Flesh*	(4) *Torah of Spirit in Christ*
Weakened by the Flesh	Gift of Righteousness
Torah of Sin and Death	Torah of Spirit of Life in Christ
Minds on the Flesh	Minds on the Spirit

Divine Decision

Redemption

Salvation

Liberation of All Creation

(4) Judgment	(5) Justification
Condemnation	Condemned Sin in the Flesh

Consequence

(5) *Death*	(6) *Life*
	Eternal Life
	Peace
	Reconciliation now and future
	Unity, Love, Welcome
	Sibling relations
	Liberation of all Creation
	Glorification
	Kingdom of God Realized

Parameters of Divine Decision

(6) Many/All*	(7) Many/All

*"Many" and "All" are synonyms.

If the intent of Romans 5–8 is this comprehensive vision toward transformation in Christ through the Spirit, then we must learn to read Romans 7 within that cosmic vision of redemption. The "I" of Romans 7 is someone exploring transformation through the Torah but fails miserably at observing the Torah. The rhetorical force of the I passage cannot be emphasized enough. Discussions often devolve into debates about who the I is—here Adam, there

Israel, now Paul, then Jewish believers—and miss the rhetorical context. We need to ask if the I of Romans 7 is the Judge whom Paul uses to represent the Weak of Rome.

Readers of Romans 7 know that the I section includes a history of debate. The Protestant view has nearly always seen the I of Romans 7 as the common Ego-Adam experience of struggling with merit-seeking pride. (Which contradicts what Paul says of himself in Philippians 3:3-14.) Others think the I is collective: Paul in his preconversion days as a representative or even superzealous Torah-observant Jew learning that the Torah is impossible to do perfectly (again, a problem for Philippians 3) or impossible to bring about the kingdom, or the I as a collective story of Israel's life under the Torah, or even Paul as a collective postconversion Jewish Christian having to learn that he cannot find spiritual formation through the Torah but only through grace and the Spirit.

We need to consider, too, the rhetorical device called speech-in-character or, in Greek, *prosopopoeia*. If we think of this text through speech-in-character, Romans 7 is not Paul's personal experience so much as a character (the Judge or the Weak)[1] whose view Paul wants to sketch before his readers—think of the Strong hearing this "I" as the Weak—so they will not pursue the "I" option for Christoformity. Who is most likely to have chosen the Torah option to become Christoform? The Weak or the Strong? The answer comes by consulting Romans 14–15, where the Weak were seeking to get the Strong to be more observant of Torah. On top of that observation, consider again Romans 7:1-6, which is aimed at the Weak. It is a smooth transition then from the Weak of 7:1-6 to the Judge, as representing (or being represented as) the Weak in Romans 2, in Romans 7:7-25. I will now call the "I" of Romans 7 *the Judge*.

We are reading Romans backwards as a heuristic exploration of what Romans looks like from the other end. The I of our chapter is the Weak's (the Judge's) demand to find Christoformity through Torah observance and, at the same time, to appeal to the Strong to be Torah observant for full conversion. Think, perhaps, of the Strong's unwillingness to do the Torah on the path to Christoformity. Clearly, the solution for the lived-theology vision of Paul is at the end of Romans 7. In other words, Paul puts into the mouth of someone what he more or less has contended throughout his mission church experiences. He preaches the gospel, gentiles come to faith, Jewish believers or Jewish nonbelievers contend with gentile converts that full conversion to the God of Israel and the Messiah entails observance of the whole Torah. Then the gentile converts who try to observe the Torah do not succeed. The I passage then becomes Paul's fullest argument against the need of the Torah for gentile converts. He shows that gentiles who try to observe the Torah will not find the path to Christoformity, and it all begins with Romans 7:1-6.

THE TWO "WE'S"

The "we" of 7:7a ("What then should *we* say?") finds a second question that clarifies it: "That the law is sin?" The answer of Paul is, "By no means!" These words and questions are typical diatribal, rhetorical, and speech-in-character moves. They counter what emerges out of 7:1-6, a passage undoubtedly aimed at the Weak. So the opening We of 7:7a and the one in 7:14a ("*we* know that the law is spiritual [or, of the Spirit]") permit Paul to identify with his (Weak) audience and lead them to his viewpoint of how best to achieve lived theology. The answer he gives in 7:7-25 is, "Not through the Torah." Romans 8 will say, "But through God's grace, in Christ, through the Spirit."

Romans 7:1-6 proposes two history-shifting ideas: the Torah is *a temporary arrangement* given by God through Moses to Israel until the Messiah, and the Torah's purpose is *to reveal sin as transgression and to magnify sin into Sin*.[2] If the Torah's days are numbered and the Torah's design is to manifest sin as Sin, then the questions of Romans 7:1 but especially 7:7 are explicable. The question in Romans 7:1 is: "Is the law sinful?" And in 7:7: "Is the law sin?" What we learn, then, from the two We's is that the Torah's days are up and the Torah's purpose is to reveal Sin, not to generate Christoformity. This is what the rest of the I passage is about.

THE PURPOSE OF ROMANS 7:7-25

Paul then creates a speech-in-character to flesh out the purpose of the Torah and therefore its temporal restriction from Moses to Christ, all with the rhetorical aim of proving that Christoformity cannot be achieved through Torah observance. Lived theology is life in the Spirit. One is reminded that in the Generic/All passage at 5:20, Paul briefly stated what is now stated in this I passage.[3] The Torah's purpose was to enter into human history, and the result was that trespasses abounded. Paul's aim in 7:7-25 is not then to tell his story or really anyone else's but to put in the words of "I" an articulation of what the Torah's purpose was (and also then what it was not). The character Paul creates here, the Judge, does not proceed step by step but instead weaves terms together so that Torah, commandment, sin, flesh, and I become a seamless cloth that exhibits the divine purpose of the Torah.

I do not pretend to have resolved this most difficult of passages iɪ but there are some observations to make. *First,* the Judge knows ... never have known sin without the Torah: "Yet, if it had not been for the law, I would not have known sin" (7:7). The Judge uses "covet" as his illustration.[4] *Second,* the Torah's commandment and Sin become a mutually reinforcing machine to bring Death to the Judge, who wants to follow the Torah: "but when the commandment came, sin revived" (Rom 7:9), and "For sin, seizing an opportunity in the commandment, deceived me and through it killed me." (7:11). *Third,* though sin was sin before the Torah's arrival with Moses, it was not until the Torah that sin was seen for what it is: sin, sinfulness, Sin. Hence, our third observation is that the Torah's purpose was to be used by Sin to make sin exceedingly sinful: "It was sin, working death in me through what is good, in order that sin might be shown to be sin, and through the commandment might become sinful beyond measure" (7:13). At work behind this blaming of Sin is that the Torah, Paul must insist, is "holy and just and good" (7:12; cf. 7:13) and "spiritual" or "Spirit-derived" or "Spiritual" (7:14). The problem is not the Torah. The problem is elsewhere. The problem, too, is that the Judge wants the Torah to do what it cannot do: transform.

Fourth, Paul shifts and blames Sin for what the Torah accomplishes for those who want to find Christoformity by its observance. The Judge is "of the flesh, sold into slavery under sin" (7:14)—so much so that the Judge can't seem to obey the Torah because Sin in him provokes the Torah to reveal sin and tempt him to sin (7:15-20)! He begins then with blaming Sin, but he pushes deeper. *Fifth,* it is not just Sin at work but something *in the Judge himself,* and his admission is astounding: "But in fact it is no longer I that do it, but sin that dwells within me. For I know that nothing good dwells within me, that is, in my flesh" (7:17-18). He says it more forcefully in 7:20: "It is no longer I that do it, but sin that dwells within me" (7:20). Sin now indwells the Judge. *Sixth,* the Judge not only points his finger at Sin and Sin-at-work-in-him, but he has become an embodied slave to Sin as a tyrant: "but I see in my members another law at war with the law of my mind, making me captive to the law of sin that dwells in my members" (7:23). He calls this the "body of death," an expression that he shares with all those who are outside of Christ (7:24). It is nothing short of shocking for Paul to tie Torah so closely to the ultimate tyrant, Death. The line of Adam is here reworked, and now Death is at work in all those who seek Christoformity through Torah observance. *Seventh,* this embodied slavery to Sin is life in the Flesh: "So then, with my mind I am a slave to the law of God, but with my flesh I am a slave to the law of sin" (7:25). The terms are now a tight knot: Adam, sin, Sin, Flesh, and Death. The Torah is part of the Death machine, but not by itself: the Torah only becomes an instrument of Death because of Sin and Flesh.

Therefore, the Torah's purpose never was and never will be to move sinners to holiness or to love or to mutual welcome among the Strong and the Weak. The purpose of the Torah—God's intended purpose according to Paul's lights—was to reveal the divine will to Israel. Contrary to the Judge's educational designs for the Strong, once the Torah was revealed, individual Israelites sinned, and sin multiplied becomes systemic Sin in both the individual and Israel, and from this point on the purpose of the Torah is to reveal both God's will and Israel's sinfulness. Paul gives no break here for the Torah being a revelation of God's will once Christ has come or once the Torah's purpose has been served. His solution for knowing God's will as something to be lived and that can be lived is not practicing Torah but living in the Spirit. (But he will curl around this one in our next section.)

Reading Romans 7 as aimed at the Judge—that is, at the one who thinks Christoformity can flow from Torah observance and sitting in judgment on the Strong for not observing Torah—leads to brief reminders of Romans 9–11: Israel has the privilege (9:4-5), the Messiah reveals that Israel's quest for righteousness through Torah observance is unenlightened (10:1-3), and Christ has radically altered Israel's story (10:4). The people of God, Israel, is redefined now to include gentile believers so that, in Rome, the Weak and the Strong are siblings. But God is not done with Israel at all: Israel's days of redemption are on the horizon.

RESOLUTION

Christoformity—speaking of the comprehensive vision—cannot be achieved by observing the Torah. The Torah is good, and it is Spiritual; the mind of the Judge knows the good and the holy and what is of the Spirit. The Flesh is at work against the Spirit's work in the Judge. The solution is to be found not in Torah but in a renewed mind, slavery to God, and surrender to the Spirit. Resolution for the Way of Christ and Christoformity is "through Jesus Christ our Lord" and through a Spirit-generated renewed mind (7:25; the same at 12:2).

Only paragraph divisions permit us to ignore what Paul says next. What Paul writes next is crucial for comprehending the rhetorical intent of the I section. In spite of the Torah's revelation-of-sin-as-Sin purpose, "in Christ Jesus" there is "now no condemnation" (8:1). But Paul curls around all he has said in Romans 7. He does not say that we are not condemned because we are justified in Christ. No, he answers, "For the law of the Spirit of life in Christ Jesus has set you free from the law of sin and of death" (8:2). Which means the Weak, the Judge, and also the Strong are liberated from being under Torah to be under grace in Christ—which does not mean they can live like hell and not worry about it. No, Paul's vision is that Christ has done for us what we cannot do for ourselves—he has died our death and *noticeably* put to death the Flesh (8:3). The purpose of the Torah was to turn Israelites into Fleshy Israel, but the purpose of Christ is to destroy sin, Sin, Flesh, and Death. Now, the comprehensiveness of Paul's chapters becomes clear: "so that the just requirement of the Torah might be fulfilled in us, who walk not according to the flesh but according to the Spirit" (8:4). That is to say, grace to us in Christ through the Spirit effects a gracious transformation into Torah-observance-and-beyond. What does this mean? Righteousness, obedience, sanctification, love, unity, peace, and reconciliation in welcoming one another to the table as siblings. Lived theology, pure and simple. Peace in the heart of the empire that begins with the Strong and the Weak, and with the Judge dropping his charges.

His comprehensive vision includes transformation of both the individual, embodied person and all of creation. All of creation groans for redemption, understood as liberation from slavery to sins, Sin, Flesh, and Death. Redemption is now clarified: it is "the freedom of the glory of the children of God" (8:21), it is "adoption, the redemption of our bodies" (8:23), and it is the completion of the chain from predestination to glorification (8:30). God's love is certain and assuring: those in Christ may suffer, but through their sufferings they will discover that nothing separates them from God's gracious love that promises glorification (8:31-39).

Only this comprehensive vision explains the I section completely: one is not going to be transformed by the Torah, which is designed to reveal sin as Sin. The transformation the Judge has learned is not the way of Torah but the way of grace through the Spirit.

CONCLUSION

READING ROMANS FORWARDS, IN BRIEF

To read Romans well, we need *to read it backwards*. The intent of Romans is Christoformity in both Jewish and gentile believers, roughly, then, the Weak and the Strong. The problem in Rome is the Judge, who speaks for the Weak against the Strong to contend that Christoformity can be achieved only by full adoption of Torah observance. The Strong counter the Weak by means of their higher social status, their total disregard and ridicule of Torah observance, and their coercion of the Weak to eat whatever is placed on the table. The Weak will not have it, and the Strong are not accommodating. Paul's message is that the Strong need to tolerate the Weak's conscience and that the Weak need to know that Torah observance is not the way to achieve Christoformity.

To read Romans well, *we need to profile both the Weak and the Strong*. The Weak are Jewish believers who are in the stream of God's election and need to be affirmed in their election, but who have questions about the faithfulness of God to that election and who need to embrace the surprising moves of God throughout Israel's history. The Weak know the Torah, practice the Torah, but, in the person of the Judge, sit in judgment on gentiles, especially the Strong in the Christian community in Rome, even though they have no status or privilege or power. Furthermore, the Weak are tempted to resist paying taxes to Rome on the basis of the Jewish zealotry tradition. In addition, the Weak—in the face of the Judge—need to apply "faith in Christ" more radically to themselves, so discovering that they are a new example of the "remnant" of Israel, and they need to see that the sufficiency of faith means that gentile believers in Christ are siblings and that Torah observance is not the way of transformation for either themselves or the Strong in Rome.

The Strong are predominately gentiles who believe in Jesus as Messiah or king, who do not observe Torah as the will of God for them, and who have condescending and despising attitudes probably toward Jews but especially to Jewish believers in Jesus, and all of this is wrapped up in the superior higher status of the Strong in Rome. Paul and Jewish believers who embrace the

nonnecessity of Torah observance are, at least at times, among the Strong in
their theological convictions about Torah observance as the way of Christoformity. But the Strong are taking advantage of their superior social status
to denigrate the Torah and holiness as the quest of the Christians in Rome,
and so they are coercing the Weak into table fellowship over nonkosher food.
The Strong, then, are as known for their position on observance of Torah and
for their status as they are for ethnicity.

To read Romans well, *all of Romans* must be read in light of the context
in Romans 14–15. Once one lets that context shape one's reading of Romans,
some of the interpretive problems are resolved, and new nuances are achieved
in that reading. I think especially of reading Romans 1–4. Those chapters—so
often taken to be simply a soteriological scheme of proving that all are in sin so
all are in need of the Savior, which in some senses is true for these passages—
are not best read that way. Once one reads Romans backwards, one finds that
the entire passage is aimed at the Judge, a Christian and not a Jew in general,
who sits in judgment of the Strong for their lack of Torah observance.

To read Romans well, *the solution to lived theology is to be found in Romans
5–8* as the theological underpinnings for the lived theology of Romans 14–15.
The relationship of Romans 5–8 to Romans 12–16 is not theology and practice
but lived theology and theology for that lived theology. Romans 1–8 is not
abstract theology that can be plopped down as the preface to any of Paul's
letters but a theology designed because of the lived theology of Romans 12–16.

To read Romans well, *a sharp profile of the lived theology of Romans 12–16
needs to be presented*. The themes of those chapters can be summarized in the
term "Christoformity," and the heart of the vision is for the Strong and the
Weak to drop their defenses and privileges and powers, to surrender them
to Christ of the cross, and to learn to welcome one another so they can live
in peace in the heart of the empire.

To read Romans well, we *read it as pastoral, ecclesial theology for a specific
church in a specific time*. To be sure, Romans fares well in other contexts, but,
until we profile those contexts and the message of Romans for those contexts,
we don't know what to make of it for other contexts. Romans, like no other
book in the entire Bible except for perhaps Philemon, is more relevant for the
churches of the United States than any book in the Bible. The message is a
lived theology of Christoformity manifested in peace among siblings—all
siblings, not just siblings like me. The message shouts to the American church
that its classism, its racism, its sexism, and its materialism are like the Strong's
social-status claims and the Weak's boundaried behaviors. They divide and
conquer. The message of Romans is that the Weak and the Strong of our

day—and I say now what I have not said, that everyone thinks that they are the Strong and that the other is the Weak—must surrender their claims to privilege and hand them over to Christoformity.

The way of Romans, however, is a challenge that seemingly most in America would rather ignore, choosing instead to fight about abstract theology.

Ken
Gary
Shengyl
Rolf

NOTES

PREFACE

1   Unless I am quoting someone, all references to scholarship are by name or by name and title; the sources are found in the bibliography.

INTRODUCTION: LIVED THEOLOGY

1   Frederick L. Downing, *Clarence Jordan: A Radical Pilgrimage in Scorn of the Consequences* (Macon, Ga.: Mercer University Press, 2017), 156–57.

§ 1
PHOEBE—THE FACE OF ROMANS

1   I am aware that some think Phoebe carried the letter but did not in fact read it aloud. Such persons think she coached someone else to read it. We don't know this for certain, but I prefer the Phoebe-reading hypothesis and will use it throughout under this proviso.

2   All translations are from the NRSV unless otherwise noted.

3   Paul Trebilco, *Self-Designations and Group Identity in the New Testament* (Cambridge: Cambridge University Press, 2012), 16–67.

4   From Abraham J. Malherbe, ed., *Ancient Epistolary Theorists* (Atlanta: Society of Biblical Literature, 1988), 33.

5   Notice Acts 15:31 and Col 4:16.

§ 2
THE GREETINGS AND THE HOUSE CHURCHES OF ROME

1   Seneca, *Ad Helviam* 6.2–3; from David Noy, *Foreigners at Rome: Citizens and Strangers* (London: Classical Press of Wales, 2000), 90.

2   Peter Lampe, *From Paul to Valentinus: Christians at Rome in the First Two Centuries*, ed. Marshall D. Johnson, trans. Michael Steinhauser (Minneapolis: Fortress, 2003).

3   Nero's character is captured by Subrius Flavus, well known in the Praetorian Guard, in these unflinchingly damning words when questioned by Nero

about his betrayal to join the conspiracy of AD 65: "Because I detested you! I was as loyal as any of your soldiers as long as you deserved affection. I began detesting you when you murdered your mother and wife and became a charioteer, actor and incendiary" (Tacitus, *Annals* 15.67, trans. M. Grant, Penguin Classics). The conspirators aimed to do the deed in the Circus Maximus, where (one reasonably suspects) Nero began the burning of Rome. Three years later, Nero, with the help of his scribe, committed suicide.

4   He "won" every contest he entered, totaling more than 1,800 first-place awards.

5   See Suetonius, *Nero* 31. This building project followed the fire that destroyed much of Rome. The scapegoating of Christians, reported by Tacitus, is at least open to question. See Anthony A. Barrett, Elaine Fantham, and John C. Yardley, eds., *The Emperor Nero: A Guide to the Ancient Sources* (Princeton: Princeton University Press, 2016), 161–66.

6   There was much discussion about how many floors were appropriate—some reaching as many as six to nine.

7   Tacitus, *Annals* 11.26–38.

8   Suetonius, *Claudius* 25.4.

9   This is confirmed, if not with certainty, by Claudius' roughly contemporary concern with another Christian concern, the problem of "tomb spoilation" in Galilee, upon whose violators he pronounced capital sentence. See A. C. Johnson, P. R. Coleman-Norton, and F. C. Bourne, *Ancient Roman Statutes* (Clarke, N.J.: Lawbook Exchange, 2003), 113 (#133).

10   Peter Oakes, *Reading Romans in Pompeii: Paul's Letter at Ground Level* (Minneapolis: Fortress, 2009), 96, cf. 87.

11   The greeting in 16:21-23 is third person and first person; these greetings are from believers in Corinth.

12   See Suetonius, *Claudius* 28; Dio Cassius, *History of Rome* 64.3.

13   Acts 18:2, 18, 26; 1 Cor 16:19; 1 Tim 4:19.

14   See Rom 16:3, 5, 7, 8, 9, 10, 11, 12, 13, 16.

§ 3

STRONG AND WEAK

1   Paul S. Minear, *The Obedience of Faith: The Purposes of Paul in the Epistle to the Romans*, Studies in Biblical Theology 2/19 (London: SCM Press, 1971).

2   The Greek word behind "Torah" is *nomos*, and it occurs more than seventy times in Romans.

3   Confirmed by Acts 21:17-24.

4   E. P. Sanders, *Paul and Palestinian Judaism: A Comparison of Patterns of Religion* (Philadelphia: Fortress, 1977).

5   Matthew Thiessen, *Paul and the Gentile Problem* (New York: Oxford University Press, 2016).

6   Esp. 1 Cor 8:1-13 and 10:14–11:1.

7   Macrobius, *Saturnalia* 2.4.11; Philo, *Legatio* 156, 361; Juvenal, *Satires* 14.96–99; Horace, *Sermones* 1.9.60–78.

8   Notice the shift to a gentile believer audience at Rom 11:11-36.

9   See Dan 1:8-21; Josephus, *Life* 14.

10 Philip Francis Esler, *Conflict and Identity in Romans* (Minneapolis: Fortress, 2003).

11 Josephus, *Antiquities* 19.290.

12 Tacitus, *Annals* 11.13.1.

§ 4
ZEALOTRY

1   Simeon and Levi (Gen 34; cf. Judith 9:2-4; Jub. 30:4-5, 8, 13-14, 17), Elijah (1 Kgs 18:40; 19:1, 10, 14; Sir 48:2-3; 1 Macc 2:58), Mattathias (1 Macc 2:23-27, 51-60), and one finds zeal at Qumran as well (1QH 6/14:14; 10/2:15). James D. G. Dunn, *The Theology of Paul the Apostle* (Grand Rapids: Eerdmans, 1998), 350–53.

2   I found this expression, here adjusted for reading Romans backwards, in Charles Marsh, Peter Slade, and Sarah Azaransky, eds., *Lived Theology: New Perspectives on Method, Style, and Pedagogy* (New York: Oxford University Press, 2016).

§ 5
CHRISTOFORMITY—PAUL'S VISION FOR A
LIVED THEOLOGY OF PEACE

1   Ben W. Witherington III, *The Indelible Image: The Theological and Ethical World of the New Testament*, vol. 1: *The Individual Witnesses* (Downers Grove, Ill.: IVP Academic, 2009); idem, *The Indelible Image: The Theological and Ethical Thought World of the New Testament*, vol. 2: *The Collective Witness* (Downers Grove, Ill.: IVP Academic, 2010).

2   Michael J. Gorman, *Becoming the Gospel: Paul, Participation, and Mission* (Grand Rapids: Eerdmans, 2015).

3   Andrew Root, *Christopraxis: A Practical Theology of the Cross* (Minneapolis: Fortress, 2014). Three terms can be used for what I mean by Christoformity: "cruciformity," which focuses on the cross; "Christopraxis," which focuses on one's behavior; or "Christoformity," which I intend to be broader than each and encompasses each.

§ 6

CHRISTOFORMITY IS EMBODIED GOD ORIENTATION

1   On mercy, notice Rom 9:15-16, 18, 23; 11:30-32; 15:9.

2   Paul does not use *kosmos* but uses *aion*, which refers to an age or epoch.

3   Episcopal Church, *The Book of Common Prayer* (New York: Oxford University Press, 1990), 211, 819.

4   Scholars are split over whether this doxology was original to Paul. Even the United Bible Society's textual judgment is a "C"—that is, the verses are not certain. The doxology of these verses is found in some manuscripts after 14:23; in others, after 15:33; in yet others, in our location; while some have it after 14:23 and here or after 14:23 and 15:33! A few manuscripts don't have it at all. There are then reasons to be suspicious of a later addition. Still, very important manuscripts have it at the end of the letter, and everything in this doxology is characteristic of the entire letter.

5   Larry W. Hurtado, *Lord Jesus Christ: Devotion to Jesus in Earliest Christianity* (Grand Rapids: Eerdmans, 2003); Richard Bauckham, *Jesus and the God of Israel: "God Crucified" and Other Studies on the New Testament's Christology of Divine Identity* (Grand Rapids: Eerdmans, 2008).

§ 7

CHRISTOFORMITY IS EMBODIED BODY-OF-CHRIST ORIENTATION

1   The term "church" (*ekklesia*) occurs in Romans only at 16:1, 4, 5, 16, 23.

2   One can tease out the theological substance of Rom 1–11 in chapters 12–16 by inference from the lived theology.

3   Robert Jewett, *Romans: A Commentary*, Hermeneia (Minneapolis: Fortress, 2007), 736.

4   More woodenly, "God has measured to each a measure of faith." In this case, the "measure" is the "gift" given to each.

5   The Latin translation is *secundum rationem fidei*, and later it becomes the *regula fidei*. I'm inclined to think Paul here wants the prophets to be constrained by the apostolic gospel teaching.

6   Gorman, *Becoming the Gospel*.

7   Notice the Peutinger map at http://peutinger.atlantides.org/map-a/.

8   David J. Downs, *The Offering of the Gentiles: Paul's Collection for Jerusalem in Its Chronological, Cultural, and Cultic Contexts* (Grand Rapids: Eerdmans, 2016).

9   Who were his partners in the collection? A maximal listing includes the Galatian region (1 Cor 16:1), Derbe (Acts 20:4), Lystra (Acts 20:4), Macedonia (2 Cor 8:1-5; 9:2,4), Berea (Acts 20:4), Thessalonica (20:4), and Philippi (cf. Acts 16:16 and 20:6). We can also add Corinth (Rom 15:26; 1 Cor 16:1-4), perhaps Mysia and Ephesus (Acts 20:4), and Troas (Acts 20:5-6). One can also wonder if Paul drew support from Tyre (Acts 21:34), Ptolemais (Acts

21:7), Cyprus and Caesarea (Acts 21:16), and even Rome (cf. Rom 12:13; 15:26 with 2 Cor 8:4; 9:13; and Rom 1:13 with 2 Cor 9:6-10).

10 The following texts are worthy of consideration as evidence for Paul's concern for the poor: Gal 2:10; 6:9-10; 1 Thess 5:14-15; 2 Thess 3:6-12; Rom 12:13, 16; 1 Tim 5:3-16; 6:18; Titus 3:14; Acts 20:35; so Bruce W. Longenecker, *Remember the Poor: Paul, Poverty, and the Greco-Roman World* (Grand Rapids: Eerdmans, 2010).

11 Scot McKnight, *Kingdom Conspiracy: Returning to the Radical Mission of the Local Church* (Grand Rapids: Brazos, 2014).

12 See Rom 6:2, 18, 22; 7:3; 8:2, 21.

13 One might well need to begin reading slowly at 15:8 to see how important "Christ" is in these verses. Other views are just as possible: e.g., Paul moves from Israelites (or the suffering Messiah himself) confessing YHWH among the gentiles (Ps 18) to an exhortation for gentiles to join in on the chorus of joy (Deut 32 and Ps 117) to the final prediction that gentiles will hope in the Messiah (Isaiah). J. Ross Wagner, *Heralds of the Good News: Isaiah and Paul in Concert in the Letter to the Romans*, NovTSup 101 (Leiden: Brill, 2000).

§ 8
Christoformity Is Public Orientation

1 Tacitus, *Annals* 13.50–51.

2 Suetonius, *Nero* 10.1.

3 Rom 12:9-13 reads as if it were a list of imperatives, but there is not one imperative in the whole list. Rather, Paul uses participles, infinitives, and what can be read as implied imperatives.

4 See Acts 14:8-20; 17:16-33; 19:11-41; 23:1-5. N. T. Wright, *Paul and the Faithfulness of God*, Christian Origins and the Question of God 4 (Minneapolis: Fortress, 2013), 2:1271–1319.

5 Any number of references could be mentioned: e.g., Gen 1–11; 1–2 Sam; Daniel; Sir 10:4; Wis 6:3; 1–2 Maccabees; 1QM; 1 Enoch; Josephus, *Antiquities*.

6 Paul uses two terms: *phoros* (roughly, a tribute tax to the emperor and Rome by noncitizens) and *telos* (common taxes like customs on imports or sales taxes).

§ 9
Know the Time Is Now

1 Tacitus, *Annals* 13.24–25.

§ 10
Where We've Been, Where We Are, Where We're Headed

1 I am unpersuaded that inclusion in Pauline churches wiped out previous identity factors: Jews remained Jews, women remained women, and slaves remained slaves. Being "in Christ" reconfigured that identity, but it did not erase it.

2   A. Chadwick Thornhill, *The Chosen People: Election, Paul and Second Temple Judaism* (Downers Grove, Ill.: IVP Academic, 2015).

3   While Gal 3:19–4:7 is similar to Rom 9–11 (though in Romans there is less focus on Moses and the place of the Torah in God's plan), different questions, names, and events then are at work in Romans. With that said, it is important to take Galatians into mind as one reads Rom 9–11.

4   See Acts 5:17; 13:45; 17:5; 21:20; 22:3; Gal 1:14; 4:17-18; 5:20; Phil 3:6.

5   I rely here on the italicized words in Nestle-Aland, 28th edition.

6   More specifically now, *Romans 9*: Gen 21:12 (Rom 9:7); Gen 18:10, 14 (9:9); Gen 25:23 (9:12); Mal 1:2-3 (9:13); Exod 33:19 (9:15); Exod 9:16 (9:17); Isa 29:16 (9:20); Hosea 2:25 LXX; 2:1 LXX (9:25-26); Isa 10:22-23 (9:27); Isa 28:22 (Dan 5:28?) (9:28); Isa 1:9 (9:29); and Isa 28:16; 8:14 (9:33). *Romans 10*: Lev 18:5 (Rom 10:5); Deut 30:12 (10:6); Deut 30:14 (10:8); Isa 28:16 (10:11); Joel 3:5 (10:13); Isa 52:7; Nah 2:1 (10:15); Isa 53:1 (10:16); Ps 18:5 (10:18); Deut 32:21 (10:19); and Isa 65:1-2 (10:20-21). *Romans 11*: 1 Sam 12:22; Ps 94:14 (Rom 11:2); 1 Kgs 19:10, 14 (11:3); 1 Kgs 19:18 (11:4); Deut 29:3; Isa 29:10 (11:8); Ps 68:23-24 (11:9-10); Isa 59:20-21; 27:9 (11:26-27); Isa 40:13 (11:34); and Job 41:3 (11:35).

§ 11
To the Weak

1   James D. G. Dunn, *Romans*, WBC 38 (Grand Rapids: Zondervan, 2015): 2:519.

2   A hermeneutical wedge must be used in reading Romans: I believe these Bible-soaked auditors are Jewish, not gentile, believers in Jesus as Messiah. For vigorous discussions, see Joshua D. Garroway, *Paul's Gentile-Jews: Neither Jew nor Gentile, but Both* (New York: Palgrave MacMillan, 2012); Rafael Rodriguez, *If You Call Yourself a Jew: Reappraising Paul's Letter to the Romans* (Eugene, Ore.: Cascade, 2014); Rafael Rodriguez and Matthew Thiessen, eds., *The So-Called Jew in Paul's Letter to the Romans* (Minneapolis: Fortress, 2016); Gabriele Boccaccini and Carlos A. Segovia, eds., *Paul the Jew: Rereading the Apostle as a Figure of Second Temple Judaism* (Minneapolis: Fortress, 2016).

3   John M. G. Barclay, *Paul and the Gift* (Grand Rapids: Eerdmans, 2015), 541.

4   Matthew Bates, *The Hermeneutics of the Apostolic Proclamation: The Center of Paul's Method of Scriptural Interpretation* (Waco: Baylor University Press, 2012), 233, with explanation at pp. 233–40.

5   These terms come from Barclay, *Paul and the Gift*, 185–86.

§ 12
To the Strong

1   Ps 106:31 then says of Phinehas' zeal that it "has been reckoned to him as righteousness."

2   It seems more than likely that this reflects Paul's experience with synagogue rejection and may well indicate alienation from synagogues where his mission churches have been formed.

3   Rom 9:6, 27, 31; 10:19, 21; 11:2, 25-26. Also at 1 Cor 10:18; 2 Cor 3:7, 13; Gal 6:16; Eph 2:12; Phil 3:5.

4   Echoing, too, Isa 27:9; Jer 31:33, 34.

§ 13
The Opening to the Letter

1   Rom 8:11 also connects the Holy Spirit to Jesus' resurrection.

2   Matthew W. Bates, *The Hermeneutics of the Apostolic Proclamation: The Center of Paul's Method of Scriptural Interpretation* (Waco, Tex.: Baylor University Press, 2012), 59–108.

3   What can't be explored here is the extensive connections of gospel to Isa 40–55.

4   See also 1 Cor 1:4-9; Phlm 4–7; and Col 1:3-12.

5   This is best explained as due to the expulsion of Jewish Christians from Rome in AD 49.

6   In Rom 5–8, Paul focuses on sin, Sin, Flesh, World, and Death. See our discussion there.

7   See also similar inclusive statements in 2:9-10; 3:22-24; 4:16; 5:18; 8:32; 10:4, 11–13; 11:32; 15:10-11.

8   The term "righteousness" or "justification" will be discussed in more depth on pp. 121–22.

9   Also cited at Gal 3:11; Heb 10:38.

10   The Hebrew text reads, "the righteous live by their [that is, "his"] faith"; the LXX reads, "the righteous will live by my faith/faithfulness"; and Paul splits the difference with "the one who is righteous will live by faith"!

11   As one sees in Gal 3:1-14.

§ 14
The Rhetoric of Romans 1–2

1   For example, T. Naph. 3:2-4 connects gentiles, creation orders, idolatry, and same-sex relations. See William Loader, *The New Testament on Sexuality* (Grand Rapids: Eerdmans, 2012); idem, *Making Sense of Sex: Attitudes towards Sexuality in Early Jewish and Christian Literature* (Grand Rapids: Eerdmans, 2013).

2   Notice, too, Rom 9:24-26, 30; 10:19-20.

3   Some think Jews are also in view and that Paul is scanning universal depravity in 1:18-32. Jewish sinners are sometimes found lurking behind "wickedness" (1:18; cf. 2:8-9; 3:5) or the golden calf incident in 1:23 (cf. Ps 106:20). Paul's argument in 1:19-23, however, fits a gentile condition since he appeals to natural revelation rather than to divine revelation in covenant and Torah and since the specific sins he dwells on are connected to idols and idolatry;

and the context of Wisdom of Solomon virtually clinches this as a description of gentile sinfulness. That Paul uses language for sin in typical Jewish categories may just as easily be explained as rhetorically appropriate: Jews typically use Jewish terms to describe gentile sins.

4   See also Sib. Or. 3:573-625 for a similar critical examination of gentiles' sins and the holiness of those who follow the Torah.

5   There are echoes of Wis 15:1 and 11:23 in Rom 2:4. This makes the case for a Jewish audience in Rom 2:1-16 stronger.

6   Diatribe is a style or mode of discourse involving hypothetical or representative opponents asking questions or making accusations that are responded to in turn. The opponents need not be fictional or purely imaginary. The opponents of Rom 2–3 are a representative realistic part of the Roman church.

7   The NRSV has "whoever you are" in 2:1, 3, while the Greek is ō anthrōpe (or "O man") and was standard fare in diatribes. There are echoes of Wis 15:1-5 in Rom 2:1-5—in particular, echoes of censoriousness rooted in privilege.

§ 15
READING ROMANS 2 AFTER ROMANS 1

1   Paul's approach to the audience of Rom 2–4 bears striking similarities to his approach to those in Rom 9:1–11:12 in this very noticeable particular: interrogation-type questions. As I listed questions in that section I will list them here:

(1)   You, then, that teach others, will you not teach yourself?

(2)   While you preach against stealing, do you steal?

(3)   You that forbid adultery, do you commit adultery? (2:22)

(4)   You that abhor idols, do you rob temples?

(5)   You that boast in the law, do you dishonor God by breaking the law? (2:23).

(6)   So, if those who are uncircumcised keep the requirements of the law, will not their uncircumcision be regarded as circumcision? (2:26)

(7)   Then what advantage has the Jew? Or what is the value of circumcision? (3:1)

(8)   What if some were unfaithful?

(9)   Will their faithlessness nullify the faithfulness of God? (3:3)

(10) But if our injustice serves to confirm the justice of God, what should we say?

(11) That God is unjust to inflict wrath on us? (3:5)

(12) For then how could God judge the world? (3:6)

(13) But if through my falsehood God's truthfulness abounds to his glory, why am I still being condemned as a sinner? (3:7)

(14) And why not say (as some people slander us by saying that we say), "Let us do evil so that good may come"? (3:8)

(15) What then? (3:9)

(16) Are we any better off? (3:9)

(17) Then what becomes of boasting?

(18) By what law?

(19) By that of works? (3:27)

(20) Or is God the God of Jews only?

(21) Is he not the God of Gentiles also? (3:29)

(22) Do we then overthrow the law by this faith? (3:31)

(23) What then are we to say was gained by Abraham, our ancestor according to the flesh? (4:1)

(24) For what does the scripture say? (4:3)

(25) Is this blessedness, then, pronounced only on the circumcised, or also on the uncircumcised? (4:9)

(26) How then was it reckoned to him?

(27) Was it before or after he had been circumcised? (4:10)

Both Paul and Phoebe are exhausted and the Jewish believing auditors are no doubt on their heels. It is a short step from Rom 9–11 to Rom 2–4 to see the same audience, and it is a step I take.

2　Rom 2:9 and 2:10 say, "the Jew first and also the Greek." Emphasis should be thrown on the word "first." Why? The Judge sits in judgment on the gentiles/Greeks and, in so doing, presumes he's safe, but Paul's shocking turnabout emerges in that word "first." Thus, this is not so much an emphasis on *all humans, both Jews and gentiles*, as it is a rhetorical maneuver to focus on the Judge himself.

3　The whole of Rom 2:17-20 is a long beginning to an incomplete sentence. Thus, "If you call yourself a Jew" is never completed with a "then" clause; 2:21 simply starts afresh and functions as the completion of vv. 17-20 but does so with questions (vv. 21-23, with v. 24 closing it all off).

4　Similar to what is found in Wis 15:1-6; 16:9-12.

5　The first reference to "law/Torah/*nomos*" in Romans is found in 2:12. I am persuaded that the term *nomos* never appears without evoking the tension between the Strong and the Weak.

6　Judaism's use of the language of debt and payment along with reward was a development in how sin was reframed from burden to debt, as Gary A. Anderson has clearly shown. Such a development was not a reflection of merit-seeking soteriology. Anderson, *Sin: A History* (New Haven: Yale University Press, 2009).

7　Ps 62:12; Prov 24:12; Jer 17:10; Matt 7:21-27; 16:27; 25:31-46; 2 Cor 5:10; 1 Pet 1:17.

8   Jas 1:22-25, 26-27; 2:8-13, 14-17, 18-26.
9   Lev 26:40-42; Deut 10:16; 30:6; Ezek 36:26-27.
10 Cf. Josh 2; 6 (Rahab); Luke 10:25-37; 11:32; John 4.

§ 16
THE FIRST QUESTION—ADVANTAGE

1   Paul says, "For in the first place," but never has a "second" place. This might
    suggest that "first" could mean "let's begin with this." The second, third, and
    more were also already seen in our backwards reading at Rom 9:4-5.
2   "They are Israelites, and to them belong the adoption, the glory, the cove-
    nants, the giving of the law, the worship, and the promises; to them belong
    the patriarchs, and from them, according to the flesh, comes the Messiah."
    Rom 3:1-8 has substantive parallels in 9:1-5, 6, 14, and 19.
3   This is the first instance, in a forwards reading of Romans, of the term "faith/
    faithful/believe/trust" (*pisteuo, pistis*), though here in its negated unbeliev-
    ing (meaning "*un*faithful") form (*apisteuo, apistis*). The Greek is often best
    translated with "allegiance to king Jesus as Lord."
4   Some think the "I" of 3:7-8 is like the "I" of 7:7-25, but "as some people
    slander us" in 3:8 makes the "I" of 3:7-8 a personal argument.
5   Paul quotes, seemingly randomly, OT texts, but some see resonances with
    themes at work in Romans elsewhere: Rom 3:10-12 mixes Pss 14:1-3 and
    53:1-3 with Eccl 7:20; Rom 3:13 cites Pss 5:9 and 140:3; Rom 3:14 cites Ps
    10:7; Rom 3:15-17 cites Isa 59:7-8; and Rom 3:18 cites Ps 36:1. There are
    reasons to think this listing of passages—notice the careful coverage of
    various body parts to show the fullness of sinfulness as well as the repeated
    expression "there is no one/no," mostly drawn (atypically for Paul) from
    the Psalms—could have been passed on to Paul (cf. CD 5:13-17), but he is
    fully capable of stringing passages like this together (cf. Rom 9:12-29 and
    15:9-12). Whoever put this connection of passages together did so with care.
6   Ps 14:1-3, which is repeated in 53:1-3; Eccl 7:20.
7   Pss 5:9; 140:3; 10:7; 36:1; Isa 59:7-8.
8   See Rom 5:12-21.
9   Notice the important parallel at 4QMMT [= 4Q394–399], which at
    4Q396.26–27 reads, "And also we have written to you some of the *works
    of the Torah* which we think are good for you and for your people," which
    concludes with language smacking of justification: "And it shall be reck-
    oned to you as justice when you do what is upright and good before him"
    (4Q396.32). Translation by García Martínez (Florentino García Martínez
    and Eibert J. C. Tigchelaar, eds., *The Dead Sea Scrolls Study Edition*, vol. 2
    [Leiden: Brill; Grand Rapids: Eerdmans, 1998], 803) of manuscript C.
10 I have watched this conversation since the days E. P. Sanders wrote his
    famous book (*Paul and Palestinian Judaism: A Comparison of Patterns of*

Religion [Philadelphia: Fortress, 1977]), including a seminar at the University of Nottingham when James D. G. Dunn invited Sanders to give a lecture. Many critics of Sanders and the new perspective on Paul have sought to show that Judaism had pockets of legalism or salvation by works, and, when that can be shown, then Paul's opponent becomes Judaism more generally. The irony is that when these scholars come to the same kinds of expressions about works in Jesus, Paul (Rom 2!), Hebrews, James, or John, their terms are explained as manifestations of grace. I quit counting when I got into the hundreds of examples of Christian scholars reframing works.

11   Many today connect the expression "no human being will be justified in his sight" to Ps 143:2, and it needs to be recalled that this expression is from an Israelite about himself. See too Gal 2:15-21.

12   See also Rom 1:17; 3:5; 10:3 and 2 Cor 5:21; Phil 3:9 and Matt 6:33; Jas 1:20; 2 Pet 1:1.

13   The Greek is *dia pisteos Iesou Christou*, and this can be translated as "humans trusting in Jesus Christ" (objective genitive) or as "the faithfulness of Jesus Christ himself" (subjective genitive). As with the CEB and the footnotes in the NRSV and TNIV, I prefer the second translation, with human trust clear at the end of 3:22 ("for all who believe"). For similar uses, cf. Gal 2:16; 3:22; Rom 3:22, 26; Phil 3:9; Eph 3:12. The Hebrew background (*emunah* as "faith and faithfulness," as "allegiance"; cf. Isa 11:5), the redundancy of 3:22 itself (why say, "faith in Jesus Christ to all who believe"?), and other instances of *pistis* meaning "faithfulness" (e.g., 3:3) convince me that "faithfulness of Jesus Christ himself" is the better understanding.

14   CEB: "the place of sacrifice where mercy is found" is a good translation.

15   Perhaps this refers to gentile sins, as some have suggested.

16   Or in the memorable words of Ps 50:21, "These [sins of injustice] you have done and I was silent" (trans. Robert Alter, *The Book of Psalms: A Translation with Commentary* [New York: W. W. Norton, 2007]).

§ 17
THE SECOND QUESTION—BOASTING IN ADVANTAGE

1   Another example of boasting can be found in Cicero, *Letters to Friends* 22.

2   Translation by Alison E. Cooley, *Res Gestae Divi Augusti: Text, Translation, and Commentary* (Cambridge: Cambridge University Press, 2009), 63.

3   Translation by George A. Kennedy, ed., *Progymnasmata: Greek Textbooks of Prose Composition and Rhetoric*, Writings from the Greco-Roman World (Atlanta: SBL, 2003), 82.

4   Notice, too, 2 Cor 10:14-15; 11:12-13, 21-23.

5   Also, 1 Cor 9:21.

6   Paul is here quoting the Shema of Deut 6:4.

7   Cf. Matt 5:17-20 and Gal 3:15-18.

§ 18

THE THIRD QUESTION—ABRAHAM, FAITH, AND ADVANTAGE

1   This is a separate question, as at 3:5; 6:1; 7:7; 8:31; 9:14, 30.

2   The parallel to Jas 2:18-24 is noticeable: both authors need to anchor their
     theory of righteousness in Abraham.

3   On which see N. T. Wright, *Pauline Perspectives: Essays on Paul, 1978–2013*
     (Minneapolis: Fortress, 2013), 554–92.

4   Though repentance (2 Cor 7:9; Rom 2:4) and forgiveness of sins (Col 1:14;
     Eph 1:7) are very common to Judaism, to Jesus, and to other NT authors,
     Paul's letters emphasize neither. Luke attributes such terms to Paul in Acts
     (13:24, 38; 17:30; 26:18, 20).

5   2 Cor 1:22; Eph 1:13; 4:30; also Col 2:11-12.

6   "For the promise that he would inherit the world did not come to Abraham
     or to his descendants through the law but through the righteousness of faith"
     (Rom 4:13).

7   There are noticeable parallels between the Jewish perception of gentile sins
     in 1:18-32 and Abraham's faith in 4:18-22: Abraham's faith in the creator
     God, in new life from God, in glorifying God, in knowing God's power,
     and in heterosexual procreation (4:17, 19, 20, 21) are in contrast to gentile
     suppression of God as creator, in dishonoring the body, in not glorifying God,
     in not worshiping God, and in dishonoring the procreative powers of the
     body. See N. T. Wright, "The Letter to the Romans," in *The New Interpreter's
     Bible*, ed. Leander E. Keck, vol. 12 (Nashville: Abingdon, 2002), 500.

8   Many point to the second benediction in the standard Jewish prayer *The
     Eighteen Benedictions* (or *Shemoneh Esreh*) as common enough parallel for
     the wording here to be considered standard Jewish belief.

§ 19

ALL

1   Barclay, *Paul and the Gift*, 501.

2   Rom 5:15-17 present how Adam and Christ are *disproportionate*, while vv.
     18-21 present how Christ's line *is abundantly greater*. Sin and Death are not
     capable of matching Grace and Life. Rom 5:12 jogs off midstream, and not
     until 5:18-21 does Paul get back to the mainstream so that 5:12 is completed.

3   The Greek for "free gift" (NRSV) or "gift" (NIV) is *charisma*, while for
     "grace" it is *charis*.

4   Paul does not seem, then, to make Adam a type of Israel; he is a type of Christ.

5   Gift and grace terms are used ten times in Rom 5:15-21, and that's not count-
     ing terms connected to justification and abundance and life!

6   See pp. 87–88 on Romans 11:26.

7   One might wonder if the same theory of emergence might best explain Adam himself.

8   The following is based on the exceptional study of Matthew Croasmun, *The Emergence of Sin: The Cosmic Tyrant in Romans* (New York: Oxford University Press, 2017).

9   In none of Paul's uses of *eph' ho* does it mean "in whom"; see 2 Cor 5:4; Phil 3:12; 4:10.

10   Miryam T. Brand, *Evil Within and Without: The Source of Sin and Its Nature as Portrayed in Second Temple Literature*, JAJSup 9 (Gottingen: Vandenhoeck & Ruprecht, 2013).

11   I have discussed Adam (and Eve) in the Jewish texts at Dennis R. Venema and Scot McKnight, *Adam and the Genome: Reading Scripture after Genetic Science* (Grand Rapids: Brazos, 2017), 147–69.

12   See, too, Rom 3:25 and 5:9.

13   Scot McKnight, *A Community Called Atonement* (Nashville: Abingdon, 2007).

§ 20
You and We

1   Haley Goranson Jacob, *Conformed to the Image of His Son: Reconsidering Paul's Theology of Glory in Romans* (Downers Grove, Ill.: IVP Academic, 2018).

2   It is unlikely this term evokes the sense of Weak in Rom 14–15.

3   Some helpfully use the term "rectification."

4   At times the standard is not the Torah, and the term "righteous" is used to describe one's relational conformity to another relational standard: Gen 38:26; 1 Sam 24:17.

5   Until English translations find a new way, we will need to explain that behind both "righteousness" and "justification" are the Hebrew *tsedek* and the Greek *dikaios/dikaioo/dikaiosyne*. Hence, "to be righteoused," while unacceptable English, creates the right impression.

6   Michael F. Bird, *The Saving Righteousness of God: Studies on Paul, Justification, and the New Perspective*, Paternoster Biblical Monographs (Bletchley, Milton Keynes, U.K.: Paternoster / Authentic Media, 2007); McKnight, *Community Called Atonement*.

7   Themes present in Barclay, *Paul and the Gift*; Michael J. Gorman, *Cruciformity: Paul's Narrative Spirituality of the Cross* (Grand Rapids: Eerdmans, 2001).

8   Jacob, *Conformed to the Image of His Son*.

§ 21
I

1   Since many would argue that imagined interlocutors in a text are both real and the same, one has to lean in the direction that the "I" of Rom 7 is the Judge of Rom 2.

2   He says something similar in Gal 3:15-25.

3   Rom 5:20-21, though, is not the only text that begged for Paul to say more about how the Torah fits in God's plans: cf. 2:17-29; 3:19-31; 4:15; 5:13-14; and 6:14-15. Those passages, then, need to be read in light of Rom 7—and we dare not ignore other letters of Paul: e.g., Gal 3:19-31 and 2 Cor 3–4.

4   Rom 7:7b stems from Exod 20:17; Deut 5:21. The term here is *epithumia*, sometimes translated "desire" or "lust," but here he's using the common Greek term in the LXX for "covet." It is not clear that the commandment chosen (desire) is anything but a random one-off choice, nor is it clear that it refers to Adam's sin in Eden. After all, according to Rom 5:12-14, Adam's sin is not against the Torah, because it had not yet been given. Seeing Adam here is to create needless tension with 5:12-14. Yet, possible echoes of Gen 3 may be found in Rom 7 (cf., e.g., 7:9 and 7:11 to Gen 3:1-5 and 3:13). Others think there are echoes to the giving of the Torah at Sinai.

BIBLIOGRAPHY

Romans intimidates many pastors, preachers, and students today. The debates are too fierce and the scholars too weighty for all but specialists to explain this letter's intricacies. Hence, many avoid Romans and preach Galatians instead. I have written this book for the intimidated. I attempted the impossible: an entire discussion of Romans with very few footnotes to scholarly discussions. My indebtedness to the following will be known to those who know Romans studies. Hundreds more could be added, which only illustrates why the first sentence above is true.

Alter, Robert. *The Book of Psalms: A Translation with Commentary*. New York: W. W. Norton, 2007.

Anderson, Gary A. *Sin: A History*. New Haven: Yale University Press, 2009.

Barclay, John M. G. *Paul and the Gift*. Grand Rapids: Eerdmans, 2015.

Barrett, Anthony A., Elaine Fantham, and John C. Yardley, eds. *The Emperor Nero: A Guide to the Ancient Sources*. Princeton: Princeton University Press, 2016.

Bates, Matthew W. *The Hermeneutics of the Apostolic Proclamation: The Center of Paul's Method of Scriptural Interpretation*. Waco, Tex.: Baylor University Press, 2012.

———. *Salvation by Allegiance Alone: Rethinking Faith, Works, and the Gospel of Jesus the King*. Grand Rapids: Baker Academic, 2017.

Bauckham, Richard. *Jesus and the God of Israel: "God Crucified" and Other Studies on the New Testament's Christology of Divine Identity*. Grand Rapids: Eerdmans, 2008.

Beard, Mary. *The Fires of Vesuvius: Pompeii Lost and Found*. Cambridge, Mass.: Harvard Belknap Press, 2010.

———. *The Roman Triumph*. Cambridge, Mass.: Harvard Belknap Press, 2007.

———. *SPQR: A History of Ancient Rome*. New York: Liveright, 2015.

Bird, Michael F. *The Saving Righteousness of God: Studies on Paul, Justification, and the New Perspective*. Paternoster Biblical Monographs. Bletchley, Milton Keynes, U.K.: Paternoster / Authentic Media, 2007.

Blackwell, Ben C., John K. Goodrich, and Jason Maston, eds. *Paul and the Apocalyptic Imagination*. Minneapolis: Fortress, 2016.

Boccaccini, Gabriele, and Carlos A. Segovia, eds. *Paul the Jew: Rereading the Apostle as a Figure of Second Temple Judaism*. Minneapolis: Fortress, 2016.

Brand, Miryam T. *Evil Within and Without: The Source of Sin and Its Nature as Portrayed in Second Temple Literature*. Journal of Ancient Judaism Supplements 9. Gottingen: Vandenhoeck & Ruprecht, 2013.

Burke, Trevor J., and Brian S. Rosner, eds. *Paul as Missionary: Identity, Activity, Theology, and Practice*. LNTS 420. London: T&T Clark, 2011.

Campbell, Brian. *The Romans and Their World: A Short Introduction*. New Haven: Yale University Press, 2012.

Campbell, Douglas A. *The Deliverance of God: An Apocalyptic Rereading of Justification in Paul*. Grand Rapids: Eerdmans, 2013.

———. *The Quest for Paul's Gospel*. London: T&T Clark, 2005.

Clarke, Andrew D. "Equality or Mutuality? Paul's Use of 'Brother' Language." In *The New Testament in Its First Century Setting: Essays in Honour of B. W. Winter on His 65th Birthday*, edited by P. J. Williams, Andrew D. Clarke, Peter M. Head, and David Instone-Brewer, 151–64. Grand Rapids: Eerdmans, 2004.

———. *A Pauline Theology of Church Leadership*. London: Bloomsbury T&T Clark, 2008.

———. *Secular and Christian Leadership in Corinth: A Socio-historical and Exegetical Study of 1 Corinthians 1–6*. Paternoster Biblical Monographs. Milton Keyes, U.K.: Paternoster, 2006.

———. *Serve the Community of the Church: Christians as Leaders and Ministers*. First Century Christians in the Graeco-Roman World. Grand Rapids: Eerdmans, 2000.

Cooley, Alison E. *Res Gestae Divi Augusti: Text, Translation, and Commentary*. Cambridge: Cambridge University Press, 2009.

Croasmun, Matthew. *The Emergence of Sin: The Cosmic Tyrant in Romans*. New York: Oxford University Press, 2017.

Donfried, Karl P., ed. *The Romans Debate*. 2nd ed. Grand Rapids: Baker Academic, 1991.

Downing, Frederick L. *Clarence Jordan: A Radical Pilgrimage in Scorn of the Consequences*. Macon, Ga.: Mercer University Press, 2017.

Downs, David J. *The Offering of the Gentiles: Paul's Collection for Jerusalem in Its Chronological, Cultural, and Cultic Contexts.* Grand Rapids: Eerdmans, 2016.

Dunn, James D. G. *Beginning from Jerusalem.* Christianity in the Making 2. Grand Rapids: Eerdmans, 2009.

————. *Jesus, Paul and the Law: Studies in Mark and Galatians.* Louisville: Westminster John Knox, 1990.

————. *The New Perspective on Paul.* Rev. ed. Grand Rapids: Eerdmans, 2008.

————. *Romans.* 2 vols. WBC 38. Waco, Tex.: Thomas Nelson, 1988.

————. *The Theology of Paul the Apostle.* Grand Rapids: Eerdmans, 1998.

Eastman, Susan Grove. *Paul and the Person: Reframing Paul's Anthropology.* Grand Rapids: Eerdmans, 2017.

Episcopal Church. *The Book of Common Prayer.* New York: Oxford University Press, 1990.

Esler, Philip Francis. *Conflict and Identity in Romans.* Minneapolis: Fortress, 2003.

Garroway, Joshua D. *Paul's Gentile-Jews: Neither Jew nor Gentile, but Both.* New York: Palgrave MacMillan, 2012.

Gaventa, Beverly Roberts. *When in Romans: An Invitation to Linger with the Gospel According to Paul.* Grand Rapids: Baker Academic, 2016.

Gorman, Michael J. *Apostle of the Crucified Lord: A Theological Introduction to Paul and His Letters.* 2nd ed. Grand Rapids: Eerdmans, 2016.

————. *Becoming the Gospel: Paul, Participation, and Mission.* Grand Rapids: Eerdmans, 2015.

————. *Cruciformity: Paul's Narrative Spirituality of the Cross.* Grand Rapids: Eerdmans, 2001.

————. *Inhabiting the Cruciform God: Kenosis, Justification, and Theosis in Paul's Narrative Soteriology.* Grand Rapids: Eerdmans, 2009.

Gray, Patrick. *Paul as a Problem in History and Culture: The Apostle and His Critics through the Centuries.* Grand Rapids: Baker Academic, 2016.

Hengel, Martin. *The Zealots: Investigations into the Jewish Freedom Movement in the Period from Herod 1 until 70 AD.* Translated by David Smith. Edinburgh: T&T Clark, 1997.

Horrell, David G. *Solidarity and Difference: A Contemporary Reading of Paul's Ethics.* 2nd ed. London: Bloomsbury T&T Clark, 2015.

Hurtado, Larry W. *Lord Jesus Christ: Devotion to Jesus in Earliest Christianity.* Grand Rapids: Eerdmans, 2003.

Jacob, Haley Goranson. *Conformed to the Image of His Son: Reconsidering Paul's Theology of Glory in Romans.* Downers Grove, Ill.: IVP Academic, 2018.

Jewett, Robert. *Romans: A Commentary*. Hermeneia. Minneapolis: Fortress, 2007.

———. *Romans: A Short Commentary*. Minneapolis: Fortress, 2013.

Johnson, A. C., P. R. Coleman-Norton, and F. C. Bourne. *Ancient Roman Statutes*. Clarke, N.J.: Lawbook Exchange, 2003.

Käsemann, Ernst. *Commentary on Romans*. Grand Rapids: Eerdmans, 1980.

Keck, Leander E. *Romans*. Abingdon New Testament Commentaries. Nashville: Abingdon, 2005.

Kennedy, George A., ed. *Progymnasmata: Greek Textbooks of Prose Composition and Rhetoric*. Writings from the Greco-Roman World. Atlanta: SBL, 2003.

Lampe, Peter. *From Paul to Valentinus: Christians at Rome in the First Two Centuries*. Edited by Marshall D. Johnson. Translated by Michael Steinhauser. Minneapolis: Fortress, 2003.

Lancaster, Sarah Heaner. *Romans*. Belief: A Theological Commentary on the Bible. Louisville: Westminster John Knox, 2015.

Levenson, Jon D. *The Love of God: Divine Gift, Human Gratitude, and Mutual Faithfulness in Judaism*. Princeton: Princeton University Press, 2016.

Loader, William. *Making Sense of Sex: Attitudes towards Sexuality in Early Jewish and Christian Literature*. Grand Rapids: Eerdmans, 2013.

———. *The New Testament on Sexuality*. Grand Rapids: Eerdmans, 2012.

Longenecker, Bruce W. *Remember the Poor: Paul, Poverty, and the Greco-Roman World*. Grand Rapids: Eerdmans, 2010.

———. *The Triumph of Abraham's God: The Transformation of Identity in Galatians*. Nashville: Abingdon, 1998.

Longenecker, Richard N. *The Epistle to the Romans*. Grand Rapids: Eerdmans, 2016.

———. *Introducing Romans: Critical Issues in Paul's Most Famous Letter*. Grand Rapids: Eerdmans, 2011.

———. *Paul, Apostle of Liberty: The Origin and Nature of Paul's Christianity*. 2nd ed. Grand Rapids: Eerdmans, 2015.

Malherbe, Abraham J., ed. *Ancient Epistolary Theorists*. Atlanta: Society of Biblical Literature, 1988.

Marsh, Charles, Peter Slade, and Sarah Azaransky, eds. *Lived Theology: New Perspectives on Method, Style, and Pedagogy*. New York: Oxford University Press, 2016.

Martínez, Florentino García, and Eibert J. C. Tigchelaar, eds. *The Dead Sea Scrolls Study Edition*. Vol. 2. Leiden: Brill; Grand Rapids: Eerdmans, 1998.

Mathew, Susan. *Women in the Greetings of Romans 16.1-16: A Study of Mutuality and Women's Ministry in the Letter to the Romans*. LNTS 471. London: T&T Clark, 2014.

McKnight, Scot. *A Community Called Atonement*. Nashville: Abingdon, 2007.

———. *Kingdom Conspiracy: Returning to the Radical Mission of the Local Church*. Grand Rapids: Brazos, 2014.

Minear, Paul S. *The Obedience of Faith: The Purposes of Paul in the Epistle to the Romans*. Studies in Biblical Theology, 2.19. London: SCM Press, 1971.

Moo, Douglas J. *The Epistle to the Romans*. 2nd ed. NICNT. Grand Rapids: Eerdmans, 2018.

Noy, David. *Foreigners at Rome: Citizens and Strangers*. London: Classical Press of Wales, 2000.

Oakes, Peter. *Reading Romans in Pompeii: Paul's Letter at Ground Level*. Minneapolis: Fortress, 2009.

Reasoner, Mark. *Romans in Full Circle: A History of Interpretation*. Louisville: Westminster John Knox, 2005.

———. *The Strong and the Weak: Romans 14.1–15.13 in Context*. SNTSMS 103. Cambridge: Cambridge University Press, 1999.

Rodriguez, Rafael. *If You Call Yourself a Jew: Reappraising Paul's Letter to the Romans*. Eugene, Ore.: Cascade, 2014.

Rodriguez, Rafael, and Matthew Thiessen, eds. *The So-Called Jew in Paul's Letter to the Romans*. Minneapolis: Fortress, 2016.

Romm, James. *Dying Every Day: Seneca at the Court of Nero*. New York: A. A. Knopf, 2014.

Root, Andrew. *Christopraxis: A Practical Theology of the Cross*. Minneapolis: Fortress, 2014.

———. *Faith Formation in a Secular Age: Responding to the Church's Obsession with Youthfulness*. Grand Rapids: Baker Academic, 2017.

Rowe, C. Kavin. *One True Life: The Stoics and Early Christians as Rival Traditions*. New Haven: Yale University Press, 2016.

———. *World Upside Down: Reading Acts in the Graeco-Roman Age*. New York: Oxford University Press, 2009.

Sanders, E. P. *Jewish Law from Jesus to the Mishnah: Five Studies*. Philadelphia: Trinity Press International, 1990.

———. *Judaism: Practice and Belief. 63BCE–66CE*. Minneapolis: Fortress, 2016.

———. *Paul and Palestinian Judaism: A Comparison of Patterns of Religion*. Philadelphia: Fortress, 1977.

————. *Paul: The Apostle's Life, Letters, and Thought.* Minneapolis: Fortress, 2015.

Shiell, William D. *Delivering from Memory: The Effect of Performance on the Early Christian Audience.* Eugene, Ore.: Pickwick, 2011.

Shotter, David. *Nero Caesar Augustus: Emperor of Rome.* New York: Routledge, 2008.

Stuhlmacher, Peter. *Biblical Theology of the New Testament.* Edited by Daniel P. Bailey and Jostein Ådna. Translated by Daniel P. Bailey. Grand Rapids: Eerdmans, 2018.

Tacitus. *The Annals of Imperial Rome.* Translated by Michael Grant. Rev. ed. New York: Penguin, 1978.

Thiessen, Matthew. *Paul and the Gentile Problem.* New York: Oxford University Press, 2016.

Thornhill, A. Chadwick. *The Chosen People: Election, Paul and Second Temple Judaism.* Downers Grove, Ill.: IVP Academic, 2015.

Thorsteinsson, Runar. *Paul's Interlocutor in Romans 2: Function and Identity in the Context of Ancient Epistolography.* Coniectanea Biblica: New Testament Series 40. Lund: Lund University Press, 2003.

Trebilco, Paul. *Self-Designations and Group Identity in the New Testament.* Cambridge: Cambridge University Press, 2012.

Venema, Dennis R., and Scot McKnight. *Adam and the Genome: Reading Scripture after Genetic Science.* Grand Rapids: Brazos, 2017.

Wagner, J. Ross. *Heralds of the Good News: Isaiah and Paul in Concert in the Letter to the Romans.* NovTSup 101. Leiden: Brill, 2000.

Watson, Francis. *Paul and the Hermeneutics of Faith.* New York: Bloomsbury T&T Clark, 2004.

————. *Paul, Judaism, and the Gentiles: Beyond the New Perspective.* 2nd ed. Grand Rapids: Eerdmans, 2007.

Wedderburn, A. J. M. *The Reasons for Romans.* Minneapolis: Fortress, 1991.

Williams, Ritva H. *Stewards, Prophets, Keepers of the Word: Leadership in the Early Church.* Peabody, Mass.: Hendrickson, 2006.

Witherington, Ben W., III. *The Indelible Image: The Theological and Ethical World of the New Testament.* Vol. 1: *The Individual Witnesses.* Downers Grove, Ill.: IVP Academic, 2009.

————. *The Indelible Image: The Theological and Ethical Thought World of the New Testament.* Vol. 2: *The Collective Witness.* Downers Grove, Ill.: IVP Academic, 2010.

Wright, N. T. "The Letter to the Romans." In *The New Interpreter's Bible*, 12:393–770. Nashville: Abingdon, 2002.

———. *Paul and the Faithfulness of God*. 2 vols. Christian Origins and the Question of God 4. Minneapolis: Fortress, 2013.

———. *Pauline Perspectives: Essays on Paul, 1978–2013*. Minneapolis: Fortress, 2013.

Yinger, Kent L. *Paul, Judaism, and Judgment According to Deeds*. SNTSMS 105. New York: Cambridge University Press, 1999.

SCRIPTURE INDEX

Note citations refer to page numbers in the text. **Bold** in the Romans section shows key index entries.

ANCIENT SOURCES INDEX

Left Dec Tue 11/29   - 30
Ret. Dec Tue 12/6